Sociocognitive Perspect
Use and Language Learı

Published in this series

Sociocognitive Perspectives on Language Use and Language Learning

edited by

ROB BATSTONE

OXFORD
UNIVERSITY PRESS

OXFORD

UNIVERSITY PRESS

Great Clarendon Street, Oxford OX2 6DP

Oxford University Press is a department of the University of Oxford.
It furthers the University's objective of excellence in research, scholarship,
and education by publishing worldwide in

Oxford New York

Auckland Cape Town Dar es Salaam Hong Kong Karachi
Kuala Lumpur Madrid Melbourne Mexico City Nairobi
New Delhi Shanghai Taipei Toronto

With offices in

Argentina Austria Brazil Chile Czech Republic France Greece
Guatemala Hungary Italy Japan Poland Portugal Singapore
South Korea Switzerland Thailand Turkey Ukraine Vietnam

OXFORD and OXFORD ENGLISH are registered trade marks of
Oxford University Press in the UK and in certain other countries

ISBN: 978 0 19 442477 6

Printed in China

Preface

The field of Second Language Acquisition (SLA) has seen a great deal of debate and disagreement in recent years over questions which have to do with the nature of language use, language learning, and their interrelationship. For many years the emphasis of much research in SLA—and particularly research into classroom interaction and its relationship to language learning—has been predominantly cognitive (e.g. Gass 1997; Doughty and Williams 1998). Interaction, for example, has been regarded very largely as a mechanism for generating 'input', which in turn triggers the activation of internal cognitive processes (Long 1996). Such a view has been subjected to heavy criticism in recent years (Block 2003). Interaction, many critics argue, is first and foremost a social phenomenon. How, then, can we begin to comprehend how interaction works without taking account of such factors as participants' identities, or the ways in which interlocutors adapt their social roles as an interaction proceeds? (e.g. Tarone and Liu 1995; Atkinson et al. 2007).

Two of the most cited critics of cognitive SLA are Alan Firth and Etienne Wagner, who argue in an article first published in 1997 that the dominant, cognitive view of discourse and communication in SLA is 'individualistic and mechanistic', and that it 'fails to account in a satisfactory way for interactional and sociolinguistic dimensions of language' (1997: 285). Firth and Wagner's concern for greater attention to the sociolinguistic as well as the psycholinguistic is reflected in the current blossoming of research in SLA across a range of perspectives. Alongside the continuing development of cognitive enquiry, there has been a notable expansion in recent years of research based on sociocultural theory (e.g. Lantolf 2000; Lantolf and Thorne 2006), into matters of identity and the relationship between identity and language (Pavlenko and Blackledge 2004; Block 2006), into second language socialization (Bayley and Schecter 2003; Morita and Kobayashi 2008), and into communities of practice (Leki 2001; Morita 2004).

However, with the significant exception of sociocultural theory, much of the research underpinning these theoretical options has been predominantly social, reflecting a tendency in much SLA research to lay emphasis either on the cognitive or on the social, and to argue for the merits of one in reference to the inadequacies of the other. No doubt such disputes have their place, but they ought not to distract us from the value of jointly looking at the social and the cognitive. It was in order to recognize and to explore this relationship further that the University of Auckland hosted an international symposium and conference on Social and Cognitive Aspects of Second Language Use and

Learning in April 2007, for which a number of chapters presented here were initially drafted (the chapters by Atkinson, Batstone, Larsen-Freeman, and Philp and Mackey were written specifically for this volume).

In keeping with the aims of the Auckland conference, this book brings together work by scholars who, although they represent a range of perspectives, have in common the belief that the processes of language use, language learning, and language teaching all involve interconnections between social and cognitive elements without which they cannot be adequately understood.

Introduction to Part One

The chapters in Part One are concerned with overall trends in SLA theorizing and with the failure in much mainstream SLA to capture the interdependence of social and cognitive elements. The authors of each chapter outline their own particular ways of framing the social/cognitive relationship.

Rob Batstone (Ch. 1) traces the recent emergence of sociocognitive debate and some if its historical antecedents, before moving on to argue that there are two ways in which the social/cognitive relationship is represented in contemporary SLA research—holistic sociocognition and analytic sociocognition. Holistic approaches are based on the view that the social and the cognitive are inseparable, whereas analytic perspectives maintain that the social and the cognitive can usefully be teased apart at a theoretical level. Batstone assesses the scope and the potential of each perspective for understanding some of the key issues for language learning and teaching, including the relationship between knowledge and performance, and the degree to which the impact of classroom interventions can be anticipated in advance.

The case for a holistic conception of sociocognition is taken up in Chapter 2 by **Dwight Atkinson**. Atkinson explains the conceptual basis for sociocognition in SLA, noting that there are three key principles which underpin his own sociocognitive approach: the inseparability principle, the learning-is-adaptive principle, and (of particular importance for language learning) the alignment principle. Atkinson then goes on to provide a sociocognitive explanation for a construct which has long been at the heart of cognitive accounts of SLA: attention. In cognitive accounts, attention is seen as a complex of internal cognitive processes. For Atkinson, though, attention as a cognitive phenomenon cannot meaningfully be separated from attention as a social phenomenon, because attention is always jointly constructed between participants who are working to bring their separate worlds into alignment.

Another scholar who places great emphasis on the notion of adaptivity (albeit in somewhat different terms from Atkinson) is **Diane Larsen-Freeman** (Ch. 3). Larsen-Freeman sees in the contemporary state of SLA theorizing a schism between theories which prioritize the cognitive and those which prioritize the social. She proposes chaos/complexity theory as a fruitful basis for challenging this schism, by arguing that the social and the cognitive work together in language use in highly dynamic and adaptive ways. Opposing the traditional distinction between a cognitive conception of knowledge and the social conditions in which knowledge is put to use, language learners in a chaos/complexity perspective are seen as continually adapting (and thus changing) their language resources to respond to new contexts. In this view, says Larsen-Freeman, 'the language system and its use are mutually constitutive'.

Like Larsen-Freeman, **Elaine Tarone** (Ch. 4) takes issue with some established constructs which fail to do justice to the interdependence of social and cognitive elements. Tarone argues that in cognitive SLA terms such as 'input' and 'output' are treated far too mechanistically, and that they 'must be treated more seriously as socio-cognitive constructs in SLA theory'. Tarone's particular focus is on the role of social setting. Reviewing a number of recent studies, Tarone's argument is that social setting strongly influences both the kind of input learners have access to, and the quantity and quality of learners' output. She then goes on to suggest that social setting can influence acquisition both in terms of rate and (more significantly) in terms of route.

Introduction to Part Two

Part Two focuses on the relationship between thinking and social context, central to any account of the social/cognitive relationship. When we think of the word 'social' in relation to language, probably the first idea which comes to mind is of language used for the construction and maintenance of social relationships. But the notion of the social does not exclude the individual, and many scholars—particularly those who take a sociocultural perspective—argue that the development of mental forms involves a shifting balance between the *interpersonal* (where language learning is achieved in interaction with others), and the *intrapersonal* (where individuals use language and gesture to think their way into a better understanding of a language-related problem).

In Part Two we consider four studies. The first two stress interpersonal aspects of language learning, emphasizing the close link between language learning, identity, and social community. **Patricia Duff** and **Masaki Kobayashi** (Ch. 5) focus on the relationship between second language socialization and language learning. Studies of socialization often have a great deal more to say about social processes than about cognition. Duff and Kobayashi, however, argue that L2 socialization research 'brings together an analysis of social, cultural, and cognitive dimensions of situated language learning' and that it is therefore 'highly compatible with a *sociocognitive* perspective'. They go on to illustrate the interplay of social, cultural, and cognitive factors in a study of how Japanese international students in Canada learn to participate in cultural practices designed to increase their L2 communicative competence in a content-based university academic exchange programme. **Lynda Yates**, **Howard Nicholas**, and **Michele de Courcy** (Ch. 6) examine the language development and experiences of three different age groups of largely Shia refugees from Iraq as they settled in a small rural town in Victoria, Australia. What makes this study unusual is the care that the authors take to correlate social issues of access and exclusion with developmental measures of their acquisition collected through a combination of structured and semi-structured tasks administered over several months. The authors argue that their study draws together the cognitive and the social because it is based on a view of learning as the internalization of 'a cognitively-represented system through participation in communities, involving agency and investment'.

The second two chapters in Part Two place greater emphasis on the intrapersonal, exploring the argument made in sociocultural theory that thinking is a process which can be brought into existence through talk and through gesture. **Merrill Swain** (Ch. 7) focuses on the use of language—or in her terms, 'languaging'—as a means of talking oneself through cognitively complex tasks. Swain illustrates her argument with a study of intermediate learners of French who are asked to read aloud and then explain a text about the concept of 'voice'. Swain's central hypothesis is that 'by having to read aloud each sentence of an explanatory text we developed about the concept of voice in French, and say what their understanding of it was, our students would learn what active, passive, and middle voice sentences were, and be able to identify and use them'. Like Swain, **Jim Lantolf** (Ch. 8) draws on sociocultural theory to examine ways in which learners talk their way into understanding, though in his case the focus is not just talk, but talk integrated with gesture. Lantolf presents a case study of an L2 learner who uses gesture integrated with speech to think her way into an understanding of how to use aspect in a French narrative. Lantolf's study is the first to consider what he refers to as 'the self-generated use of gesture to think through and resolve an L2 language problem'. The arguments made by Swain and by Lantolf draw on a view of the interdependence between the social and the cognitive which lies at the heart of sociocultural theory. When Swain's learners engage in languaging and when Lantolf's learners talk and gesture their way into an understanding of aspect, they are engaging in an activity which has a cognitive dimension (and, indeed, a cognitive pay-off) because it is through talk and gesture that new understandings emerge. But languaging and the use of talk/gesture are also social processes. Even in the absence of an interlocutor with whom meanings are co-constructed, these *intra*personal uses of language are also *inter*personal, because—as Lantolf argues—they are forms of dialogue, albeit dialogue which is 'I–me' rather than 'I–you'. At the same time, talk/gesture draw together the cognitive and the social in a broader, developmental sense. In sociocultural theory, communication begins as a social process which eventually takes on psychological status. This connectedness between the cognitive and the social reflects a defining belief in sociocultural theory: those cognitive, higher-level processes of reasoning are brought into existence through socially mediated action.

Introduction to Part Three

All the chapters in Part Three involve second language classroom-based research, and they all deal with the same fundamental topic: the social and cognitive factors which orient learners' attention to form.

The vast majority of second language learning theories presume that class-room learning requires learners to engage with language through meaningful interaction of one sort or another. In mainstream cognitive SLA, however, the role of interaction is limited to that of a mechanism for generating 'input'—a starkly cognitive view which marginalizes the role of social factors. In con-trast, sociocognitive perspectives on interaction are based on the argument that cognitive processes cannot be understood without examining how they are brought about or changed through the joint construction of social con-texts, a process in which the cognitive and the social work together in tightly integrated ways.

The chapters in this part represent a variety of sociocognitive perspectives on the relationship between interaction and second language learning. The first three chapters investigate interaction between teachers and learners, with particular emphasis on the provision of corrective feedback. **Rod Ellis** (Ch. 9) examines three theoretical perspectives on corrective feedback: the cognitive, the social, and the psychological. Ellis argues that a theory of cor-rective feedback needs to take account of all three perspectives and that the only available theory with the capacity to do so is a sociocultural theory. In such a theory, corrective feedback is framed as 'a collaborative endeavor' that must be adapted to both the individual learner and to the social/situational context in which the corrective feedback occurs. Ellis concludes with a set of general pedagogic proposals for conducting corrective feedback, drawing on all three of the perspectives he examines in his chapter.

The theme of corrective feedback is continued in the chapter by **Neomy Storch** and **Gillian Wigglesworth** (Ch. 10), with their empirical study of the effects of different forms of teacher feedback on learners' writing. They begin with a quantitative and largely cognitive analysis of their data which indi-cates that feedback in the form of editing symbols elicited a higher 'depth of processing' than feedback in the form of reformulations. They then under-take a fine-grained qualitative analysis of the talk of two pairs of learners which indicates the important role played by agency in mediating learners' decisions about how to respond to the different forms of feedback. Taken as a whole, Storch and Wigglesworth's study shows how constructs such as depth of processing (most often treated as a cognitive construct) may be best understood as sociocognitive (or as socially mediated cognition).

The chapter by **Paul Toth** (Ch. 11) also deals with matters of corrective feedback, together with other forms of form-focusing assistance provided during teacher-led classroom interaction. Drawing on a study of L2 Spanish instruction, Toth shows how types of classroom interaction traditionally favoured in cognitive L2 theory—in particular, the emphasis on linguistic accuracy as a response to corrective moves—depend for their effectiveness on the degree to which the aims and procedures involved in the wider discourse are shared by all participants. Toth refers to this kind of shared understanding as 'cohesion'. Drawing in particular on Relevance Theory, Toth goes on to argue that cohesion 'maximizes the cognitive and social benefits of teacher-led interaction for second language acquisition'.

In Chapter 12, **Jenefer Philp** and **Alison Mackey** examine the interactions between university students learning French in a foreign language context. They discuss how learners' peer interactions can be mediated by the social relationships the learners have with each other, as well as by their perceptions about the instructor and the instructors' expectations. Philp and Mackey present their data as part of a wider argument for incorporating some social insights into the traditionally cognitive 'interaction approach'. Interaction, they argue, might usefully be seen as a 'potential forum for combining some of the new perspectives that are emerging within the broader field of SLA, both the more cognitive, and the more social'.

Acknowledgements

I am much indebted to Rod Ellis for his advice, support, and encouragement. Editing this volume would have been a great deal more difficult without his guidance and wise counsel.

I would also like to thank Cristina Whitecross, who provided editorial energy and commitment to the publication of this book at a critical time.

Contents

List of Contributors

Dwight Atkinson (Purdue University, USA)
Rob Batstone (University of Auckland, New Zealand)
Michele de Courcy (University of Melbourne. Australia)
Patricia Duff (University of British Columbia, Canada)
Diane Larsen-Freeman (University of Michigan, USA)
Rod Ellis (University of Auckland, New Zealand)
Masaki Kobayashi (Kanda University of International Studies, Japan)
Jim Lantolf (The Pennsylvania State University, USA)
Alison Mackey (Georgetown University, USA)
Howard Nicholas (La Trobe University, Melbourne, Australia)
Jenefer Philp (University of Auckland, New Zealand)
Neomy Storch (The University of Melbourne, Australia)
Merrill Swain (University of Toronto, Canada)
Elaine Tarone (University of Minnesota, USA)
Paul Toth (Temple University, USA)
Gillian Wigglesworth (The University of Melbourne, Australia)
Lynda Yates (Macquarie University, Australia)

PART ONE
Theoretical perspectives on sociocognition

I

Issues and options in sociocognition

ROB BATSTONE

Section 1 What is sociocognition and why is it important?

Introduction

The chapter is divided into four sections. In the first section I review recent debates in SLA which have a strong bearing on the evolution and possible future course of sociocognitive accounts of language use and language learning. In Section 2 I introduce two forms of sociocognition: holistic sociocognition and analytic sociocognition. Holistic approaches are based on the view that the social and the cognitive are inseparable, and that making any kind of theoretical distinction between them will misrepresent the nature of a highly integrated system. Analytic perspectives on sociocognition are based on the belief that whilst the social and the cognitive are inseparable during the moment-by-moment dynamics of language use, they can usefully be teased apart at a theoretical level, the better to scrutinize ways in which elements of cognition and aspects of social context act upon and modify each other.

The focus of Sections 3 and 4 is more critical and argumentative. In Section 3 we examine the contrasting claims of holistic and analytic sociocognition in relation to a topic which has long been of central concern in SLA: the relationship between knowledge of language and language use, and the debate about how flexible and responsive the mind is when language learners encounter new forms of classroom discourse. In Section 4 we turn to look at a similarly contentious question: to what extent can we predict the outcome of classroom tasks? This is a question of central importance for language teaching. We examine the competing claims made for holistic and analytic sociocognition and consider the implications for future classroom research.

Three perspectives on the social and the cognitive in language use/learning

Language learning is primarily cognitive

The essence of sociocognition is the belief that neither language use nor language learning can be adequately defined or understood without recognizing that they have both a social and a cognitive dimension. This might seem a relatively uncontentious assertion. Few if any applied linguists or language teachers would want to deny that language learning engages the mind in one way or another, or that a person's engagement with language is influenced by their social context. However, if we examine the issue a little further it soon becomes apparent that there are at least three possible positions which can be taken on this issue.

The first position is that although social factors are certainly involved in language acquisition, their role is at best somewhat marginal—language acquisition is primarily a cognitive process. Such cognitive accounts of language acquisition have been very influential over the past thirty years or more, both amongst theorists and in reference to language teaching (e.g. Gass 1997; Doughty and Williams 1998). Superficially, such accounts appear to have a strongly social orientation, because they argue that language acquisition has its genesis in processes of turn-taking in language use. However, interaction in cognitive accounts of language acquisition is understood somewhat asocially, as a mechanism for generating 'input', thereby activating the various cognitive mechanisms involved in information processing. Central to many such accounts is the concept of negotiation, either of meaning (Long 1996) or of form (Lyster and Ranta 1997). In the case of negotiation of meaning, learners are understood to pay attention to linguistic errors to the extent that they lead to misunderstandings which call for clarification (Long and Robinson 1998). In the negotiation of form (Lyster and Ranta 1997; Lyster 1998), teachers provide learners with cues whose corrective function is made more explicit than is the case with the negotiation of meaning, because it 'draws attention to students' non-target output in ways that encourage them to peer or self-repair' (Lyster 2002: 383). From a cognitive perspective, it is not possible to explain L2 acquisition without acknowledging that 'the result of communicative experience…remains, memory permitting, in the form of a modified, individual, partly idiosyncratic, internal mental representation of the L2' (Kasper 1997: 319).

Language learning is primarily social

The second possible view is diametrically opposed to the cognitive perspective we have just considered. Many scholars argue that although the mind is undoubtedly involved in the processes of language use and language learning, it is perfectly viable to elaborate theories which focus principally or entirely on the role of social factors and the importance of social participation in learning. Wagner (2004: 614), for example, put the case in these terms:

The theory of learning as participation simply avoids statements about the participants' inner states. The participants are socialized into practices, but the description has no means to show what kind of inner states are related to the process of becoming a member in a social group. *This argument does not claim that there are no inner states but leaves its description to a different methodology.* Increasing participation in social life is the main object of description of a social theory of learning. (italics added)

This essentially social perspective has become increasingly popular in recent years, with a great many articles and books devoted to such issues as identity (e.g. Norton 2000*a*), to communities of practice (Lave and Wenger 1991), and to second language socialization (Morita and M. Kobayashi 2008). Whilst it would be wrong to characterize the work of these scholars as entirely social, their overall focus is clearly sociolinguistic rather than sociocognitive.

Language learning is sociocognitive

The third view, and the one which forms the basis for this volume, is socio-cognitive. Sociocognition is based on the view that neither language use nor language learning can be adequately defined or understood without recognizing that they have both a social and a cognitive dimension which interact.

Framed this way, sociocognition is by no means a new phenomenon. For example, SLA researchers have long been interested in how the mind stores information not merely about language but also about the social world (e.g. Hymes 1972). SLA researchers also have a well-established and ongoing interest in a learner's relationships with the social world and the degree to which these relationships influence second language learning (e.g. Schumann 1978*a*).

In language teaching, too, the question of how the social and the cognitive affect each other will not be new to most language teachers, although they may not have thought about it in quite these terms. One has only to observe the behaviour of learners working in pairs or groups—how their levels of participation fluctuate depending on who else is in the group and how well they work together with them—to know that such 'cognitive' questions as whether and how learners pay attention to new linguistic forms through interaction is influenced by social context and by social relationships.

Nonetheless, with the significant exception of sociocultural theory, socio-cognitive perspectives remain relatively underexplored in SLA compared to the sheer volume of research which takes a rather more cognitive perspective.

Section 2 Analytic and holistic sociocognition

Introduction

In this section I divide the concept of sociocognition into two, making a broad distinction between 'analytic' and 'holistic'. Both holistic and analytic perspectives on sociocognition start out with the view that the social and cognitive elements in language use and language learning are ultimately inseparable, and that as a result any attempt to construct a theory to explain language use which diminishes the role of the one at the expense of the other is unlikely to carry conviction. But they view this interdependence in strikingly different ways. In holistic sociocognition we emphasize the indivisibility of the social and the cognitive, whereas in the case of analytic sociocognition we regard them as interacting but also as theoretically separable. Couched in these terms, holistic and analytic sociocognition reflect very different ways of looking at language use and language learning, and they carry quite distinct implications for how we might think about instructed second language learning.[1]

Holistic sociocognition

Defining holistic sociocognition

Scholars who argue for a holistic view of sociocognition do so in order to emphasize the inseparability of the social and the cognitive at every level, so that any attempt to examine them as separate entities is destined to fail, as by definition it will misrepresent the nature of the very phenomenon it aims to illuminate. The scholar who has done most to elaborate on this view from an explicitly sociocognitive perspective is Dwight Atkinson (Atkinson 2002; Atkinson et al. 2007). Atkinson's argument is that the social and the cognitive interweave at every level and in many domains—in linguistic description and in first and second language acquisition as well as in language use. Atkinson (2002: 527) argues that 'language never occurs apart from a rich set of situational/sociocultural/historical/existential correlates, and to separate it out artificially is to denature it'.

In addition, a number of scholars argue that language use involves such a sociocognitively complex array of features that we cannot hope to make reliable predictions about the trajectory which any particular discourse might take. This belief has important implications for language teaching, as we shall see in Section 4.

Key themes in holistic sociocognition: the mind/world unity

The idea that the social and the cognitive are inseparable has a long history in philosophical thinking, where it is talked about in terms of the essential unity between the mind, the body, and the world. John Dewey (1896), for example, denied that there is any significant metaphysical distinction between mind, body, and world. For Dewey, such superficially separate concepts as awareness and action become inseparable within a wider and coherent experience, and much of what we think of as features of a purely mental life (including beliefs, ideas, and desires) ought to fall within the scope of social psychology (Dewey 1985/1917: 54). Dewey, in his turn, has strongly influenced the thinking of (amongst others) Vygotsky, Wittgenstein, and Bruner.

A number of related theoretical paradigms deal with issues of precisely this kind, including the notion of 'embodied cognition' (Lakoff and Turner 1989;

Varela, Thompson, and Rosch 1993; Clark 1999; Fauconnier and Turner 2002), situated cognition (Brown, Collins, and Duguid 1989; Greeno 1989; Lave and Wenger 1991; Greeno 2006), theories of learning as participation (Sfard 1998), and ecological perspectives on language use and language learning (van Lier 1996, 2000, 2004).

Reduced to its essentials, the idea that there are fundamental links between mind, body, and world encapsulates the view that cognition is not situated exclusively in the individual human mind. Rather, our thinking is linked to, and often enhanced by, our use of gesture (Lantolf, Ch. 8 below) and features in our environment (Atkinson, Ch. 2 below). This idea that the mind, body, and world are interconnected has obvious implications for language teaching. Probably the best-known example is the sociocultural belief that the mental processes of language learning cannot meaningfully be separated from the support a learner receives from another interlocutor (Lantolf 2000: 13–18).

Key themes in holistic sociocognition: language use is language learning

A key question which sociocognition aims to answer is: 'what are the socio-cognitive conditions for language use which are most beneficial for language learning?' In cognitive SLA the social conditions of language use and the cognitive processes of language acquisition are dealt with as almost entirely separate phenomena. The purpose of interaction is to create 'input' to activate learners' attentional processes and thus to provide the linguistic 'data' that learners can process internally in order to advance their interlanguages. Interaction serves simply as one of a number of means by which learners can obtain input. In holistic sociocognition, however, no clear distinction is made between the processes of language use and those of language learning, because it is precisely those processes of using language which constitute the essence of learning. Swain and Lapkin (1998: 321) put the case in these terms:

In much socio-cultural discussion, the co-construction of new language and its immediate use in discourse is equated with learning. Unlike the claim that comprehensible input leads to learning, we wish to suggest that what occurs in collaborative dialogues *is* learning. That is, learning does not happen outside performance; it occurs in performance. Furthermore, learning is cumulative, emergent, and ongoing.

Key themes in holistic sociocognition: the importance of common ground

Proponents of holistic sociocognition recognize that there are certain conditions on the kind of language use which is the most productive for language learning. One such condition has to do with the importance of language users achieving a measure of convergence on a common understanding of the nature, procedures, and goals of the activity in which they are engaged. This central idea tends to be elaborated through a sometimes bewildering range of terms, but they have in common a concern with the need for participants to share common ground, and (in cases where such common ground is absent) actively to negotiate an agreed perspective. Thus sociocultural theorists often refer to the concept of 'intersubjectivity' to talk about a shared subjective understanding of a particular activity (e.g. Donato 1994). Similarly, Atkinson (2002 and Ch. 2 below) refers to the processes involved in constantly adjusting to a changing sociocognitive environment using the term 'alignment'.

Illustrating holistic sociocognition: Nassaji and Swain (2000)

In Vygotskian sociocultural theory, scaffolding is seen as a fundamentally situated process of collaborative dialogue which 'anchors' learning in social activity (Lantolf 2000: 13) by providing learners with just sufficient assistance to enable them to accomplish through collaboration what they could not accomplish on their own (Antón and Di Camilla 1998; Antón 1999; Nassaji and Cumming 2000; Ohta 2001). Nassaji and Swain (2000) discuss and illustrate this process in their study of two adult L2 learners, both native speakers of Korean, who were enrolled in a five-week intensive intermediate writing class in an ESL programme in a university in Canada. The authors provide data based on an interaction between one of these learners and a tutor who is providing scaffolded corrective feedback on the learner's written work. In the extract which follows, we see how a tutor focuses on one learner's failure to produce the definite article (writing 'most of Korean' rather than 'most of *the* Koreans'). Nassaji and Swain note that the tutor starts with the most indirect feedback and then provides progressively more help:

1	T	'Most of Korean have same name'. So do you see anything wrong with this sentence?
2	S	uhm...I imagine that...uhm but...in this position...I imagine that...I think it's OK [laughing]
3	T	It's OK?
4	S	Yes.
5	T	ah...what about this part, 'most of Korean'. Do you see...Do you see anything wrong with this phrase?
6	S	Most of a Korean...Korean [whispering]...mmm...
7	T	Anything wrong within this part [referring to the place of the error]?
8	S	Korean?
9	T	No.
10	S	No? uhm...
11	T	Yes there is something wrong with this [referring to the word 'Korean']
12	S	Yes. I think...ah...Korea means Korean people, yes?
13	T	OK.
14	S	Yes?
15	T	But grammatically, is there anything wrong?
16	S	Of the? No?
17	T	Yes, what?
18	S	Of the?

19	T	The, yeah
20	S	Yes.

In this episode the learner made two errors, one having to do with the need to use the definite article 'the' before the word 'Korean(s)', and the other concerning the use of the definite article before the phrase 'same name'. Nassaji and Swain (2000: 40) describe the correction procedure thus:

> The tutor started with the most indirect way of correcting the error, which was reading the section containing the error, and as needed, provided more help in a gradual and progressive fashion. [This] episode shows the negotiation between the tutor and the tutee on the first encounter of the error. It illustrates the amount and the quality of help the ZPD learner elicited from the tutor in order to overcome the error. As can be seen, the learner needed several levels of help before she was able to discover and overcome the error.

In fact, the authors note that the learner was not able to overcome the error until she received the tutor's prompt at turn 15, indicating that the error is a grammatical one. However, the next time a similar error occurs, the learner was able to recognize the nature of the error with much less elaborate prompting from the tutor:

1	T	'Most of the Koreans have same name'. Do you see anything wrong with this?
2	S	Have the . . . same name?
3	T	Ok, yes.
4	S	I'm . . . my article is bad [laughing].

Illustrating holistic sociocognition: Atkinson, Churchill, Nishino, and Okada (2007)

Atkinson and his colleagues argue that a sociocognitive understanding of the processes of language learning requires us to pay careful attention to what they refer to as the 'full array of sociocognitive affordances' (Atkinson et al. 2007: 171), including not only the roles and identities of interlocutors but also 'associated tools' (including pens, books, and learning materials such as a textbook), and 'embodied tools' (such as physical orientation, eye gaze, and gesture). In their study of interaction between Ako (a young Japanese learner) and Tomo (her aunt) as they work together on an exercise on Ako's EFL worksheet, the authors provide a detailed, moment-by-moment account of how such tools are put to use as Tomo scaffolds Ako towards a better understanding of the target form (the present perfect in the model sentence 'have you ever' + past participle).

Atkinson et al. identify numerous instances where Tomo's scaffolding involves the provision of corrective feedback. The notion of corrective feedback has been the subject of much cognitive research in SLA, with a great many studies investigating how teachers provide more or less explicit feedback to learners as they 'negotiate meaning' (e.g. Long 1996) or 'negotiate form' (e.g. Lyster and Ranta 1997). As was indicated earlier in this chapter, such research focuses on patterns of interaction and the use of specific forms by teachers and learners, but has very little to say about the impact of social context on these processes.

One could hardly find a stronger contrast to this than the study by Atkinson and his colleagues. We have already seen how holistic sociocognition views learning as a process which occurs across the whole mind/body/world spectrum, and which is co-constructed as participants work to create mutual alignment. Both these processes are very evident in Atkinson et al.'s careful analysis. Tomo scaffolds Ako's understanding of the workbook exercise not merely by providing corrective feedback, but also (and at the same time) by providing affective encouragement and support, and she does both these things by drawing on a range of sociocognitive tools. Early on in the interaction, for instance, Ako reads the first part of the exercise quietly under her breath. Tomo responds with a confirmation ('right') and she then repeats part of Ako's utterance in what the authors describe as 'a softness of voice and intonation pattern closely mirroring Ako's' (ibid. 176). This apparently straightforward exchange involves Tomo in quietly mirroring Ako's volume, intonation, and gestures, putting her hand to her forehead in a way which 'softly shadows' Ako's own movements. The authors argue that Tomo's behaviour is managed in tight coordination with Ako's, a process which simultaneously guides her and aligns Tomo's bodily posture with that of Ako.

Atkinson and his colleagues note how the ongoing alignments which Ako and Tomo co-construct lead to Ako having a firmer grasp of the target language form in her workbook. Initially, Ako required extensive scaffolding from her aunt in order to formulate a correct response, but later on she is able to offer '*have you eva r/i/du*' (Line 9) with only minimal prompting. This development, the authors argue, illustrates 'the developing repertoires of participation that we claim characterize second language acquisition from a sociocognitive perspective' (ibid. 182).

Analytic sociocognition

Defining analytic sociocognition

There are two factors which distinguish analytic perspectives on sociocognition. The first is that although the social and the cognitive are interdependent whenever they are in process, they can usefully be analysed at a theoretical level as separable elements. This is a very different perspective from the holistic one, where there is a strong emphasis on the inseparable unity of the social and the cognitive. In separating out the cognitive from the social, analytic perspectives enable us to investigate how elements act upon one another and how, in doing so, they change one another. For example, we can see how the social acts on the cognitive in the sense that different social settings or different social relationships influence a learner's capacity to pay attention to new language, or to take risks by using more elaborate or complex language at the outer limits of their current ability (see Tarone 2000*a* and below, Ch. 4). Similarly, we can see how the cognitive influences the social when teachers make unjustified assumptions about learners' knowledge of particular classroom interactive routines, leading to forms of misunderstanding on both the teacher's and the learner's part which can all too easily go unnoticed (we will examine examples of exactly this kind of eventuality later in the chapter).

The second distinguishing feature of analytic sociocognition is the view that particular elements or combinations of elements act upon one another to lead to partially predictable outcomes, and that at least some of these elements can be influenced by careful pedagogic intervention.

The historical roots of analytic sociocognition

Analytic conceptions of sociocognition draw upon a very different view of the mind/body/world relationship from the one presupposed in holistic sociocognition. Part of Descartes's legacy to cognitive science was a view of mind and body as being entirely separate entities, a view often referred to as 'mind/body dualism'. The philosopher John Locke built on Descartes's work by arguing that when we elaborate ideas which are increasingly complex, we necessarily find ourselves generalizing and abstracting, and thus we leave the physical trappings of the here-and-now world behind. Rules, abstractions, and generalizations are often seen as defining features of traditional notions of cognition.

Illustrating analytic sociocognition: variationism

One area of research which is concerned with the study of how social context impacts on a learner's cognition is variationism. Variationists typically regard context as something which, at least for theoretical purposes, is divisible into a variety of subcomponents. One scholar who has worked to draw on the relevancy of a variationist perspective for SLA is Tarone (1988, 2000*b*, and below, Ch. 4). Tarone argues that different social contexts, and particularly different forms of social relationship between interlocutors, can create conditions which vary quite dramatically in the degree to which they are favourable for acquisition. Tarone works within a conceptual framework which includes a number of key constructs from cognitive SLA, including attention, noticing, and input, arguing that these essentially cognitive processes of language acquisition are strongly affected by the type of relationship between interlocutors (Philp and Mackey, below, Ch. 12, make a similar argument). The impact of social relationships on cognition is well illustrated in Tarone and Liu's (1995) longitudinal study of a 6-year-old Chinese boy (called Bob) learning English in Australia. Liu collected data from Bob's interactions with three different addressees—his classroom teachers, his classroom peers, and a familiar adult. Tarone and Liu note that the interactions in these three contexts varied greatly in qualitative terms. For example, they found that Bob initiated interactions with the familiar adult and produced much more complex structures than in either of the other two contexts. Using Pienemann and Johnston's

(1987) proposed set of stages for the acquisition of interrogative structures, Tarone and Liu were able to show that new forms appeared in Bob's interlanguage first with his interactions with the researcher, and only later in the other two contexts. More significantly, the authors also demonstrated that the order in which Bob acquired these forms contradicted the order proposed by Pienemann and Johnston. Tarone and Liu (1995: 122) argue that 'the social demands can be so strong that they can cause an alteration in internal psychologically motivated sequences of acquisition'. Tarone and Liu's study offers us an intriguing glimpse into the possibilities for a sociocognitive account which (by definition) would argue that acquisitional sequences, if they exist at all, are a reflection of *socio*cognitive constraints on developmental sequences. Nonetheless, it is important to stress that the wealth of evidence for some form of predictable developmental sequence which has come from cognitive studies far outstrips anything which more socially sensitive theories have yet offered.

Section 3 Knowledge of language and language use: sociocognitive perspectives

Introduction

In the final two sections of this chapter, the focus moves more towards a critical discussion of some key issues raised by sociocognition. In this section I look first at the ways in which knowledge of language is represented in the mind. A sociocognitive perspective stresses that knowledge is structured in ways which reflect the multiple social purposes to which it is put. For example, scholars regularly talk about knowledge of how turns are patterned in particular discourses. However, there is very little grounded research to demonstrate how such knowledge is learnt. We then move on to consider the dynamic relationship between knowledge of language and language use. Sociocognitive perspectives emphasize the highly adaptable ways in which knowledge is continuously changed through experiences in language use, and how it then becomes available as a resource for subsequent interactions. The issue of adaptability raises important questions about whether and how language learning is a potentially lifelong process.

Knowledge

Competence and performance

The relationship between knowledge of language and its application in language use has traditionally been explained by drawing a clear distinction between 'competence' (understood as an idealized account of a person's knowledge of linguistic regularities) and 'performance' (understood as engaging with language in actual discourse). Many researchers argue that descriptions of competence amount to little more than a set of rather abstract taxonomies which, whilst they may be neat and orderly, have little if anything to say about how the mental storage of knowledge equips the language user to deal with the pressures of real-time language use (e.g. Widdowson 1989; Carr and Curran 1994), or with the 'messy, ambiguous, and context-sensitive' nature of much actually occurring discourse (Bruner 1996: 5).

Issues for sociocognition: the merging of the cognitive and the social

Some scholars are so strongly opposed to this distinction between competence and performance that they reject any notion of cognition as a resource for learning which is distinct from the dynamic unfolding of language use. Johnson (2004), for example, maintains that the workings of the mind are so closely interwoven with the intricacies of situated meaning-making that the very notion of cognition or competence as distinct from performance in social contexts is rejected. In effect, Johnson argues that there is no significant theoretical difference between what goes on intrapersonally (within the minds of individual interlocutors) and what goes on interpersonally (between interlocutors). She puts her case in these terms: 'A dialectal interaction between the interpersonal and the intrapersonal planes leads to the merging of language performance and language competence: they represent two sides of the same coin' (ibid. 172). In effect, Johnson's argument is that we ought to equate the cognitive with the social. As she says, interaction 'is viewed not as a cognitive issue but as a social issue'. The equation of cognition/competence with social/performance is problematic, however, because it is difficult to see how learning could proceed very far without being able to draw on generalizations of one sort or another.

Issues for sociocognition: the importance of knowledge generalization

Sfard (1998: 9) clearly sees the generalization of knowledge as an issue which will not go away:

Not even the most zealous followers of the [participation metaphor]-based line of thought would deny that something does keep repeating itself as we move from situation to situation and from context to context. Our ability to prepare ourselves today to deal with new situations we are going to encounter tomorrow is the very essence of learning. Competence means being able to repeat what can be repeated while changing what needs to be changed. How is all of this accounted for if we are not allowed to talk about carrying anything with us from one situation to another?

It would be hard to overstate the significance of Sfard's remarks here. When we 'repeat what can be repeated', we draw on knowledge which we have generalized to some degree. The most obvious and pervasive example of generalized knowledge is grammar, because grammar provides us with information about how to construct a potentially limitless number of sentences on the basis of a relatively small number of economical rules. If our knowledge of language was completely lacking in generalization, what would it look like?

The very question feels somehow contradictory, because knowledge without generalization would effectively mean there would be no significant difference between what we know about language and what we do with language. It would be like having a vast but completely unedited mental store of things we have heard, read, written, or spoken. We could hardly refer to such a store as 'knowledge' at all, because it would fail to provide us with any of the functions we routinely associate with a knowledge base, such as indications about how particular stretches of language can or cannot be modified to fit particular conditions of use. Johnson appears perilously close to this position with her suggestion that competence and performance can effectively be 'merged'.

This is an argument of central importance for holistic and analytic sociocognition. Because analytic sociocognition allows us to examine how social and cognitive elements act upon each other, it is well equipped to handle the distinction between cognitively generalized knowledge and the social conditions particular to language use. The holistic sociocognition position involves arguing that the social and the cognitive are inseparable. As a result, some holistic scholars regard knowledge either as highly functional (e.g. Atkinson 2002), or they argue that we must think of knowledge not as distanced from context but as fundamentally 'local' (e.g. Young 1999; Young and Miller 2004).

But even 'local' or 'functional' knowledge must be generalized if it is to do its proper job and act as a resource for language use, and to the extent that generalization necessarily involves a degree of detachment from context, these holistic arguments acknowledge—albeit implicitly—a distinction between the cognitive and the social, leading to a potential contradiction for those who wish to maintain that the social and the cognitive are indivisible.

Issues for sociocognition: demonstrating the learning of situated knowledge

This is not to say, however, that sociocognition more generally cannot make a useful contribution to the debate. Scholars working in the field of interactional competence, in particular, routinely stress the importance of knowledge of the patterns which underlie particular forms of discourse. Thus Hall (1997: 303) talks about 'the patterned ways in which turns are taken, and the linguistic and other interactional means by which typical opening, transitional, and closing turns are accomplished'. Such constructs are often talked about in ways which imply an awareness of the importance of generalizations. Young (1999: 119–20), for example, defines interactional competence as involving 'the structure of *recurring* episodes of face-to-face interaction' and he argues that interactional competence will gain considerably in explanatory power when we have pedagogical studies which indicate 'the degree to which interactional competence in a given practice can be *generalized* to other practices' (italics added).

As an illustration, we might think of the forms of knowledge a learner might need in order to participate in the scaffolding interaction we looked at earlier (Nassaji and Swain 2000). Arguably, classroom learners could benefit from knowing something of the way in which a teacher's prompts begin with very inductive forms of questioning, and how they systematically shift towards more explicit help.

Knowledge of this sort is well suited to sociocognitive analysis. Scholars such as Atkinson are strongly opposed to any form of knowledge which would lead us into a view of language as becoming 'progressively more decontextualized and autonomous in the course of its acquisition' (2002: 532). But knowledge of discourse patterns is, arguably, a form of knowledge which is generalized without at the same time losing its essential grounding in language use. Learners who have internalized generalizations about scaffolding come to expect particular rhetorical patterns (such as the move from implicit to explicit questioning), but their expectations are a great deal more contextualized than, say, grammatical knowledge can be. They may associate patterns of scaffolded turn-taking with particular roles—for example, they know that it is the teacher who initiates the routine, and that implicit questions call upon learners to make every effort to formulate their own solutions to the problem at hand.

Yet despite the many appeals to knowledge of this sort, we still have very little practical demonstration of how a learner might develop her awareness of 'the structure of recurring episodes of face-to-face interaction', and this despite widespread recognition that to demonstrate learning we need to show 'the transcendence of a particular time and space' (Larsen-Freeman 2007: 783). In a similar vein, though somewhat more specifically, R. Ellis (forthcoming) suggests that in order to demonstrate change we ideally need to show the following:

1 The learner could not do x at time a (the 'gap').
2 The learner co-adapted x at time b ('social construction').
3 The learner initiated x at time c in a similar context as in time b ('internalization/ self-regulation').
4 The learner employed x at time d in a new context ('transfer of learning').

What is needed is much clearer definitions attached to empirical work which explicitly seek to show how cross-contextual knowledge is developed in one context and transferred to another.

The relationship between knowledge and use: prior knowledge and adaptability

Introduction

I noted earlier on that a key belief in holistic sociocognition is the importance of establishing common ground between interlocutors in language use. Block

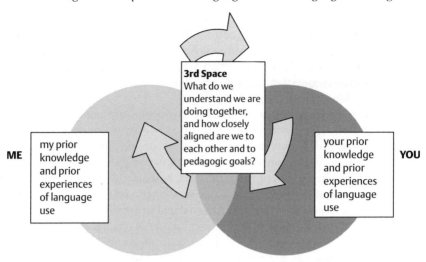

Figure 1.1   A sociocognitive 3rd place

(2003: 104) uses the term '3rd place' to point to the importance of what goes on between participants. In this section we investigate this 3rd place in terms of how it is shaped by the individual cognitions which resource it. This is very much a sociocognitive inquiry, because it has to do with how an individual's cognition contributes to what Atkinson (2002) calls 'joint cognition'. I provide a very general picture of the 3rd place and something of its immediate context in Figure 1.1.

Prior knowledge as a resource for scaffolding: an analytic perspective

I referred earlier to the importance attached in interactional competence to what Young (1999) refers to as 'the structure of *recurring* episodes of face-to-face interaction'. How do learners come to know such things, and how easy is such knowledge to acquire? In addressing these questions, we can usefully return for a moment to the data we examined earlier from Nassaji and Swain's (2000) study of scaffolding. In order for both interlocutors to participate effectively in scaffolded interaction, they need to have at least some degree of common access to an underlying frame. However, Nassaji and Swain's data is ambiguous in this respect since at least two possible interpretations can be applied to it.

One interpretation would be that the learner is familiar with the tutor's intended script from the outset, so that her failure to detect the nature of her error until line 15 can be taken as evidence that she 'needed several levels of help before she was able to discover and overcome the error' (Nassaji and Swain 2000: 40).

A second rendering of the data might run thus: the cues the tutor deploys at the outset of the interaction are simply too oblique to be understood, with the consequence that the learner is struggling to determine just what it is that the tutor wants from her, until the cues finally become more explicit. In addition, some of the learner's utterances are themselves open to misinterpretation. In line 8, for example, the learner may be asking the tutor whether the problem the tutor is referring to is the word 'Korean'. The tutor replies in line 9 by saying simply 'no'. This is in itself an ambiguous utterance which leads the learner to signal her uncertainty in line 10 ('No? uhm...'). The tutor then attempts to clarify in line 11. Then in line 12, for example, we find the learner wondering whether the tutor is querying her meaning (rather than her use of linguistic form), and so she attempts to clarify by saying that she is using the word 'Korea' to refer to the Korean people, rather than to Korea as a geographical entity. When the tutor finally clarifies that he wants to focus on grammar (line 15) the learner *immediately* self-corrects in line 16 ('of *the*? No?').

The immediacy with which the learner provides the correct form in line 16 suggests that she may have known the solution to this problem all along. If this is the case, the fact that the learner is able to indentify and correct the same error more quickly in her next encounter with the tutor (ibid. 41–2) may not be evidence of the tutor's prior scaffolding (as is suggested by Nassaji and Swain), but simply a reflection of prior knowledge combined with a clearer understanding of the goal of enterprise as a whole.

This second interpretation of Nassaji and Swain's data applies an analytic perspective because it sees the cognitive (in the guise of prior knowledge) and the social (in terms of social interaction and the pursuit of common ground) as separable, at least for the purposes of theoretical analysis. Furthermore, it does this in a way which allows us to examine how the cognitive influences the social, either in terms of a resource for the successful co-construction of mutual understanding in a 3rd place, or as a constraint which may prevent such an understanding from being reached.

Sociocognitive responsiveness

One possible reaction to this discussion of Nassaji and Swain's data would be to play down the possibilities for an absence of joint cognition, on the assumption that even if there is a lack of convergence, it is likely to be only a temporary one, because language learners very quickly learn the 'rules of the game'.

The notion that language learners can quickly adapt or adjust their knowledge in relation to experience, and that there is a close and ever-changing relationship between what learners know about language and how they experience language, is strongly associated with connectionism. Connectionists argue that knowledge exists only in the form of associations between neurons which, as soon as they are activated, combine in potentially limitless ways to perform specific activities, including both the production and comprehension of discourse (Rumelhart and McClelland 1986; N. Ellis 1998). The more frequently a learner encounters a particular sequence, the stronger the association becomes, and the easier to activate. Thus connectionism networks are seen as highly responsive to a person's experiences of language use: what we say and do is flexibly resourced by neural networks, whilst at the same time social interaction is endlessly creative and neural networks are responsive to this creativity through being continuously updated. As Larsen-Freeman (2007: 783) puts it, 'every use of language changes the language resources of the learner/user, and the changed resources are then potentially available for the next speech event'.

A somewhat different account of the relationship between knowledge and use is associated with the notion of the cognitive schema. Schemas reflect our recognition of recurring patterns in language use, and so include such matters as 'what topics will be raised, how they should be interpreted, and...the different orientations and discourse roles of the participants' (Bremer et al. 1996: 14). What marks them as distinct from connectionist networks is that schemas are seen as prototypically cognitive constructs which, (in contrast to the flexibility inherent in connectionism networks) can become strongly entrenched and therefore difficult to modify.

The issue of the degree to which the cognition and social context are flexibly and mutually modifying is an important one. Very roughly speaking, the greater the emphasis on flexibility, the more we are moving towards a holistic position which stresses the mutual dependency of cognition and language use in social contexts. Conversely, the more emphasis we place on a clear division between cognition and social context—such as might arise when particular schemas are resistant to change irrespective of the social conditions of language use—the more we find ourselves drawing on an analytic perspective.

The question of how easily learners are able to adapt to (and hence learn) new patterns of discourse is a very important one not only for sociocognition in general, but for language teaching and learning in particular. Hall (1995*a*: 218) argues that 'our [i.e. learners] becoming [effective] participants [in language use] involves three processes: the discovery (other- and self-guided) of interactive patterns in the practices in which we engage with others, observation and reflection of others' participatory moves and the responses to these moves; and our own active constructions of responses to these patterns'. The issue for language pedagogy is whether such learning is fast and flexible (so that one learns largely through observation and active involvement) or whether it requires careful and explicit teaching procedures. Slembrouck (2006) is one who takes this latter view, arguing that knowledge of how a particular form of discourse is structured 'may be taken for granted by one party but remain unknown to the other'. Similarly, Batstone (2006, 2007) argues that whilst some classroom interactive routines are simple and likely to have been learnt from an early age by the vast majority of learners, there are other forms of structured interaction, including some which involve the implicit provision of corrective feedback, which are a great deal more opaque, and which may well require explicit teaching.

Section 4 Sociocognition perspectives on the predictability of classroom tasks

Introduction

One of the defining beliefs underlying all forms of language teaching is that there is something about what teachers can do with learners—the kinds of methodological interventions they make, the ways in which they construct classroom cultures—which are distinct from and potentially improve upon what learners could do in naturalistic environments. And one of the aims of SLA theorizing, of course, is to suggest optimal forms of pedagogic intervention.

Over the past thirty years, the most influential strand of SLA theory in this regard has been cognitive SLA. To take just two examples (and to simplify things somewhat), research in cognitive SLA suggests that learners who engage either in pre-task planning or in task repetition are said to use language which is likely to be improved in terms of accuracy and/or complexity and/or fluency (R. Ellis 2003). As a result, planning and task repetition are now strongly recommended as important tools for task-based language teaching (e.g. Thornbury 2001). Underlying such recommendations is the belief that there is a causal link between engaging in certain forms of pre-task planning on the one hand, and the use of more accurate, fluent, or complex language on the other.

How reliable are recommendations of this kind? In a great many language classrooms across the globe, language teaching is structured in ways which presume that, generally speaking, the outcomes of classroom tasks can be predicted with reasonable accuracy. But what if the outcomes of tasks are not, generally speaking, as predictable as we might suppose? Even amongst those who work within a cognitive framework, there is concern that the generalization of static data has a way of masking very significant differences in the way individual learners handle a particular task (Foster 1998).

Sociocognitive approaches (whether holistic or analytic) would reject the idea that we can make predictions about the impact of a task per se as simplistic and unrepresentative. A sociocognitive view of language presupposes that interaction is a complex process where cognition is interdependent with social context, and it is this very interdependence which is the source of so much variation in the ways that language learners interpret classroom tasks.

I begin this section by reviewing some of the general theoretical claims made about causation and predictability from both a holistic and an analytic sociocognitive stance. I then turn to examine the different implications of these positions for language teaching, focusing in particular on the negotiable impact of tasks on learners' performance. I conclude by making some suggestions for future research.

Sociocognitive perspectives on predictability

Holistic claims for predictability

If we are looking for a theory rooted in holistic sociocognition which makes strong claims about the unpredictability of classroom tasks, we need look no further than complexity theory. Complexity theorists argue that complex systems—including the dynamics of language use and language learning—are non-linear. This means that the effects which result from a cause will not be proportional to that cause, with the consequence that 'a minor change can have global effects' (Larsen-Freeman 2002: 39). In complexity theory, says Larsen-Freeman (1997: 159), interaction is viewed as a complex system, and complex systems 'are comprised of many interacting parts, the behaviour of which (even the tiniest), when combined, is unpredictable'.[2]

A somewhat different perspective on change and the predictability of dynamic interaction comes from activity theory and the incorporation of insights from activity theory into sociocultural theory. Whereas complexity theory emphasizes that there is no difference in principle between biological and non-biological systems, activity theory stresses the central role played by human agency in striving to bring about particular outcomes in relation to personal goals.

Analytic claims for predictability

In analytic sociocognition we choose to focus on particular elements because we believe that the presence or absence of particular social and cognitive elements (or combinations of elements) act upon one another in ways which have discernible consequences or outcomes. We examined various manifestations of this earlier on in the chapter. We saw, for example, how learners' capacity to participate in mutually intelligible ways in a scaffolded interaction is aided or inhibited to a significant degree depending on the prior cognitive resources which they have at their disposal. We also looked at variationist perspectives which are quite clearly based on the view that particular aspects of a discourse such as social setting can exert a disproportionate effect, as Tarone persuasively argues in Chapter 4 below.

What distinguishes analytic sociocognition from holistic sociocognition, then, is the belief that there are certain elements within a dynamic and interactive system which have a disproportionate (although never entirely predictable) impact on the overall direction a discourse may take. Thus when Tarone (Ch. 4) talks about the impact of social setting, she is careful to point out that it is not the impact of the social setting per se which is of any interest, but the potential impact of social setting on the perceptions of those who interact within it.

Similarly when I argue that prior knowledge of discourse makes a major difference to a learner's capacity to participate in scaffolded interactions, it is not the presence or absence of knowledge per se which is significant. Clearly, this can only be true when a scaffolded interaction of this kind is underway, and only to the degree that a lack of prior knowledge of scaffolding procedures continues to have an impact on participants' capacity to co-construct an interactive scaffolding frame as the discourse proceeds (as was argued earlier). The analytic claim would be that the system is not as highly or as quickly responsive as scholars such as Larsen-Freeman would maintain.

Investigating the predictability of pedagogic interventions

Holistic sociocognition and pedagogic intervention: 'task' and 'activity'

Activity theorists discuss how the direction of classroom events emerges as participants negotiate a shared understanding of the ends and means of the activity they are engaged in—a process strongly influenced by each person's personal history, goals, and current abilities (Coughlan and Duff 1994; Roebuck 2000; Seedhouse 2005). Roebuck (2000: 84) neatly summarizes the task/activity distinction by noting that 'the task represents what the researcher... would like the learner to do, and activity is what the learner actually does'.

Coughlan and Duff illustrate the distinction between task and activity by drawing on data from structured interviews with four Hungarian students learning EFL at a secondary school in Hungary and one Cambodian immigrant to Canada. They focus on a task where the interviewer showed each learner a picture of a seaside beach scene and asked him or her to describe it. The authors note how their participants responded to the 'same' task in a variety of ways, with some providing a descriptive account of what they see in the picture, whilst others refer the picture to personal experience, hypothesizing about the identities of the people involved. They conclude that 'even with a single, relatively controlled task, a range of discourse types may result from subjects' multiple interpretations of that task' (Coughlan and Duff 1994: 185).

Analytic sociocognitive perspectives on pedagogic intervention

I suggested earlier that the 'task' perspective—i.e. the idea that we can make reasonably sound predictions about the effects of certain task designs—is likely to reflect a cognitive viewpoint, because it assumes that social factors play a negligible role in shaping the way learners respond to tasks. One could argue, though, that tasks do indeed often lead to a particular outcome in terms of learner behaviour, not because of any feature inherent to the task, but as a reflection of a tendency for learners to interpret a task in similar ways when classroom conditions (including teacher interventions) successfully encourage them to do so.

Much of the data provided in the study by Coughlan and Duff (1994) could very well be taken as evidence of the analytic position. One needs first to point out the obvious—that presented with a picture of a seaside resort, all the participants involved in the study referred (albeit selectively) to what they could see in the picture, suggesting that they had in common a sense of the limits governing how the task could reasonably and relevantly be interpreted. More specifically, it is interesting to see how responsive the participants were to comments made by the interviewer. Coughlan and Duff comment on how the Cambodian participant (known as 'JDB') constructed a discourse which was essentially an elaborated description—rather than, say, a narrative—producing 'what most researchers would consider a model picture description, rich with detail' (ibid. 180).

One factor which appears to have been instrumental in encouraging JDB's decision to emphasize the descriptive was the comments made by the interviewer. Coughlan and Duff explain: 'The interviewer...tells JDB that she wants him to "describe—a picture," and after a two second pause she adds "tell me, or make a story, about the picture." After another three second pause, she adds the word "anything"' (ibid. 179). The interviewer's comments are hardly extensive, yet they appear to have a very marked effect in orienting JDB. What possible implications might there be here for language teaching? The way the interviewer introduced the task parallels an important but much underrated role for classroom teachers in 'contextualizing' tasks before they are undertaken. I use the term 'contextualizing' advisedly, mindful of its meaning in discourse as something which is co-constructed (together with related goals and strategies) rather than something which pre-exists and has self-contained meaning (Gumperz 1982).

The analytic argument, then, is that tasks are always interpreted, but that learner interpretations of tasks can be influenced to a significant degree by teachers, not merely by announcing their purpose but by engaging in a process of co-contextualizing tasks in order to create a kind of 'pedagogic 3rd place' between teacher and learners where the aims and means of classroom tasks are negotiated and clarified.

Research issues arising for sociocognition

Second language teaching is based very largely on the assumption of a fairly clear relationship between classroom tasks and their outcomes. A comparison of cognitive with various forms of sociocognitive claims for the predictability of classroom tasks, however, suggests a range of opinions, many of which challenge current practice quite radically. Given the importance of the issue, we need a great deal more sustained and focused research which addresses the question of task predictability. We need to know more about the extent to which variation in the ways that learners interpret various kinds of task is beyond the reach of current pedagogic practices. We need to know more about how and to what extent teachers contextualize tasks and about the impact of different types of contextualization. We also need to investigate in a more coordinated fashion to what extent learners' personal sociohistories and goals are amenable to pedagogic direction, and whether the answer to such questions varies more or less significantly from one sociocultural setting to another.

Conclusion

Theorizing in SLA is currently at a crossroads. From a sociocognitive perspective, the time is very ripe for the development of new ideas and ways which ought to strike a chord with those many scholars over the years who have lamented the polarizing of our field into positions which are diametrically opposed (Larsen-Freeman 2007). And there is no better example of this than the gulf which exists between advocates of cognitive SLA and advocates of sociolinguistic approaches to understanding how second languages are learnt. Sociocognition provides a rich basis upon which to search for new areas of synthesis along the nexus between 'incommensurate' schools of thought, and thus it provides impetus for new research without becoming immediately vulnerable to cynical claims (not least from language teachers) that what we are doing here is simply pushing the pendulum one more time from one extreme to another.

Notes

1. The distinction between holistic and analytic sociocognition inevitably involves a degree of idealization. Both holistic and analytic elements, for example, can be found in sociocultural theory. Thus Lantolf and Thorne (2006: 165) argue that sociocultural theory is characterized by 'analytic dualism', in which 'it is possible to sustain an ontological unity of individual-world while at the same time allowing for analytical separability'.
2. It should be noted that Larsen-Freeman's treatment of complexity theory has elements of both holistic and analytic sociocognition. Holistically there is a strong emphasis on unpredictability, but this is coupled with the analytic view that we can look at language use in terms of the complexity of its interacting constituents.

2

Sociocognition: what it can mean for second language acquisition

DWIGHT ATKINSON

Imagine two people walking (Tomasello 2008). They are walking in the same direction, at the same pace, and close to each other. Suddenly Walker 1 slows down and turns into a doorway. What does Walker 2 do?

If Walker 2 *just happens* to be walking in the same direction, at the same pace, etc. as Walker 1, she will probably just keep walking, since both people exist in their own (more-or-less[1]) private worlds. If they are 'walking together', however, Walker 2 will almost certainly behave differently: she may slow down and follow Walker 1, or stop and call out, 'Where are you going?' or simply murmur, 'See you in 10,' and keep walking. Likewise, Walker 1 will almost certainly reciprocate—e.g. by holding the door open, stopping to explain, or murmuring back. To make a long scenario short, if both people are walking together, they inhabit the same social world—they are performing *social action* in a *social relationship*.

For pioneer sociologist Max Weber (1922/1978: 30), 'a social relationship may be said to exist when several people reciprocally adjust their behavior to each other with respect to the meaning...they give...it, and when this reciprocal adjustment determines the form...it takes'. In this chapter I aim to suggest how social relationships, so defined, along with certain other relationships I will describe, operate in the species of sociocognitive action known as SLA. More specifically, I: (1) review the conceptual basis of a sociocognitive approach to SLA; (2) introduce three core principles of this approach; (3) present three examples of potential sociocognitive activity in SLA; and (4) examine a mainstream SLA studies concept—attention—from a sociocognitive perspective.

Conceptual basis of a sociocognitive approach to SLA

The approach to SLA I support is based largely on *extended* and *embodied* conceptualizations of cognition. Given the relative newness of these views and their lack of influence on SLA studies to date, I summarize them here, connecting them to SLA later on.

Extended cognition sees everyday thought as deeply embedded in the ecosocial environment (A. Clark and Chalmers 1998). It is a response to *cognitivism*, the doctrine that the mind/brain is the sole (or solely important) source of cognition—a view which has dominated Western thought for the last four centuries, and especially the last fifty years (Atkinson forthcoming *a*). Significantly, two major expressions of twentieth-century cognitivism—cognitive psychology and generative linguistics—originally inspired SLA studies (e.g. Corder 1967) and continue to influence it today (Larsen-Freeman 2007).

Extended approaches to cognition help us rethink the mind–world relationship. Thus, ponder the physical environment's role in each of the following sociocognitive activities—i.e. activities in which mind, body, and ecosocial world function integratively:[2] We wake to a ringing alarm clock or sunlight peeking through the curtains; we grab our robe 'without thinking' from its usual spot in the closet; our toothbrush, toothpaste, hairbrush, soap, and washcloth come almost magically to hand in the bathroom, requiring minimal cognitive effort to locate them; back in the closet, the day's wardrobe is easily chosen from the highly organized array of clothes; once dressed, we check our watch to confirm we're on schedule and then follow the hallway (rather than navigating a series of rooms) to the kitchen, itself a virtual material mnemonic: the cereal is in the cupboard by the stove, the bowls in the cupboard above it, the spoons in the counter drawer below the first cupboard, and the milk on the top shelf in the fridge. Finishing breakfast, we peek outside to know if we need a coat or umbrella, grab our keys and wallet from the stand by the door, and head to work.

Such examples can be multiplied endlessly—e.g. cognition-for-driving-to-work relies on the road grid, traffic lights, signage, traffic reports, and actual flow of traffic—but I hope the implications are clear: Everyday cognition is pervasively integrated with a broad array of *cognitive technologies* (A. Clark 2001) and natural *affordances* (Gibson 1979)—worldly phenomena which initiate, organize, and enhance our cognitive processes.

A second sense in which cognition is extended—and one especially important for SLA—is through communicative practices. Conversations and meetings, for example, deeply complement our naked cognitive resources by enabling the shared construction of meaning and knowledge. Thus, we commonly 'talk out our problems' in conversation with friends and 'put our heads together' in meetings to reach group decisions. In fact, a nearly infinite variety of socially constituted groups help us think and act better/differently than we usually can alone: support groups, advocacy groups, work groups, study groups, reading groups, writing groups, meditation groups, therapy groups, research groups, hobby clubs, political parties, and academic associations, to name a few. None of this is to argue that humans *can't* (sometimes) solve their problems individually—or, for that matter, survive without well-ordered closets or kitchens. But the fact that everyday cognition pervasively incorporates the environment is surely more than incidental. In short, we think *with* the world, not in isolation from it.

Embodied cognition is the understanding that: 'The brain is … part of an integrated dynamic system devoted to the moment-to-moment embodied dynamics of everyday life. Viewing the brain simply as an information-processing or computational device, as the center of cognition, ignores the centrality of animate form in human thought' (Gibbs 2005: 6). Cognition, in brief, is fundamentally embodied. If its main evolved function is to maximize environmental adaptivity (e.g. Barselou 2008), then cognition serves directly to keep our bodies viable. Conversely, our bodies inform our cognitive processes at every turn, or, to put it more radically, are an inextricable part of cognition.

There is a great deal of empirical evidence for embodied cognition, starting with the finding that, far from being independent systems, perception, cognition, and motor action are complexly intertwined. An important discovery in this regard has been *mirror neurons*—neurons in the premotor and parietal cortex of the brain which fire both when observing actions being performed by others, and when performing those same actions oneself (Rizzolatti and Craighero 2004; Iacoboni 2009). This suggests a neural mechanism for directly comprehending others' actions and intentions, versus the cognitivist assumption of elaborate, abstract, and decontextualized cognitive representations or world models. Mirror neurons may further provide a neural basis for imitative learning and behavioral synchronization.

In fact, the most relevant evidence for embodied cognition vis-à-vis SLA/learning may concern behavioral synchronization. There is plentiful evidence that human interaction is intimately coordinated, especially face-to-face. Thus, we: smile, laugh, frown, and talk in close entrainment with others; alternate turn-taking in speech and other cooperative endeavors; adopt congruent postures; tune our emotions sensitively to those of others; and accommodate our language styles to those of our interlocutors (Collins 2004; Giles and Ogay 2007; Semin and Smith 2008; Kinsbourne and Jordan 2009). Reasons underlying such synchronization are clear: It is the social manifestation of moment-to-moment environmental adaptivity. In a complex and ever-changing ecosocial environment, we must constantly be prepared to make common cause, whether in performing collaborative social action (e.g. moving a large boat, planning a family reunion), defending against mutual danger (e.g. by speeding up or slowing down synchronously on the freeway), or simply acknowledging the existence of socially meaningful others (e.g. via daily greetings), thus enhancing the future likelihood of cooperation when needed.[3] Similarly, being sensitively attuned to others' responses to the non-human environment helps guide our own (e.g. if the car ahead swerves to avoid something I can't see, I will likely swerve too, or at least slow down).

Although the physiological mechanisms for behavioral synchrony are not yet well understood, recent theories give mirror neurons a central role (e.g. Semin and Cacioppo 2008). That is, if many of the same neural circuits are dedicated to both perceiving others' actions and performing similar actions ourselves, a neurological basis exists for highly tuned behavioral synchrony.

Other forms of cognitive representation[4] doubtless also participate in complex synchronization, but the discovery of mirror neurons suggests that cognition is significantly less abstract, decontextualized, top-down, and significantly more embodied and distributed than traditionally assumed.

Three principles of a sociocognitive approach to SLA

In Atkinson (submitted) I present three principles of a sociocognitive approach to SLA: (1) the *Inseparability Principle*—mind, body, and world work together in SLA; (2) the *Learning-is-adaptive Principle*—the main purpose of SLA/learning is to support adaptivity to complex and dynamic ecosocial environments; and (3) the *Alignment Principle*—the processes by which we continuously adapt to our environment constitute a major engine of SLA. Here, I briefly review Principles 1 and 2 before focusing on the Alignment Principle—the key principle since it posits actual learning mechanisms.

The Inseparability Principle, as Batstone put it in an earlier version of his Chapter 1, describes a 'holistic' approach to sociocognition in which 'the social and the cognitive are indivisible and can only be properly understood by keeping their essential unity intact'. This fairly captures the Inseparability Principle, if 'body' and 'environment' are added to 'social' and 'cognitive'. The resulting formulation might be: 'Mind, body, and ecosocial world are inseparable contributors to SLA processes, so to understand such processes these elements must be considered together.' The standard scientific strategy of decomposability (Haugeland 1998) is therefore ruled out—extracting one or another element from mind-body-world denatures the whole. Extended and embodied approaches to cognition represent the main conceptual basis for this principle, which also has roots in continental philosophy.

The Inseparability Principle causes all-too-apparent difficulties for the study of SLA. Treating mind-body-world as a functional unit radically alters cognition conceptually and our means of studying it methodologically. We do not even possess an agreed-upon descriptive vocabulary, forcing terminological reliance on the very paradigms we seek to 'trouble'. Yet if mind-body-world really is a functional unit in SLA—or we just wish to test this claim—then SLA must be studied as such despite the obvious difficulties (see Atkinson forthcoming *b* for conceptual and methodological approaches, and Kingstone, Smilek, and Eastwood 2008 for a defense of holistic sociocognitive research).

The Learning-is-adaptive Principle: This principle extends the claim that cognition's main function is ecological—i.e. subserves adaptive action. That is, if extended, embodied cognition enables humans to adapt to their ecosocial environments, and if learning is a cognitive process, then learning is adaptive. This is, of course, mere common sense—learning is largely a process of better adapting to our ecosocial environments. Yet mainstream learning theory, including in SLA studies, seems to tacitly assume the opposite—that learning occurs largely for its own sake. This, at least, is the message I take from rigid dichotomies of acquisition vs. use and competence vs. performance, as well as from radically internalist models of SLA (e.g. Gass 1997). More generally, mainstream learning theory conceptualizes learning as progressive extraction/separation of knowledge *from* the environment, rather than as building and deepening connections *with/in* it.

The Alignment Principle: Weber's (1922/1978) definition of 'social relationship', quoted above, provides crucial conceptual support for this principle. Erickson (1986: 128) elaborates: 'Standing somewhere...is a behavior. Standing in line, however, is social action, according to Weber's definition, because it is meaningfully oriented to the actions of others in the scene.' Other participants in the social scene are therefore 'part of ego's social ecology'—participants 'constitute environments for each other'. Weber's insight, then, is that social meaning is radically *co-constructed*: the intelligibility (and effectiveness) of social action relies on the ongoing framing and negotiation of meaning *across* social actors, as well as cognitive technologies and affordances, regarding 'what it is that's going on here' (Goffman 1974/1986: 8). Meaning is thus a property of the whole ecological system rather than of individual cognition.

But *how* is such meaning constructed—what are the mechanisms behind social meaning? Obviously, language plays a central role, yet language is just the crowning achievement of a profound interactive meaning-making capacity developed over our whole species-history, without which language is impossible. Levinson (2006; see also Tomasello 2008) dubs this capacity the 'interaction engine'—the evolutionarily accumulated suite of abilities which make us the 'spectacularly social species' (Kinsbourne and Jordan 2009: 104) that we are. These include: (1) *theory of mind*—our ability to attribute 'minds like ours' to others and to act on that basis; (2) *mutual salience-producing simulation*—our ability to know what others know about our knowing, thereby enabling 'mental coordination without communication' (Levinson 2006: 54); (3) *Gricean intentions*—'intentions that drive behaviors whose sole function is...having those intentions recognized' (ibid.); and (4) *multimodal interactive practices*—behaviors such as turn-taking and repair (recall that Levinson claims these phenomena *preexist* speech) which promote communication through close temporal sequencing of behavior, as well as provide opportunities to backtrack, question, and clarify behavioral meaning.

The interaction engine notion is a powerful one—it explains crucial elements of communication in all its forms. At the same time, it is 'cognitively rich' (Tomasello 2008) and 'ecosocially poor', insufficiently acknowledging the importance of sociocognitive practice. If meaning is substantially shared, public, and participatory, as Weber argues, it must also be (at least partly) visible, or at any rate perceivable. Put specifically in terms of embodiment, 'the positioning, actions, and orientation of the body in the environment are crucial to how participants understand what is happening and build action together' (Goodwin 2003: 20). Yet the body is just part of a complex multimodal signifying capacity: 'Rather than being lodged in a single modality...many forms of human action are built through the juxtaposition of quite diverse materials, including the actor's body, the bodies of others, language, structure in the environment, and so on' (ibid. 22–3).

Alignment, then, is the means by which social actors participate in the ongoing construction of social meaning and action in public/sociocognitive space. In mutually attending, negotiating, sharing information and emotions, solving interactional/communicative problems, building participation frameworks, interacting with their extended cognitive surroundings, etc., social actors dynamically adapt to their environments, creating shared meaning in mind-body-world. Behavioral synchrony—the ability to align our thoughts and actions inter-individually so that they become *shared* thoughts and actions—is a sociocognitive ability; it involves both the cooperative skills comprising the interaction engine and extended, embodied cognition.

My colleagues and I have proposed that alignment, so conceptualized, is a major mechanism of SLA (Atkinson et al. 2007). By participating in the ongoing construction of meaning in sociocognitive space, we learn *how* to mean in an L2. That is, we learn 'the differences that make a difference' (Bateson 1972: 459)—the social signifying practices particular to the ecosocial environment of which the second language is part. But we do this not as *tabulae rasae*—we bring powerful interaction engines to the task.

Examples of alignment for sociocognitive SLA

Space does not permit detailed exemplification of sociocognitive SLA here (see Atkinson et al. 2007, Churchill et al. in press, Atkinson forthcoming *d* for such examples). This is unfortunate, because the essence of alignment is in the details. I nevertheless provide three brief illustrations which suggest processes and mechanisms of SLA 'in flight'—i.e. as it may occur in meaning-*full* interaction.[5]

The first illustration, although emanating from a non-SLA context, shows one means by which L2 features may become publicly 'visible' and thus learnable in the course of natural conversation. Goodwin (1980, 1981) discovered that speakers construct their utterances in sensitive alignment with conversational partners, resulting in significant modifications to those utterances. For example, speakers tend to break off speaking when, as they start an utterance and gaze at their interlocutor, they find the latter not gazing back in return. They then 'restart' their utterance, apparently as a means of attaining the interlocutor's gaze. Restarts, which also typically involve 'self-repair' (Schegloff, Sacks, and Jefferson 1977), therefore represent a means of orienting listeners to the message being produced. Consider the following, wherein the 'IG' marks the initiation of interlocutor gaze, and the solid line its continuation:

(1)   A   We went t- I went to bed really early last night
       B   IG _____

                                        (Goodwin 1980: 275, 2006: 101)

Here, the speaker presumably stops short on *t-* after having brought her gaze to the interlocutor and found him not gazing back, and then continues with *I* as she attains his gaze.[6] Apart from its role in conversation management, this procedure has twofold potential as a learning device (Goodwin 2006): (1) The constituent structure 'X went to' is indicated by a break in the utterance's intonation contour (not shown in example), thus addressing the basic language learning problem of how to deduce constituent structure from a continuous speech stream (Doughty 2003);[7] and (2) Contrasting options for the same grammatical slot are presented: *We* and *I* are both offered as subjects of *went to*, thus exemplifying both the grammatical slot and two of its candidate fillers. Of course, such learning would likely take place across many tokens/repetitions and be probabilistically based (Seidenberg and MacDonald 1999), but the main point for present purposes is that language learning can occur as a natural consequence of interaction—interaction which makes the formal structure of utterances publicly available. It should likewise be noted that such learning opportunities are the product not of single, isolated cognitive apparatuses,[8] but of two individuals performing joint action as a sociocognitive unit.

My second illustration comes from the English as a Foreign Language (EFL) tutoring session analyzed by Atkinson et al. (2007: 175). Here, a Japanese junior high school student ('Ako') is completing a grammar worksheet assignment with the help of her aunt ('Tomo'), an experienced EFL teacher. In (2) below, they translate a sentence into English in which the target structure is the present-perfect construction, 'Have you ever X'. Of interest here again is the public structure of the interaction, and how it allows Ako to participate fluently and in fact (co-)arrive at the correct translation.

(2)[9]

1   A   ((Reads first part of exercise item quickly under her breath))
        >°Anata wa ima made ni eigo de tegami°< (2.0) Ima made ni=
            [Lit: You [SUBJ] ever in English letter]   Ever

2   T   ((Softly shadowing A's volume, intonation, and bodily
          orientation))
        =°Un ima made°
            Right, ever

3   (1.0)

4   A   [Ne:ba:
            Never

5   T   [>Sakki no tsukaeba iin janai?< ((Searching unsuccessfully for
          earlier item on worksheet, using pen as pointer))
            Why not use the one you used before?

6   A   Ima made (.8) ne- e:va ka
            Ever.   Ne- ever?

7   T   Have you ever toka nantoka=
            Have you ever blank

8   A   =Have you eva writu, written=
        Have you ever write, written
9   T   =Un.
        Right.

In line 1 Ako begins by reading part of the sentence aloud from the work-sheet and then repeats the time adverbial *ima made ni* ('ever'); by so doing she 'externalizes' her cognitive activity/attentional focus into public, socio-cognitive space, thereby enabling extended cognition across herself, Tomo, and the grammar worksheet. In line 2, Tomo confirms (and thereby further co-constructs) Ako's focus in a highly public, synchronized, and multi-modal way, i.e. by mirroring her words, intonation, volume, and physical orientation. In line 4, Ako takes her first stab at translating the adverbial, venturing the inaccurate *neba* ('never'), to which Tomo responds not by directly flagging the error but by suggesting a form of extended cogni-tion—that Ako look for the answer in a previously completed exercise item—while simultaneously embodying her solution in physical space by searching for the item with her pen. But Tomo is unable to find the item, and in line 6 Ako produces the adverbial's correct translation, *eva* ('ever'). Tomo responds by radically reducing the sociocognitive 'problem space' for translating the sentence—she builds Ako's answer into a sentence stem complete with a blank to be filled with the correct principal part of the verb (an especially difficult part of this exercise, at least for Ako, as other episodes in the tutoring session reveal): *I have never toka nantoka* ('I have never blank'). Ako instantaneously responds by repeating the sentence stem and filling the blank, first with the inaccurate (but still targetlike) *writu* ('write'), and then with the correct *written* (line 8). In proceeding in this way, it is notable that Ako employs the same basic process she used in line 6 of first externalizing a candidate answer into sociocognitive space and only then adjusting it for accuracy.

This too-brief and coarse-grained description is nonetheless suggestive for sociocognitive SLA. Ako is a low-level learner, yet she actively and success-fully participates in translating the sentence. She does so, obviously, in part through the expert scaffolding of her aunt. But what is particularly interest-ing is *how* she does it—by continuously aligning in sociocognitive space with her aunt and the item on the worksheet. More accurately, all three collude in enabling convergence on the correct answer, the production of which must therefore be attributed to the full mind-body-world ecology in which Ako, Tomo, and the worksheet are major elements.

My third and final illustration again concerns the tutoring session between Ako and Tomo, but this time involves meaning-focused (vs. grammar-based) interaction. During the session, and immediately upon completing a work-sheet item, Tomo sometimes tried to engage Ako in real-world communication using the target form. This is the case in (3), where the answer to the just-completed item was the question, 'How long have you been busy'?

(3)
1   T   Been busy un. (3.5) ((Speaks with great feeling)) ∘For a long
        time ne? (2.8) Kotaeta no kizuita. ((Leans toward A, laughing
        slightly)) I have been busy for a long time.∘
        Been busy, right. For a long time, right? Did you realize that
        I answered? I have been busy for a long time.
2   A   ((Nods and chuckles while writing down answer on worksheet))
        For a long time ∘kaku no ka to omotta∘
        I thought I was supposed to write 'for a long time.'
3   T   ((Laughingly)) >Chigau chigau chigau< ((A laughs slightly)) How
        long have you been <u>busy</u>. ((Points to A with pen)) (.8) <u>Chitt</u>omo
        I have never been busy desho. (1.5) How long have you been busy.
        (.5) ((Pokes A with pen)) ∘Ako-san.∘
                No, no, no! How long have you been busy?
                'Never ever, I have never been busy,' right? How long have you
                been busy, Ako-san?
        (1.5)
4   A   ((Still looking at exercise sheet)) I havu been busy for two/i/ weeks
        ((Shifts gaze to T and laughs energetically))
5   T   Nande nani de, for whatto. (.5) How come [why
        Why? From what? For what? How come?   Why?
6   A   [I am sleep
7   T   Sleep de, hai.
        Ok, from sleeping
8   A   Yes yes ((laughs))   (Atkinson forthcoming *d*)

In line 1, Tomo attempts to shift the 'definition of the situation' (Goffman
1972) from grammar-exercise completion to conversational sharing of personal information and feelings. Thus, after a lengthy pause, she answers the
question they have just co-constructed ('How long have you been busy'?)
with great feeling, probably reflecting her extremely stressful personal life
(see Atkinson forthcoming *d*). When Ako doesn't respond, Tomo leans close
and asks if Ako realizes that she (Tomo) has just answered the question. Ako
responds that she thought she was being told to write something, thus indicating that she is still operating in the situational domain of the grammar
exercise. Tomo answers with an energetic and playful denial in line 3, eliciting
a slight laugh from Ako, and then poses the question to Ako: 'How long have
you been busy?' while pointing at her with her pen. But Ako, her gaze still
fixed on the grammar worksheet item, does not answer. After a short pause,
Tomo then answers *for* Ako, also apparently teasing her for her lazy reputa-
tion: *Chittomo I have never been busy desho* ('Never ever I have never been
busy, right?'). She then pauses, apparently expecting an answer, but none
comes. Finally, Tomo restates the question, pauses for half a second, and
pokes Ako with the non-writing end of her pen while addressing her with the
notably formal *Ako-san*.[10]

After a longish pause, and still gazing at the worksheet, Ako answers *I have been busy for two/i/ weeks*, shifts her gaze to Tomo, and laughs energetically. Tomo follows up in line 5 with *Nande nani de, for whatto. How come why* ('Why? From what? For what? How come? Why?'), to which Ako answers *I am sleep*. Tomo then acknowledges Ako's answer with *Sleep de, hai* ('Ok, from sleeping'), which Ako confirms with *Yes yes*.

The main points of interest in this example are: (1) Tomo's various strategies for gaining Ako's alignment vis-à-vis the question she is asking, which are perhaps the more evident for Ako's unwillingness or inability to align. Thus, Tomo begins by answering the just-constructed grammar-item question with emotion, apparently trying to signal a redefinition of the situation and engage Ako, then seeks Ako's acknowledgment of her action. She next poses the same question to Ako while pointing at her with her pen, and, on receiving no response, proceeds to answer the question *for* Ako. She then restates the question, and with no answer forthcoming, pokes Ako with the pen and addresses her with marked and distancing politeness. It is only then that Ako responds and a brief conversation ensues; (2) although seamless alignment is not exemplified here, it is noteworthy that Ako, a low-level learner of English, ends up engaging in real-world L2 communication, however slowly and perhaps effortfully—she therefore eventually aligns; and (3) having stated that Ako's alignment is slow and seemingly effortful, I must add that in virtually all other ways *except* answering Tomo's question in English, A is a fully aligned participant in the interaction—she nods, chuckles, and answers in line 2, laughs slightly in response to Tomo's laughing denial in line 3, and then responds to Tomo in English in lines 4, 6, and 8. This is therefore a prime example of the workings of Levinson's interaction engine, revealing the vast machinery that underlies communication, and on which, I would claim, SLA is also built.

A sociocognitive approach to cognitivist SLA concepts: the case of attention

So far, I have presented the sociocognitive approach to SLA I favor largely on its own terms. The question might arise, however, as to what this approach can offer *other* perspectives on SLA. Here, I explore this question by taking a major concept from cognitivist/mainstream SLA studies, *attention,* and subjecting it to sociocognitive reanalysis. Naturally, doing so can only be suggestive of broader applications of my approach as I treat but a single example.

The twin concepts of noticing and attention—major theoretical contributors to current mainstream/cognitivist SLA studies—were developed by Schmidt (e.g. 1990, 2001) on the basis of two self-conducted case studies and reviews of the cognitive psychology literature. Schmidt's claim is that noticing and attention are necessary for virtually all aspects of SLA, with 'noticing' signifying conscious awareness of linguistic surface feature characteristics. For Schmidt, noticing is the subjective correlate of attention, which is a collection of internal cognitive processes. As Schmidt (2001: 3–4) explains, one important goal of his work on attention is:

> To provide some details of the role of attention as that fits within a broader cognitive approach to understanding SLA, one that relies on the mental processes of language learners as the basic explanation of learning. I am particularly concerned with those mental processes that are conscious, under the working hypothesis that SLA is largely driven by what learners pay attention to and notice in target language input and what they understand the significance of noticed input to be.

It is incontrovertible that attention involves internal mental processes, and is sometimes at least conscious (Koch and Tsuchiya 2006). But focusing *only* on these aspects leaves aside much of interest and importance. In the following two subsections, I explore attention from a sociocognitive perspective.

Attention is adaptive

We devote attentional resources to something not because it exists, but because it is potentially important for our survival and prosperity—i.e. attention is adaptive. Put differently, attention is an *ecological relationship* rather than a 'lonely' mental phenomenon, connecting minds via bodies to (attentionally selected aspects of) ecosocial worlds. Put differently once again, 'attention is preparatory for action' (Kinsbourne and Jordan 2009: 105).

Kingstone et al. (2008) discuss personal (i.e. whole-person-in-ecosocial-context) vs. subpersonal (i.e. brain-internal) perspectives on attention in suggesting what ecologically valid cognitive research can add to laboratory-based experiments. They point out that subpersonal perspectives cannot answer questions regarding *why* attentional processes operate as they do in the real world, or *how* these processes relate to other human processes (ibid. 325).

As evidence that attention needs to be studied at the personal as well as subpersonal levels in SLA research, one might reverse the order of Schmidt's research trajectory and return to the case studies that initially inspired his theory. Schmidt (1983) first introduced noticing to explain the SLA of 'Wes', a 33-year-old Japanese man learning English 'naturalistically' as he gradually relocated from Japan to Hawai'i over a three-year period. Wes adopted a striking L2 learning strategy, appearing to learn multi-word formulas (e.g. *So, what's new? You know what I mean?*) over morphological and syntactic rules, and relied on those formulas to communicate with undeniable effectiveness in his extremely active personal and professional life.[11] Yet, for Schmidt, Wes was ultimately an unsuccessful language learner—he learned relatively few rule-governed aspects of English, which Schmidt speculated was due to his unwillingness to attend to that core part of language.[12]

Schmidt followed up this study by investigating his own learning of Brazilian Portuguese during a five-month stay in Brazil (Schmidt and Frota 1986). Starting three weeks after his arrival, Schmidt attended 50 hours of language classes, and throughout his stay he interacted intensively with Brazilians in Portuguese. Simultaneously, Schmidt kept a detailed language learning diary, and recorded four 'conversations' with his Brazilian co-author over the five-month period.

Perhaps unsurprisingly, Schmidt and his co-author found that many of the linguistic forms he noted being exposed to in his diary also turned up in their conversations. This may be unsurprising because, as Schmidt himself admits, he approached learning Portuguese as a professional linguist—he tried to learn the language system consciously and explicitly. This is well exemplified in excerpts from his diary:

Week 4: At the end of class, [the teacher] put the paradigm for SER on the board.... Great! This is better than *bom dia* ['Good day'—the students had been asked to greet and introduce themselves to each other] and then silence. (243)

Week 6: The last thing he corrected was *estava* (ESTAR + imperfect) *meu aluno* to *era* (SER + imperfect) *meu aluno*. I know I have problems with that. How does a permanent state of affairs become past tense? (260)

Week 7: Since we don't have a real grammar book [in class]...I've been organizing my own, mostly verb tables, vocabulary lists, and whatever comes up in class that's interesting. I review these every day on the bus. (245)

Week 9: I had no idea that I had been leaving out my copulas! Why haven't I been aware of it? Why hasn't someone corrected me? Why am I forgetting them anyway? I suppose it's the influence of Arabic again. Damn it, why can't I keep these two languages apart? (261)

Week 19: G told a joke.... What I don't understand is why *era* would be the preferred form in the first place. If it's got to be a form of SER, why not *fui* (SER + perfect)? (260)

Week 22: In our session S told me she was robbed last week at knife-point. I just told M about that and said *ela tada assaltada*? Probably not *foi*. I think the only time I've ever heard *foi* as the past of SER is in *foi um barato*. (260)

In its own way, Schmidt's approach to SLA seems as radical as Wes's, suggesting as it does that language learning is a matter of consciously understanding rules. In fact, Schmidt's approach seems *more* radical in that it assigns equal weight to linguistic analysis and communication—surely few L2 learners have any particular interest in linguistics. Nor are they professional linguists undertaking natural experiments in language learning.

Given the above, it is perhaps no coincidence that Schmidt and Frota's results—and the attention-based theory that followed—fit hand-in-glove with Schmidt's 'professional linguist' approach to L2 learning. To say that noticing/attention is necessary for SLA is to confirm, practically speaking, Schmidt's approach to learning Portuguese: that explicit attention to linguistic detail matters. And herein lies the crux of my point: What really matters to a person—what is *adaptive*—is what gets attended. In this sense, attention is outward-looking—an ecological relationship, as mentioned above. Both

Schmidt and Wes learned their target languages in ways that were personally relevant and personally adaptive.

Attention is jointly constructed and distributed

In social relationships, including teaching and learning, attention is socially tuned and socially constructed—it is more than the product of individual minds. In fact, all forms of sociality are marked by 'mutual orientation in a rich interactive environment' (Goodwin 2006: 97); indeed, this is largely Weber's point in his definition of social relationships discussed earlier. To interact with someone, we need to share a common 'definition of the situation' (Goffman 1972) and 'joint attentional frame' (Tomasello 2008), and these frameworks for understanding are interactively constructed. This leads to self and other being, to use different researchers' terms, *jointly committed* (H. Clark 2006), *mutually oriented* (Goodwin 2006), *intersubjective* (Zlatev et al. 2008), *synchronized* (Semin and Cacioppo 2008), or *aligned* (Atkinson et al. 2007). Semin and Cacioppo (2008: 123), for their part, define synchronization as:

jointly and simultaneously recruited sensorimotor processes that are evident in a neurophysiological mirroring of the producer by the perceiver. . . . These processes link two or more human agents, thereby putting them on a similar footing. It is jointly recruited processes with overlapping 'identities' that facilitate understanding (co-cogitation) and adaptive co-action (co-regulation) between two or more individuals. In other words, such mechanisms facilitate reaching a state of correspondence between the individuals. What counts for the one member may not have initially counted for the other, but through interaction these two become synchronized to approach being on the same page—that is . . . what counts for one individual also counts for the other. Such synchronization can occur without the presence of explicit intent or goals.

While synchronization processes doubtless include more than joint attention, such attention is necessary for successful social interaction. That is, social actors must orient to the environment in the same general way if adaptive social action is to occur: To perform cooperative social action, one must be attending to the same stimuli at the same time in the same basic fashion— they must be meaningful in the same basic way.

Two examples may make this point clearer. The first comes from Herbert Clark's (2006) research on social commitments, in which two individuals ('Burton' and 'Ann') are asked to assemble a wooden television stand together. Besides the general definition of the situation and participation framework which Burton and Ann need to negotiate and jointly maintain, they must also ensure the 'joint salience' (p. 135) of situational features, as in (4):[13]

(4)   BURTON   ∘Now let's do this one∘ ((picks up top piece))
      ANN   Okay   (p. 135)

While Clark provides few multimodal details of this interaction, a likely scenario can be constructed based on other empirical work (e.g. Goodwin

1981, 2000): as Burton speaks and picks up the top piece, his gaze likely shifts from the piece itself to Ann, and then back to the piece in preparing to work with it. As Ann answers *Okay*, she likely focuses her gaze first on Burton and then on the piece. Once mutual attention has been established by such means, assembly using the piece can begin. Through the participants' co-actions, as well as more general mutual orientation to performing the larger action they're engaged in, shared attention is produced within a participation framework.

As a second example of sociocognitively constructed joint attention—and one directly featuring L2 teaching/learning—consider again the first episode from the Ako–Tomo tutoring session, given in (2) above. As suggested previously, this episode involves the construction, maintenance, and development of shared attention. Thus, in line 1 Ako commences work on the sentence to be translated by reading the first part of it aloud from the worksheet. By so doing, she focuses not just her own attention but also Tomo's on the sentence, thereby creating a joint or shared attentional focus. Ako then narrows this focus to a single grammatical element—the sentence's time adverbial—by repeating it. It must be added that Ako had previously been taught to use time adverbials as cues for determining English verb tenses, the latter activity (along with choosing the verb's proper form) being the main pedagogical point of the exercise item here being worked on. Ako's attention has thus already been 'socialized' (Zukow-Goldring and Ferko 1994). Her immediate focus on the adverbial has been further promoted[14] by the grammar worksheet section immediately preceding the one she is currently working on—there, the task was to convert sentences with simple past tense verbs into sentences with present perfect verbs, using highlighted time adverbials as prompts.

In lines 3 and 4, Tomo plays her own substantial part in constructing/confirming the shared focus of attention: She multimodally confirms Ako's choice of the time adverbial as a good place to start translating, as described previously. Much of the rest of this episode involves the ongoing focusing of shared attention on various aspects of the grammar-translation task; e.g. in line 7, Tomo projects a proposal—that Ako use an already-answered exercise item as a model for the current one—into physical space by tracing the path of her search for the item with the tip of her pen. In so doing, she further directs and focuses their mutual attention.

While this example deals directly with L2 teaching/learning, it might still seem distant from Schmidt's position. Schmidt's claim is that SLA results not just from *any* attention, but a particular type: attention to linguistic features wherein learners at least sometimes identify mismatches between forms held in long-term memory and forms in the input. Two points can be made here: (1) As argued above, different kinds of attention may result in different kinds of language learning. Thus, Wes's attention, which certainly appears to have facilitated strong communicative skills, was focused not on discrete grammar but on socially useful formulas. It therefore appears that our concept of attention-for-language-learning may need to be expanded; (2) Even Schmidt's own notion of grammatically focused attention certainly needs to be broadened to include more than simple comparison of forms. How can one know, for instance, that two forms are directly comparable without also being aware of correspondence in their meaning/use? It therefore seems that meaning and form in attention cannot simply be separated. If this is true, then the ecosocial context's contribution to meaning will have to be factored in.

A final point—and one which Schmidt (2001) alludes to in passing—is that attentional resources can be externally augmented, thereby ameliorating if not bypassing the problem cognitive psychologists identify at the heart of attention—its severely limited and therefore highly selective character. Extended cognition, in fact, is a substantive response to such cognitivist claims—if cognition (including attention) can be offloaded onto the environment, then onboard cognitive resources can be devoted to other things. The grammar worksheet used by Ako and Tomo—not to mention Tomo herself—is just such an extended attentional device: it incorporates techniques such as textual highlighting which allow its users to focus their attention on other things. Simply the literate character of the worksheet makes it a formidable attention-enhancer—the printed word allows enhancement and freeing of attention that would otherwise be difficult or impossible without it.

Conclusion

In this chapter, I have sketched an SLA approach which attempts to study the mind as it extends into the body and ecosocial world. Most uses of the term 'sociocognitive' stop well short of this point, still relying in one way or other on the old and inadequate cognitive/social division. Descartes's substance dualism is alive and well in SLA studies, even as it is actively being rejected across large parts of cognitive science. To move forward in understanding the complexly reticulated ecological phenomenon of SLA, we should follow suit.

Notes

1. I add 'more-or-less' because even mere proximity activates pro-social awareness, as noted by Collins (2004: 53).
2. The 'sociocognitive activities' I mention here are obviously culture-specific. This has little bearing on my larger point.
3. It is therefore significant that unconscious behavioral 'mimicry' increases the mimicker's trustworthiness and likeability (van Baaren et al. 2004).
4. The concept of 'representation' is a controversial one in cognitive science. Kinsbourne and Jordan's (2009 n. 1) position is basically the one I adopt here.
5. The standard (if ideal) acquisition criterion in SLA studies is of course a 'smoking gun' or final proof of acquisition, typically as measured by a discrete-point test. While simply dismissing this criterion would be unwise, it appears to have serious problems as currently operationalized, as discussed in Doughty (2003) and Norris and Ortega (2000).

6. I write 'presumably' here because Goodwin does not give complete information on this example in either of the two articles in which it appears. The example is therefore partly reconstructed from these two articles.

7. Goodwin (2006) points out that one need not know a language to be sensitive to intonation contour breaks in it. This appears to be an example of Levinson's interaction engine at work.

8. This is exactly how false starts and other speech dysfluencies have been treated in mainstream language processing research—as indicators, for example, of insufficient cognitive planning (Goodwin 1980).

9. This transcript uses the transcription conventions developed by Gail Jefferson for conversation analysis (see Ochs, Schegloff, and Thompson 1996: 461–5). Here is a basic list:

,	Non-final/continuing intonation followed by short pause
.	Final falling intonation followed by pause
?	Final rising intonation followed by pause
:	Phoneme lengthening
(( ))	Non-linguistic event descriptions
( )	Transcriber doubt
(0.6)	Pauses timed by 10ths of second
=	'Latching', i.e. second speaker's turn begins without pause after first speaker's
[	Overlap of one speaker's turn by another's
>No<	Diamond brackets enclose talk which is faster than surrounding talk
∘No∘	Degree signs enclose talk which is quieter than surrounding talk
<u>No</u>	Underlining marks various kinds of 'voice quality', e.g. emphasis and stress

CAPITAL LETTERS Notably high volume.

10. The *–san* suffixed to Ako's name is an honorific suffix in the 'polite style' of the Japanese honorific system.

11. It is not the case that Wes learned *no* discrete grammar over the three-year period of study. Over the first two years, for instance, five of the nine morphemes measured in Wes's interlanguage moved in the direction of 'nativelike' performance, although Schmidt (1983: 146) suggests that these measurements 'may overstate Wes's actual competence with respect to these morphemes'.

12. In this regard it is interesting that, while grammatical rules play no real part in Schmidt's later (1990, 2001) theory of noticing/attention, Schmidt (2001: 10) mentions Skehan's (1998) tripartite schema of language aptitude as including 'the ability to retrieve chunks from memory'.

13. Clark's (2006) transcription conventions are different than those used elsewhere in this chapter (see n. 9). I have therefore taken the liberty to retranscribe these two lines, applying the conventions used in the rest of the chapter.

14. To put it in more standard cognitive processing terms, Ako's response has been *primed*—i.e. biased in the direction of the adverbial by recent/previous experience.

3

The dynamic co-adaptation of cognitive and social views: a Complexity Theory perspective

DIANE LARSEN-FREEMAN

Introduction

From its founding, the field of second language acquisition (SLA) has focused primarily on the cognitive dimension of language acquisition. More recently, there have been renewed calls for broadening this focus to include a more socially situated view of the acquisition process. Some researchers have rejected the call, maintaining that SLA is essentially a cognitive process, involving the acquisition of a mental grammar. Other researchers have placed particular emphasis on the impact of the social context for its primacy in the SLA process and/or because the social context plays a fundamental role in shaping both the SLA process and its outcome. Still others have favored an inclusive sociocognitive approach, in which the social and psychological form a unity.

While I place myself in this last group, what is of interest to me is not only that both social and cognitive positions are represented, but also that we interrogate how they intersect. It will be the purpose of this chapter to highlight a theory that inspires such a perspective, Complexity Theory. Not only can Complexity Theory accommodate both social and cognitive dimensions, but it can also provide a principled way to connect them.

I begin by briefly discussing the cognitive origins of the SLA field. I then show how Complexity Theory (hereafter CT) is compatible with a cognitive understanding of SLA. I next turn to the social dimension. I demonstrate how CT can accommodate the varying levels of commitment to a social account of SLA as well. I conclude by discussing how CT makes a connection between the two dimensions.

SLA: a cognitive beginning

Most second language acquisition researchers date the origin of modern-day interest in the language learning process to the cognitive revolution that was launched in the early 1970s. Although it had various sources and manifestations, the most influential theory in our field was undoubtedly that of Noam Chomsky's nativist generative linguistics. While not all SLA researchers accept the need for positing an innate language faculty, as Chomsky does, many concur with generative linguists' claim that language is rule- or principle-governed. As such, it is assumed that the process of language acquisition involves learners internalizing a mental set of rules/principles or grammar. Most SLA researchers date this cognitivist beginning of modern-day interest in SLA to Pit Corder's 1967 article 'The Significance of Learners' Errors'. Overgeneralization errors (e.g. the use of the third person singular present tense inflection on English modal verbs: *'She cans play the piano') were thought to offer convincing evidence of learners' attempts to formulate a rule at a point when the learners were not yet aware of the limitations of their generalizations. Rather than being problematic, then, such errors were interpreted as signs that learners were cognitively active and engaged in a hypothesis-testing process through which they would induce the rules of the language they were learning. Second language learners' errors were thus 'windows on the mind', useful for both teachers and researchers. Early SLA work, based in part on Roger Brown's (1973) now-famous study of three children acquiring English as their native language, contributed to the observation that the SLA process was truly one of 'creative construction' (Dulay and Burt 1973), rather than one in which learners struggled to overcome native language habits.

For the decades since, the basic view of the learner as a hypothesis tester has been the mainstream position. Complementing the centrality of cognition were key concepts, such as comprehensible input (the idea that learners must be able to understand the language they encounter in order to acquire it), noticing (the idea that learners' attention needs to be directed to particular features of the target language), and the negotiation of meaning (the idea that learners learn through working to communicate meaningfully). These three, and other similarly oriented cognitive concepts, have been extremely influential in shaping the SLA research agenda.

Thus, even as Chomsky's influence in SLA has waned over the years, SLA's commitment to a cognitive account remains strong. I believe that this position is justified. However, it is important to acknowledge that all along, there have also been SLA researchers who have made the case for the social dimension to the SLA process. Citing just a few of these researchers, Tarone, Beebe, and R. Ellis have maintained the importance of social context in accounting for variation in learners' production, and researchers such as Lantolf, Thorne, and Kelly Hall have pointed to the primacy of social interaction in the SLA process. There have also been SLA researchers who have investigated identity and language socialization processes (Duff, Norton, Rampton) and conversational interaction (Kasper, Markee, Firth, and Wagner). While some of these researchers have charged that their ideas have not been taken up by mainstream SLA researchers, socially oriented researchers certainly have, in my opinion, made significant contributions to our understanding of second language acquisition.

Reconciling cognitive and social points of view

It is not uncommon for multiple theoretical perspectives to coexist in a field, especially when they are seen to be incommensurate. Some researchers feel this to be true of the cognitive-social points of view. Thus, it may well be that the more cognitively oriented researchers and the more socially oriented researchers will each pursue their own research agendas independently, never identifying a common ground. This is what seems to be happening today.

It is also possible that in the future one position will 'win out', making the other position marginal. This possibility rests on the assumption that empirical research will adjudicate which of the two perspectives explains SLA more adequately. This is not as likely as it may seem at first, though, because the prospect of determining which position is more powerful may be confined to the perspective through which the questions were posed and the data gathered.

A third possibility is for the field to broaden its theoretical commitment and to embrace both perspectives. This is indeed what has happened in the SLA field historically (Larsen-Freeman 2002). For instance, in the early 1970s, it was realized that a priori contrastive analysis (where the L1 and the L2 were systematically compared) could not be relied on to account for all learners' errors. In its stead, the field adopted a more comprehensive approach, error analysis, in which contrastive analysis played one part. This process was iterated when it became clear that we needed to view learners' total performance, rather than focusing narrowly on learners' errors. Performance analysis was later further subsumed by discourse analysis in order for researchers to consider not only what learners were producing, but also what was being said to them (Larsen-Freeman and Long 1991).

So perhaps at this juncture in its evolution, the field of second language learning and teaching would benefit from a broader approach to understanding SLA, one that makes room for both cognitive and social perspectives. I think CT inspires such a position.

Complexity Theory

CT has its roots in the physical sciences, but it has been applied to many social sciences, such as economics, epidemiology, and organizational development. This is because CT affords a transdisciplinary (Halliday 1990) perspective. What is of interest to complexity theorists is the dynamics of self-organization in complex, dynamic systems (Larsen-Freeman 1997). Rather than seeing the world through a deterministic, reductionist, Newtonian lens, complexity theorists adopt a more holistic perspective. What this means is that they adopt a systems perspective and look for interconnections among components or subsystems of the system that researchers have previously studied separately. Furthermore, they study patterns that emerge from the interaction of the components. Oft-cited examples of self-organization are bird flocks and fish schools, which emerge out of the interaction of individual birds or fish.

Complex systems are dynamic. In the topological vocabulary of CT, it is said that over time, a complex system moves through a sequence of states or modes of behavior; particular states or modes that the system 'prefers' are called attractors. Some of these may be quite stable, though they are never static. The stable patterns emerge through an iterative process. The system visits the same or similar territory over and over again. At other times, because of the changing relationships within the components of the system, or due to the openness and connection of the system to its environment, change can happen quite precipitously. At this point there is a great deal of instability in the system. The relation between stability and variability becomes an important aspect of system dynamics, reflecting potential for more dramatic change or for long-term stability.

Much more could be said about CT (see e.g. Larsen-Freeman and Cameron 2008), but perhaps this introduction is sufficient to see the conceptual potential of CT. Since complex, dynamic systems involving language exist on every level of scale from the neural system within individuals, to the interlanguage of second language learners, to the shared dialect of the sociocultural group, to the society of the speech community, CT has relevance for our understanding of these systems. It also has the scope to embrace both the cognitive and the social, and, importantly, a way to connect the two. Before taking up this last point, I turn next to how CT can accommodate both cognitive and social perspectives.

CT from a cognitive perspective

Extending a CT-inspired view to language and language acquisition helps us to see both as dynamic processes—relentlessly changing. Continuing with lessons from CT, it can be inferred that if language is a complex, dynamic system, sometimes referred to as a complex adaptive system (N. Ellis and Larsen-Freeman 2009), then the language system of a speech community and the interlanguage system of language learners, like other dynamic systems, emerges in a 'bottom-up' process through use. As speakers communicate, they soft assemble their language resources. Soft-assembly refers to processes involving the articulation of multiple components of a system, where 'each action is a response to the variable features of the particular task' (Thelen and Smith 1994: 64). The assembly is said to be 'soft' because the elements being assembled as well as the specific ways in which they are assembled can change at any point during the task.

From such repeated soft assemblies, stable language-using patterns (Larsen-Freeman and Cameron 2008) emerge. Usage leads to these becoming entrenched in the speaker's mind and for them to be taken up by members of the speech community. Thus, a usage-based (e.g. Tomasello 2003) or emergentist (N. Ellis and Larsen-Freeman 2006) view of language acquisition aligns well with CT. According to this view, language has the shape that it does because of the way that it is used, not because of an innate bio-program or internal mental organ. As for acquisition, it is the frequency of patterns in language use that promotes learning. Such patterns exist at every level of scale from phonemes to lexical items, phrases, idioms, non-canonical collocations, grammar constructions, conversational structures, etc. As learners revisit the same territory again and again, they perceive and begin to recognize patterns at these levels of scale; they register them in memory. With subsequent encounters, the pattern is strengthened in memory (in neural networks we speak of the connection weights being increased). However, it is not merely numerical superiority that privileges certain forms above others and leads to their earlier appearance in learners' production. For one thing, there is the contingency factor. Certain forms are uniquely associated with a meaning or with a use.[1]

Such forms are more readily learnable than forms that are polysemous or multifunctional, especially since learners are thought to initially subscribe to the 'one to one principle' (Andersen 1984), where they associate one form with one meaning or one function. For another thing, L2 learners' evaluation of the usefulness of a form will also affect the rate at which it is acquired. The learner has agency in the SLA process. So frequency and contingency and learners' assessments are all important. Beyond these, also contributing to a learner's mastering a form is the form's perceptual saliency (Goldschneider and DeKeyser 2001). Retarding learning are other psychological factors, such as the processes of blocking and overshadowing (N. Ellis 2002), both of which refer to learner inattention due to the fact that once an association has been reliably established in a learner's mind, new associations are blocked or overshadowed, the latter when the more salient association overshadows the less salient one.

Although never static, with increasing use, there is a stable attractor of language-using patterns that develops. Slobin (1996) supports this with his 'thinking for speaking' hypothesis. Typological difference patterns between the learners' native language and the language they are studying may cause the learners to express themselves differently even when they are at a high level of target language proficiency. One example of this in SLA is Negueruela et al.'s (2004) study of advanced learners of Spanish. Negueruela et al. found that English-speaking learners tended to express manner in Spanish as they did in English, which did not result in an error of form but which led the learners to mark motion events in Spanish differently than Spanish speakers do. In other words, the stable attractor of Spanish blocked new associations from being made.

Complex systems such as language are characterized by a Zipfian profile (Larsen-Freeman 1997). According to Zipf's law (1935), the more common words in a language account for geometrically more word tokens than do the less common words in the language. Goldberg's (2006) research demonstrates the value of this fact for first language acquisition. Goldberg and colleagues analyzed a corpus of mothers' speech to their 28-month-old children. The researchers searched the corpus for the verb-argument patterns that mothers and children used. The analysis revealed that for each verb-argument construction they investigated, one verb, in particular, occurred with far greater frequency than any other verb.

Goldberg suggests that the frequently occurring verb facilitates the learning of a particular verb-argument pattern.[2] Indeed, child language acquisition researcher Ninio (2006) maintains that individual verbs are the seeds around which verb-argument patterns form. The child first learns these 'pathbreaking' verbs and later adds other verbs that fit the same pattern. Ninio also observes that subsequent to generalization is abstraction. Children abstract the meaning of a particular construction from the verbs that are used with it. For instance, the 'caused motion' construction conveys the meaning of 'X causes Y to receive Z, where Z = a path or location'. This explains why verbs such as 'hit' ('She hit the ball over the fence'), 'drive' ('She drove the car into the garage'), and 'spread' ('She spread jam on the bread') readily enter into this pattern. Abstraction also explains why verbs that do not normally occur in this pattern can take on a caused-motion meaning when they do, even in novel contexts. For example, Goldberg (2006) suggests that an intransitive verb such as 'sneeze' would not be expected to occur in a caused-motion verb-argument construction. None the less, when it does, as in 'She sneezed the napkin off the table,' we can make sense of it. 'Sneeze' has inherited the semantics that allows it be interpreted as having a causal meaning.

Motivated by this work in first language acquisition, SLA researchers N. Ellis and Ferreira-Junior (2009) analyzed verb-argument structures used by English language learners and native speakers as recorded in the European Science Foundation Second Language Database (<http://www.mpi.nl/world/tg/lapp/esf/esf.html>, accessed 30 October 2009). The researchers focused upon seven ESL learners living in Britain whose native languages were Italian (n = 4) or Punjabi (n = 3). Elicited and spontaneously produced data from 234 sessions across a range of activities were gathered and transcribed for these ESL learners and their native-speaker conversation partners. Searches of the corpus enabled the researchers to identify the patterns of use of the constructions in which they were interested. This investigation led them to conclude that second language learners also had skewed access to prototypical verbs. The use of these verbs may facilitate comprehension in the moment, which results in acquisition of their verb-argument constructions in the long run.

As the patterns are increasingly apprehended, they achieve some level of stability among users' language resources. Of course, stability does not mean stasis. It might be better to think of stabilized dynamic language-using patterns or a 'dynamic ensemble' (see also Cooper 1999). This is because even with stability, there is quantitative change taking place. With every use of language some forms increase or decrease in strength and thus availability to the language user. The result is the increasing or decreasing likelihood of forms being accessed the next time. Usage is probabilistic, not determined.

Furthermore, since one's experience with language differs (the context being part of a complex system), each of us constructs his or her own unique stable patterns/language resources. In addition, because we build our language resources experientially, they are accompanied by somatic, affective, and situational memories. The other important point to note is that each speaker demonstrates the ever-present potential for linguistic creativity, just as we saw with the example of 'sneeze'. This point of view is consistent with a view of language as being an open system, as CT tells us, its patterned predictability balanced with its potential for innovation when its users forge new combinations and new meanings by analogizing from older ones.

In sum, as can be seen from the preceding discussion, CT suggests a bottom-up process to language acquisition. Complexity emerges from iterations in a variety of subsystems and from their interactions. Acquisition takes place probabilistically, whereby initial language acquisition is accomplished through a process of soft assembly, in which the learning of frequently occurring and perceptually salient exemplars is facilitated by the natural skewing of the input due to its Zipfian profile. What results, what might have been called 'competence', is instead a network of contextualized dynamic language-using patterns.

CT from a social perspective

More could be said from a cognitive perspective, but perhaps this brief treatment of emergentism is enough to support my contention that CT is compatible with a cognitive perspective. Thus, it would be good at this point to consider what exactly needs to be accounted for on the social side of the sociocognitive compound. My answer here has to be more nuanced, since there are diverse levels of commitment to a social perspective within the SLA field. Here I will discuss only three positions:[3]

1 SLA is dependent on social interaction.
2 SLA production varies with social context.
3 The patterns of interest in language are primarily social, such as the turn-taking patterns in conversation.

I will address each one by one.

1. *SLA is dependent on social interaction.* Most learners are not autodidacts who acquire language by reading books. Most learn language from interacting with others. In fact, some would claim that the interaction is indispensable, and that it is instinctual (Lee et al. 2009). That is why most learners cannot learn only from watching target language television shows, for example. Learners need, or at least derive considerable benefit from, interaction with others and the opportunities that it affords them. In fact, even the most ardent cognitivists pointed out that they are proponents of the idea that SLA takes place through social interaction (Long 1997; Gass 1998) because it

is through such interaction that learners gain access to comprehensible input. However, a CT approach would not see social interaction solely as a source of 'input'. A significant contribution of social interaction, from a CT perspective, is the possibility it affords for co-adaptation. Recall that complexity theorists are interested in the interaction between components of complex systems. Such components can be elements or subsystems of language or can be agents in human systems. Thus, interactions between agents take place in L1 development between an infant and an 'other', early on its caregiver. As a child and its caregiver interact, the language resources of each are dynamically altered, as each adapts to the other. Dynamic systems theorists[4] refer to this as the 'coupling' of one complex system to another.

This is not about the acquisition of rules, nor is it about conformity to uniformity (Larsen-Freeman 2003). It is also not about the acquisition of a priori concepts, which cannot be known separately from our perception of their emergence in the ongoing flow of experience (Kramsch 2002). Rather, it is about alignment (Atkinson et al. 2007), or the term Cameron and I prefer, 'co-adaptation' (Larsen-Freeman and Cameron 2008). Co-adaptation is an iterative, reciprocal process, with each partner adjusting to the other over and over again. It is 'learning-in-interaction' (Firth 2009). Gleitman, Newport, and Gleitman's (1984) early work showed how the quality of child-directed speech changes as the child grows, coming to approximate more closely adult-directed speech—importantly, though, never becoming isomorphic with it. Here is evidence that caregiver speech and the child's developing patterns of language use are mutually constitutive, with each changing to accommodate the other through co-adaptation. This characterization of environmental language is different from static depictions that tend to regard the environment as a triggering mechanism, fostering the maturation of innate structure. It also differs from theories that regard the input as primary and which suggest that the communicative context and highly structured input propel the system forward (Tucker and Hirsch-Pasek 1993).

Dale and Spivey (2006) also showed how the child and his or her caregiver produce sequences of words or syntactic phrases during a conversation that match those being heard, a process they call 'syntactic coordination'. Interestingly, the researchers found a Zipf-like distribution in the patterns that were shared with each child and caregiver pair. In other words, there are highly frequent sequences of word classes guiding the recurrent patterns in conversation (Larsen-Freeman and Cameron 2008). We have already seen how a Zipfian profile was hypothesized to explain how learning verb-argument constructions can be facilitated. A Zipfian distribution gives learners access to a skewed sample of exemplars. From Dale and Spivey's work, we can add a Zipfian distribution of conversational patterns. Elio and Anderson (1981, 1984) have shown how learning is optimized by the introduction of an initial, low-variance sample centered upon prototypical exemplars, which allows learners to get a 'fix' on what will account for most of the category members. We know that in second language acquisition, co-adaptation also takes place[5]—between conversation partners (Firth 2009), and presumably between teachers and students in classrooms, which enhances the possibility that learners receive an optimal sample of language from which to learn.

2. *SLA production varies with the social context.* The influence of the social context has been a theme in SLA for many years. A Labovian quantitative analysis of learners' production of context-dependent forms was first done by L. Dickerson (1974), and early on, Tarone (1982) made use of Labov's stylistic continuum in her continuous competence model. Schumann (1978*b*) and Andersen (1983) applied ideas on social variation from studies of pidginization and creolization to second language acquisition, and there have been others, too numerous to mention here.

From a CT perspective, the fact that there will be performance differences in different social contexts is without question. Context is part of a complex system. We perform differently in the presence of different others. This has been shown convincingly most recently in the work of Kramsch (2008) and Kramsch and Whiteside (2008: 646). They write, 'successful communication comes less from knowing which communication strategy to pull off at which point in the interaction than it does from choosing which speech style to speak with whom, about what, and for what effects'. The critical question is whether performance at one time and one place can be linked with development over time.

The rationale for CT's affirmative answer to this question brings us back to the construct of 'soft assembly' (Thelen and Smith 1994). Larsen-Freeman and Cameron (2008) propose that at one timescale, the immediate context, language use is 'soft-assembled' by individuals—a real-time process, taking into account options and constraints, the intrinsic dynamics of the speaker, the individual's language-using history, the affordances (or what resources the learner perceives are available) of the context, and the communicative pressures at hand. When two individuals soft assemble their language resources on a given occasion and then interact and adapt to each other, their language resources change as a result of co-adaptation. This can be seen in the phenomenon of priming, where the use of a particular pattern by one conversation partner triggers the use of the same or similar pattern in the other. The changed resources mean that on another occasion, they are more available for use. In other words, using language on some local timescale is simultaneously a part of language change/learning on longer timescales (Lemke 2002: 80).

As van Lier (2000: 246) puts it, 'an ecological approach asserts that the perceptual and social activity of the learner, and particularly the verbal and nonverbal interaction, in which the learner engages, are central to an understanding of learning. In other words, they do not just facilitate learning, they *are* learning in a fundamental way.' Thus, a learner's language resources are the way they are because of the way the learner uses language. The language resources are variegated stabilities (language-using patterns of various forms) emerging out of interaction. Practices and patterns typically used in early development coexist with more recently produced patterns and are differentially present in different contexts. Since the resources are enacted in different contexts at different times, the emergent stabilities are variable and heterochronic (Lemke 2000).

Moreover, viewing language development as self-organization in a dynamic system, as CT does, means that different learners may develop different language resources even when the ambient language is similar (Mohanan 1992). No matter which variationist approach is applied, then, we would want to know how variation works at the level of the individual as well—why individuals conform and why they do not—to expected patterns (de Bot, Lowie, and Verspoor 2007).

However, the conventional variationist approach will not work from a CT point of view, at least not without modification. That is because the conventional approach is to look for correlations between individual variables and the use of particular linguistic features in particular contexts. This in itself can be useful for descriptive purposes, but, of course, correlation does not indicate causality. More seriously, taking the variables one by one misses their interaction, whereas the complexity in the language-using system arises from components and subsystems being interdependent and interacting with each other in a variety of different ways. What is evident at any one time is 'the interaction of multiple complex dynamic systems, working on multiple timescales and levels' (Larsen-Freeman 1997; Lemke 2000; Cameron and Deignan 2006).

For an explanation, rather than a description of the variability in different speakers' language performances, a different methodology is called for. The variability is not 'caused' by contextual differences. In complex systems (Byrne 2002: 105) 'we do not see causes as single factors whose presence inevitably generates an effect and whose absence means that the effect does not occur'. This is because what matters is the connections the learners will make with their own prior knowledge and experience through their 'histories of participation' (Rogers 2004: 52). It is important to note, however, that while our histories may constrain our responses, they do not determine them. What we learn when we learn a new language is 'Knowing how to negotiate our way through a world that is not fixed and pre-given but that is continually shaped by the types of actions in which we engage' (Varela et al. 1991: 144).

3. *What we actually study is different.* SLA got its start, as I pointed out earlier, by following the lead of L1 acquisition researcher Roger Brown, who studied the acquisition of grammatical morphemes, among other linguistic forms. Ever since then much of the interest in SLA has centered on understanding how the various subsystems of language—phonological, morphological, syntactic, lexical—have been acquired. Even socially oriented SLA researchers see the different effects of social context on 'the linguistic outcomes of the process' (Tarone 2007*b*: 837).

However, there are other SLA researchers who do not focus on the linguistic features of learner production, bur rather study, for example, how learners are socialized through the use of language and how they are socialized to use language (Swain and Deters 2007: 824). Still others apply conversation analysis to study the participation structures of learners (Markee and Kasper 2004).

From a CT perspective, whether formal linguistic features or participation structures are in focus is not so much an issue as it is a reflection of the diversity in the theorists' locus of explanation. However, if different features are to be the focus of study, there are some considerations from a CT point of view. Here, I will discuss five of them:

1. Patterns of language use operate at different nested levels of scale. Depending on the researcher's focus, morphosyntax, discursive routines, turn-taking patterns, etc. are all potential objects of interest. From Marr's (1982) theory of vision, we know that the same object may be represented at different levels of detail. At one extreme, what is of interest can be treated in a very abstract way (such as a generative rule); at another level, the focus of inquiry is treated with great detail, for example, specific exemplars stored in memory. At the lowest level of scale, it could be seen as patterns of connectivity in a neural network. A consequence of this is that we cannot simply talk about some language-using pattern having some property; rather, we must talk about whether, given a certain level of detail and a certain locus of explanation, it is seen to have this property.

2. Patterns are dynamic. No matter what level of scale one focuses upon, language is dynamically adaptive vis-à-vis its environment (Atkinson 2008: 6). For after all, 'language is not a fixed code' (Harris 1996) that exists independently of its users, and that is ready-made for users before they start using it, but rather it is created, or at the very least assembled from conventional units, each time it is used. This is no less true of the basic units of language as it is for the larger discursive routines.

3. Language-using patterns emerge through interaction. Because language is conceived as a complex, adaptive, dynamic system (N. Ellis and Larsen-Freeman 2009), its emergent stabilities arise from language use. This means that no matter what the locus of explanation, the emergent patterns are 'a vaguely defined set of sedimented…recurrent partials whose status is constantly being renegotiated' (Hopper 1998), what I earlier referred to, using Cooper's words, as a 'dynamic ensemble'.

4. The patterns that we study are not necessarily psychologically real for language learners. Furthermore, there is no consistent level at which patterns are fixed—their boundaries may or may not coincide with the constituent boundaries of linguists' descriptions. After all, language is a normative fiction (Klein 1998). As methodologically convenient as it is, it is not helpful to analyze our data with ready-made categories.

5. And finally, as I wrote earlier, language-using patterns are not only heterogeneous; they are also heterochronic. What a learner produces at any one time reflects the learner's history with the pattern. This also means that

using a language pattern at one time may simultaneously change the learner's language resources on a longer timescale.

CT: the connection between the cognitive and the social

As I indicated earlier, I favor an integrated sociocognitive approach, and I see in CT a way to integrate the social and the cognitive rather than segregating them (Larsen-Freeman 2002, 2007). Certainly there are some researchers who choose to work either on the social side of language or on the cognitive side with little attention paid to the other. Although dealing with one apart from the other may allow for rigorous descriptions, it must be recognized that the description of SLA can only be partial. More problematic from a CT point of view is that the dichotomizing leaves open the issue of how the two, cognitive and social, are connected—the issue of interconnectedness being central to complex systems and an issue of enormous importance when dealing with language development, language teaching, and language use.

By looking at only one side or the other, a dualistic view of phenomena is promulgated and reinforced. For example, we use such dualisms as language structure and language use. Such dualisms get in the way of seeing that members of each pair are two perspectives on the same underlying process. Language structure is shaped by the way that language is used, and its use in turn fuels further structural development. 'Structure-process', Bohm calls it (in Nichol 2003). As such, the dualistic thinking is unparsimonious and perhaps unnecessary. Clearly, then, speakers/learners of a given language are constrained to some degree by the language resources they have developed, but just as clearly, language resources are altered in a social context, sometimes much more rapidly than supposed, despite their self-reproducing natures. For instance, it is often thought that grammar patterns change rather slowly; however, it is true today that many grammar structures are being transformed rapidly, at least in English. It is therefore helpful to look closely at the interconnections between the patterns in language and how language is used in order to gain a more thorough understanding of how people both reproduce and transform language.

Before I conclude, then, the nature of the relationship between cognition and social interaction needs to be explored. Complexity Theory characterizes this relationship by suggesting that cognitive and social forces operate simultaneously, albeit on different levels and at different timescales. The natural state of the linguistic system can be 'defined as a dynamic adaptedness to a specific context' (Tucker and Hirsch-Pasek 1993: 362).[6] As they adapt their language resources to new contexts, learners change their language resources. Thus, the language system and its use are mutually constitutive. 'The act of playing the game has a way of changing the rules' is how Gleick (1987) put it when discussing naturally occurring complex systems. The rules referred to by Gleick are not linguistic rules; nevertheless, the analogy is useful for representing the self-evident fact that we learn a language by using it. Much of this process is continuous, and so it escapes our conscious attention. That language use leads to language learning is not revelatory; after all, how else could language learning occur? However, by focusing on the nexus between use and learning, rather than imposing artificial dichotomies, we come to understand that they are manifestations of a common dynamic process operating in different time frames.

Of course, it should also be acknowledged, as Leather and van Dam (2003) do, that the course of language acquisition cannot be separated from the specific circumstances of acquisition. As they write, 'there is *always* a context of acquisition that must be taken into account, and it is always complex, dynamic and in principle emergent' (ibid. 19). While it is possible, of course, to separate context and person for the purpose of analysis, such separation requires the untenable assumption that the two are independent (van Geert and Steenbeek 2005).

Certainly a fundamental difference when it comes to second language learning is the contrast between instructed and uninstructed contexts of development (overlooking for the moment the great variety of conditions and experience that exist within each of these types). I should make it clear that when it comes to SLA, few generalizations hold across different learning contexts. This goes for second language instruction as well. While I have spent considerable time making a case for language-using patterns emerging from social interaction, it is also likely important in adult SLA, at least, to recruit learners' attention and consciousness through promoting their noticing with explicit instruction. However, what would be true for teaching from a CT point of view is that, in addition, language learners must be given abundant opportunities to use language. As I have advised language teachers (Larsen-Freeman 2003), 'Teach grammaring, not grammar.' In a grammaring approach, not only is the dynamism of language learning and use acknowledged, so is the use of a psychologically authentic approach, where the construction of meaning is paramount.

Conclusion

From the CT point of view I have adopted here, 'Emergence of language abilities and real-time language processing are the same phenomenon differing only in the timescales at which they are observed' (Evans 2007: 131). Learners soft assemble their language resources interacting with a changing environment. As they do so, certain connections are strengthened, others weakened, and their language resources change.

Learning is not so much the taking in of linguistic forms by learners as it is the constant adaptation and enactment of language-using patterns as learners/users make meaning and respond to the affordances that emerge in a dynamic communicative situation. Thus, this view assumes that language development is not about learning and manipulating abstract symbols, but is enacted in real-life experiences, such as when two or more interlocutors co-adapt during an interaction. During co-adaptation, the language resources of both are transformed. A developing system functions as a resource for its own further development.

That there are differences among learners is not striking, but is rather a natural part of dynamically emergent behavior assembled by individuals with different orientations, grounded in social relationships with other people, and in keeping with historical contingency. From a Complexity Theory perspective, flux is an integral part of any system. It is not as though there was some uniform norm from which individuals deviate. Variability stems from the ongoing self-organization of systems of activity. To honor this, we need to take into account learners' histories, orientations and intentions, thoughts and feelings. We need to consider the tasks that learners perform and to consider each performance anew—stable and predictable in part, but at the same time, variable, flexible, and dynamically adapted to fit the changing situation. Learners actively transform their linguistic world; they do not just conform to it.

Notes

1. Many researchers adopt a binary view and speak of 'form and meaning', or 'form and function'. I believe that a ternary view of what needs to be learned is more appropriate, and therefore I write of form, meaning, and use (Larsen-Freeman 2003).
2. Also, more frequently used verbs tend to be shorter than less frequently used ones.
3. For others, see Larsen-Freeman (2007) and Tarone (this volume).
4. Dynamic Systems Theory and Complexity Theory afford similar views, the difference between them lying in their origin.
5. SLA researchers have known for a long time about the adjustments made by some native language speakers with learners, sometimes referred to as 'foreigner talk discourse'. Co-adaptation adds that the language resources of *both* interlocutors are altered in the interaction.
6. Of course, the context is also changing.

4

Social context and cognition in SLA: a variationist perspective

ELAINE TARONE

Introduction

Variationist second language acquisition (SLA) researchers study the systematic impact of contextual variables such as the identity and role of interlocutors, topic, and task, as well as contextual linguistic forms, on the learner's *perception*, *production*, and *acquisition* of specific aspects of the second language system. For this purpose, they find it essential to examine SLA by diverse learner types across a wide range of social contexts (Bayley and Tarone forthcoming). Many non-variationist SLA researchers are increasingly becoming interested in the impact of social context on cognitive processes of SLA.[1] This chapter will review variationist SLA research which shows how social setting systematically influences both the kind of second language (L2) input learners receive and their cognitive processing of it; the speech production of L2 learners; and even, upon occasion, the stages in which learner language (or interlanguage) forms are acquired. In this chapter, I will present arguments and evidence in support of the idea that 'cognitive' constructs such as 'input' and 'output' must be treated more seriously in SLA theory as being 'sociocognitive' in nature: in these constructs we see the influence of social variables on cognition. (For example, Wong's (2005: 119) definition of 'input' includes the stipulation that input always occurs in a 'communicative context': 'input refers to samples of language that learners are exposed to in a communicative context or setting'.)

However, too many SLA researchers have allowed the investigation of crucial concepts such as 'input,' 'output', and even 'context/setting' to be too narrowly restricted to the laboratory-like environment of the academic world, which is more conducive to psycholinguistic than sociolinguistic thinking. Psycholinguistic views of language are limited in predictive power, even in mainstream linguistics.[2]

As in mainstream linguistics, so too in SLA research it is time for theorists to see what adjustments are needed if its psycholinguistic constructs are to make any sense in the socially embedded experiences of L2 speakers in their own worlds (cf. Bigelow and Tarone 2004; Tarone, Bigelow, and Hansen

2009; Bayley and Tarone forthcoming). The present chapter proposes that SLA scholars seek guidance in the research and scholarship of mainstream sociolinguistics (e.g. Labov 1972; Bell 1984), as well as in research in 'variationist' SLA (e.g. Beebe 1977, 1980; Tarone 1979, 1988, 2000a, 2007a, 2009; Eisenstein 1989; Young 1990; Bayley and Preston 1996; Preston 2000, 2002; Lybeck 2002; Rehner 2002; Geeslin 2003; Rehner, Mougeon, and Nadasdi 2003; Bayley and Langman 2004; Gatbonton, Trofimovich, and Magid 2005; Geeslin and Guijarro-Fuentes 2006; Fasold and Preston 2007; Rau, Chang, and Tarone 2009; and many others). The variationist approach to research on learner language (or interlanguage: IL) is superior to more unstructured approaches to the study[3] of sociocognition in SLA. The variationist approach builds on a large body of research in sociolinguistics which allows us to generate a range of testable hypotheses targeting the impact of specific social variables (interlocutor, task, topic, accompanying linguistic context) on variation and development in learner language, as well as the operation of attested sociolinguistic processes such as 'change from above' and 'change from below'.[4] In addition, variationists have the capacity to avail themselves of well-established and sophisticated sociolinguistic methodologies for data collection and quantitative and qualitative analysis, including computer modeling using VARBRUL software that is specifically designed for research on language use related to complex linguistic and social variables.

Attention, or noticing

In considering the cognitive processes applied to L2 input and involved in interlanguage production, a core construct to begin with will be *attention*, or *noticing*. Here, sociolinguists have an important point to make, one that has been insufficiently considered by SLA researchers. Tarone (1979) extended Labov (1972) in postulating that the cognitive process of *attention* to language form is an important cause of learners' variable performance when using an interlanguage in different task conditions; the more attention paid to speech under different task conditions, the more 'formal' or 'accurate' the learner's language generally is. However, Bell (1984), in discussing variation in the speech of native speakers of a language, made the crucial point that attention to language form (and here I would include noticing) is actually both a cognitive and a social construct. Attention to language form is itself a complex construct. (For example, the individual's metalinguistic awareness, as embodied in the L2 learner's recall of certain types of corrective feedback, is significantly improved by alphabetic print literacy (Bigelow, delMas, Hansen, and Tarone 2006; Tarone, Bigelow, and Hansen 2009).) But whether the focus of attention is on language form or language meaning—this choice is made based on social factors—Bell's Style Axiom states that the core underlying social variable that causes attention to be directed to one or another linguistic variant is the people present in the social setting—the *audience*—and most powerfully, the interlocutor. According to Bell, all other characteristics of social setting in some sense derive from the central importance of the audience: their roles, status, and power relationships with the speaker are the factors directing speaker attention to meaning or form, and to one linguistic variant as opposed to another. Bell's Style Axiom now is widely supported in sociolinguistics. 'Variationist' SLA researchers assume that social setting (particularly the social role and identity of the interlocutor), affects learners' attention to differing aspects of L2 input, and also differentially affects learners' attentional processes in producing interlanguage. For sociolinguists, attention is an important social and cognitive construct for the learner in both processing L2 input and producing interlanguage (IL).

Impact of social setting on L2 input and interaction

The social setting systematically affects the *L2 input* the interlocutor provides, the degree to which L2 learner and interlocutor *negotiate meaning,* and the L2 learner's processing of *negative and positive evidence on L2 form, including corrective feedback.*

Social setting affects L2 input provided

Social context affects the kind of L2 input learners get. Obviously, it affects the social variety learners hear; if learners are only exposed to one social setting, the language variety used in that setting is the only one they learn. If learners need other varieties of L2, their overall acquisition can be affected. In immersion classroom settings, where L2 input consists only of an academic variety, learners say they need another: an age-appropriate vernacular variety of the L2. This is the conclusion drawn by Tarone and Swain (1995: 172) after interviewing Suzannah, a French immersion graduate who says:

I don't know if it's slang or just the way kids speak...I speak differently to my friends than I do to my parents. It's almost a whole different language, and...they [immersion teachers] don't teach us how to speak [French] that way'.... The French immersion program gave her the French she needed to talk to her parents and other adults but not the 'whole different language' that she needed to talk to her fellow adolescents in French. In sociolinguistic terms, she was given input in the L2 for adult purposes but was not given the vernacular L2 she needed for adolescent purposes.

This need affects learners' willingness to use the L2. Tarone and Swain suggest that it is in part the need for a teen vernacular that causes pre-adolescents to start using their first language with one another in 4th and 5th grade immersion classes, where previously they did not. Their unwillingness to stay in the L2 clearly will affect acquisition long-term.

Social setting also affects whether interlocutors adjust the input they provide to L2 learners. Long (1980) argued that native speakers universally make linguistic and conversational adjustments when learners signal difficulty in comprehension. But subsequent research suggests this is not true. In social contexts other than classroom or university settings, learners are less likely to receive adjusted input (see e.g. Varonis and Gass 1985). Interested in Long's claim, Bondevik (1996) conducted a controlled study of interactions between salesmen and shoppers in a Minnesota electronics store. He contrasted interactions in this social context with those in the social setting of Long's dissertation study: a room on the UCLA campus, with interactions between ESL students and ESL teachers or teacher trainees. Bondevik showed that four electronics salesmen in Minnesota did not use foreigner talk at all with three different (clearly) non-native speakers (NNSs) of English. After the NNSs said they were not native speakers and did not understand something the salesmen said, the latter did not make the linguistic and conversational adjustments to L2 input that are postulated by Long to be universally provided by proficient speakers to L2 learners. One salesman even complexified his syntax. In a subsequent interview, the salesman said that he felt it would have been insulting to simplify his speech to his customers. Although all the listeners in the setting studied by Long (1980) did use foreigner talk, using now well-known linguistic and conversational adjustments to the L2 input they provided, interlocutors in different social settings made different choices as to whether and how much they negotiated meaning or provided adjusted input to L2 learners (see Varonis and Gass 1985 for similar findings). Since adjusted L2 linguistic input, provided during negotiation of meaning, is now argued to be essential in aiding learners' cognitive processing and SLA, the finding that some people do not accommodate at all to L2 learners by simplifying linguistic input is important because it may affect second language acquisition.

Social setting affects negotiation of meaning

Social context does not just affect the L2 input that interlocutors provide learners. It also affects the way L2 learners themselves behave in negotiating meaning or focusing on L2 form. Exploring Batstone's (2002) suggestion that individuals orient differently to L2 form in input in communicative contexts than in learning contexts, Lafford (2006) reviews research on L2 learning in study abroad (SA) contexts (primarily communicative) as opposed to classroom 'at home' (AH) settings (primarily learning). Her review of an impressive body of research concludes that these settings have a significant but complex impact on individual learners' focus on L2 form in the input as opposed to meaning, depending on such factors as their proficiency level and (following Selinker and Douglas 1985, and Douglas 2004) their perception of key social factors in those settings:

It is not the context of learning alone, but rather individual learner perceptions of specific characteristics of the contexts (*setting, participants [status and roles], end/purpose, norms of interaction and interpretation*) that interact with cognitive factors (*controlled vs. automatic processing, working memory*) to account for differences in linguistic performance among L2 learners in classroom and study abroad contexts.   (Lafford 2006: 18)

Lafford concludes that large-scale quantitative studies are unlikely to tease apart these factors as effectively as qualitative explorations of individual learners in social context.

One question we might ask is, how, specifically, might factors of social context affect an individual L2 learner's willingness to negotiate meaning? Studies by George Yule and his students (Yule 1990; Yule and Macdonald 1990; Yule, Powers, and Macdonald 1992) have documented the impact of social role and relative L2 proficiency on L2 learners' negotiation of meaning. The researchers assigned speakers of English L2 to dyads in which one member was high proficiency and the other was low. The two students in each pair had similar information—most commonly maps of city streets, where one student (the sender) had a map with a delivery route to ten locations, and had to tell the other student (the receiver) this route. The task design examined the influence of proficiency level and sender vs. receiver role on the learners' negotiation of meaning. The study design set up four referential problems involving specific differences between the maps of the sender and the receiver, which the partners had to resolve, through negotiation of meaning, in order to have the receiver successfully mark a route on his or her map. Successful negotiation required that both members of the dyad recognize that their worlds of reference (i.e. their maps) were different; through negotiation of meaning they had to arrive at this conclusion and develop a solution to deal with this difference.

Results showed that *twice as much language, and three times as much negotiation of meaning* occurred when the lower-proficiency learner was placed in the role of sender (Yule and Macdonald 1990: 545). High-proficiency members in the dominant sender role tended not to negotiate meaning. They ignored attempts by low-proficiency receivers to negotiate, or even contradicted those attempts. Some low-proficiency receivers tended to be passive, not attempting to negotiate at all when the high-proficiency sender's directive was simply impossible on the receiver's map.

In the first example below, when a low-proficiency member in the receiver role (L-R) tries to negotiate with their high-proficiency partner in the sender role (H-S), the L-R's message is flatly contradicted by the sender, who asserts his own world of reference; in the second example, the L-R's unwelcome message is simply ignored:

(1)   H-S   you go into the Office and you come out of the Office
      L-R   oh—there are many Office
      H-S   no there is only one Office there
      L-R   oh
      H-S   you come out of the Office and you go back.
(Yule 1990: 57)

(2) H-S turn to the—east—you have a building—Office – do you
          have it?
     L-R em—Office yeah
     H-S okay give a package there
     L-R okay—I have three Office
     H-S do you find the Office—it is just opposite to the Church?
     L-R the Church—yeah—okay
     H-S go out of the Office—for a while we have to walk to the west.
(Yule and Macdonald 1991: 547)

Sometimes the low-proficiency receiver (L-R) just acknowledges an H-S directive without telling H-S that the directive is impossible to follow on L-R's map:

(3) H-S okay go out of the Records building—and follow the same
          path to the south
     L-R uh huh
     H-S and again from the first corner—turn to the west—in other
          words to the left okay?
     L-R okay—turn—okay.
(ibid. 546)

Yule (1990) suggests that the high-proficiency senders often seemed to believe that all problems in this task were the fault of their lower-proficiency level partners:

In those interactions where the more fluent speaker is in charge, there is a much greater incidence of meta-commentary such as *let me tell you*, *okay I tell you*, and *I will explain you*. . . . In their attempts to simplify what begins to feel like a very complex referential problem, the fluent senders often use repetition and paraphrase of even the simplest lexical items, further compounding the impression that the receiver's incompetence is the cause of their interactive difficulties. This strategy can range from simple repetition of almost every direction, as in extract (7), to the kind of explanatory statements with paraphrase shown in (8):

(7) . . . come out again—come out of the Bookstore—go up again—go up
     again
(8) . . . let me tell you one thing—all whites—all white is road—street—
     and all black is—black is not road—okay? [describing the symbolism
     of the map to the L-R partner].
(Yule 1990: 57–8)

Far more negotiation, and far more success in task completion, takes place when the low-proficiency learner is in the sender role (L-S) and the high-proficiency learner is in the receiver role (H-R):

(4) L-S you stop by the Office
     H-R now there are many Offices
     L-S the first Office

H-R   ah the first Office—I mean which Office? The one Office is to
the north—one to the south—one to the east
L-S   east—east side is the Office.
(Yule and Macdonald 1990: 549–50)

Here we see that dominance in a social relationship—in this case, a
dominance established both by speaker role and by relative perceived proficiency level—had tremendous impact on negotiation of meaning: whether it
occurred at all, and whether it was effective. The socially dominant senders
disregarded messages from the less socially dominant receivers that said that
the receivers' referential world (i.e. the map) was different from the senders'
own. In this way, social relationships between learners strongly impacted
key cognitive processes involved in the *negotiation of meaning*. And as we
shall now see, disregard for an interlocutor who is less socially dominant or
significant to the learner may also cause a learner to ignore or discount that
interlocutor's *corrective feedback* on their L2 form.

Social setting affects L2 learner's noticing of L2 form

Bell's (1984) Style Axiom, described above, suggests that audience—those
others present in the speech situation—may influence the L2 forms that
second language learners pay attention to. Much current SLA research on
noticing of L2 form has ignored the possibility that it matters to the learner
who the audience or interlocutor producing that input is.

Current SLA research posits that one central cognitive process in SLA
is learners' 'noticing' of key forms in the L2 input provided by others (e.g.
Schmidt 1993). Scholarly work on input processing (VanPatten 1996) and
focus on form (Long and Robinson 1998) suggests that acquisition occurs
when second language learners notice the difference between their own
interlanguage form and a corresponding target language form. A common
assumption is that noticing is a referential, logical, and essentially asocial act,
one for which social setting is irrelevant (e.g. Long 1997, 1998). This asocial
model of SLA implies that providing corrective feedback is rather like feeding
data into a computer: the social relationship between learner and feedback
provider is irrelevant. But we have already seen that human interlocutors are
influenced by social setting: they don't make linguistic adjustments for learners in certain social settings, and task role and proficiency level of human
interlocutors affect their negotiation of meaning.

In the same way, research findings in several studies show that social
context affects learners' noticing of L2 form.[5] Kormos (1999: 330) reviews
findings of several studies on error detection and repair, and concludes that,
as Bell's Style Axiom might have predicted, 'speakers will strive to produce
well-formed repairs not only because their original speech plan needs to be
encoded again, but also because they want to aid their interlocutors'. Kormos
concludes that error detection depends not just on psycholinguistic factors

such as availability of attention, but also on factors of social context such as the 'accuracy demand of the situation' and 'various listener-based discourse constraints' (p. 324). A similar review of research studies on L2 learners' awareness of negative feedback also concludes that such awareness is affected differently by different social contexts:

> there are differences between the findings of laboratory and classroom studies, differences between primarily structure-focused and primarily content-focused classrooms, and differences between observational studies of naturally occurring feedback patterns in classrooms and experimental studies that focus on specific linguistic features and feedback types.
>
> (Nicholas, Lightbown, and Spada 2001: 751)

For example, Lyster and Ranta (1997) showed that learners' noticing of implicit corrective feedback was different depending on whether that feedback occurred in a classroom focused on meaning (e.g. an immersion classroom) as opposed to a classroom focused on form (e.g. a grammar-focused class). If it is true that learners must notice the difference between their own and new language forms in order to acquire a new L2 form, and social setting affects this noticing, then social setting must also affect acquisition.

Of course, noticing may not always result in uptake; social context affects learners' willingness to accept the corrective feedback that they notice and use it in their own speech. Here we must come to terms with an obvious fact: all corrective feedback on linguistic form is inherently value-laden and social, by its very nature. Correction is about getting someone else to align more closely to one's own standard; doing this involves the corrector's assumption that he or she has the right and the power to direct the correction. Acceptance of a correction is also acceptance of the corrector's right to correct. It is hard to imagine corrective feedback provided by a human that does not involve this kind of assertion and negotiation of social power in a social relationship. Corrective feedback on form provided by a computer program (e.g. spell-checks) could be argued to lack that kind of social message, but not feedback provided by humans.[6]

Rider (2005) documents in a university Italian class the complexity of the social negotiation involved in giving and receiving corrective feedback when learners are asked to provide this to one another in pairs as they review the essays they are writing. Learner R in the following example is somewhat overbearing; she enjoys prestige in this class, being generally recognized as the most proficient in Italian, but learner M also is recognized as having considerable ability in the language. In the following exchange, R requests feedback from M on her (in fact incorrect) use of passato prossimo tense (*ha lavorato*), but M fails to provide feedback.

(5) R: *Il primo…È un uomo vecchio…Faceva bel tempo,* um *(7) Uomo vecchio, ah, <u>ha lavorato</u>? Nel giardino, sì?*
(The first [frame]…It's an old man…It was nice weather, um (7) Old man, ah, <u>worked</u>? In the garden, yes?)

M: Ah, *ucio can-canta?*
(Ah, [bird] si-sings?)

R takes M's silence as tacit approval, and indeed, in their later essays both of them used the incorrect *passato prossimo* form, so this failure to negotiate was unfortunate, from an SLA perspective. In later stimulated recall sessions about this exchange, R 'reported that she was worried that Michael would not contribute to the conversation, so she kept talking to "fill the space"'. This comment suggests that R feels that she, as the more proficient one, has the right to keep talking, and not pause to get M's input. In his reflection on this exchange, M reported that he was silent not because he approved but because he thought R 'seemed to have the story all worked out in her head already'. M's comment suggests acquiescence but also perhaps some resentment at R's presumed right to assert that the grammatical form she proposes is correct without waiting for him to consider it; the subtext is that she does not really need him to tell her what he thinks. As a result of subtle and complex social negotiations around the giving and receiving of corrective feedback, R's 'request for feedback' does not successfully elicit any feedback from M, corrective or otherwise. Their perceptions of one another's right to dominate in deciding what is 'correct' Italian in this exchange, and perhaps also their perceptions of one another's ability to make that decision, prevents any negotiation of form. In this way it results in lack of uptake and their use of incorrect verb forms in the final essay.

To summarize, we have seen that social setting systematically affects the L2 input provided to learners in three ways:

1 social setting affects L2 input, both the language variety and amount of linguistic or conversational adjustment provided;
2 social setting affects whether in speech production learners focus on linguistic form or meaning, and whether negotiation of meaning occurs in the L2; and
3 social setting affects learners' noticing of corrective feedback and their willingness to incorporate the corrective feedback that is provided.

Impact of social setting on learner language production

Impact of audience on L2 production

We turn now to consider the systematic impact of social variables on L2 learners' language production. The question of whether the L2 learner identifies with the interlocutor as a model of L2 use, leads us naturally into a consideration of Accommodation Theory.

Accommodation theory

Beebe and Giles (1984) explain learners' second language acquisition processes in terms of Speech Accommodation Theory (SAT). This theory predicts that L2 learners will adjust their production of IL forms to align them with forms used by their interlocutors. L2 learners may choose to converge, to sound more like interlocutors they wish to identify with, or they may choose to diverge from the speech patterns of interlocutors they do not wish to identify with. Beebe (1977, 1980) demonstrates that as L2 learners move from one interlocutor to another at a single point in time, some interlanguage forms they produce will shift, converging to become more similar to forms of their interlocutors. Beebe documents such short-term shifts, lasting only for the duration of the conversation. Rampton (1995) documents the divergence that is also predicted by SAT; he shows that Pakistani adolescents in London deliberately used a non-standard 'me no + verb' construction with their English teacher, when they were perfectly capable of saying 'I don't + verb' with other interlocutors; the 'me no' construction conveyed to their teacher their divergent identities as Pakistani Britons. Both convergence and divergence constitute strategies of short-term identification with the communicative norms of some reference group, either present or absent at the time of speaking.

Interlocutors can clearly provide learners with powerful models for language use in a wide range of social settings, and L2 learners make surprisingly sensitive adjustments in their speech production, either for accommodation or divergence, when they converse with different interlocutors. This sensitive and systematic impact of interlocutor on L2 use was documented, for example, by Broner (2001), in a detailed quantitative VARBRUL analysis showing that different interlocutors significantly influenced L2 learners' use of either L1 or L2 in the course of daily immersion classroom discourse, in an intricate interplay of accommodation to some peers and divergence from others. Other useful sociolinguistic studies documenting the impact of extra-linguistic[7] factors in L2 learner language production include Regan (2004), and Uritescu et al. (2004).

But can short-term accommodation or divergence in response to one or another role model or social group result in longitudinal change—that is, acquisition? There is growing evidence to support this. So, for example, Gatbonton, Trofimovich, and Magid (2005) find that the ethnic group affiliation of Chinese and francophone learners in Canada is directly related to the accuracy of their English L2 pronunciation. Lafford (2006), Segalowitz and Freed (2004), and Thomas (2004) show that study abroad contexts and classroom learning contexts have differential impact on second language acquisition over time.

A fine-grained longitudinal study showing social influences on interlanguage development over time is Lybeck's (2002) longitudinal study of American women sojourning in Norway. These learners' progress in acquiring L2 phonological forms is directly related to their acculturation and formation of new sociocultural relationships and roles. They were interviewed twice during one year, once in the fall and again in the spring, at which time their production of several Norwegian phonological features was judged for nativeness by native phonologists. Their social networks (cf. Milroy 1980), comprised of both Norwegians and other American expatriates, were also mapped at Time 1 and Time 2. Most of them established good social networks with Norwegians and showed progress over time, improving their production of target L2 Norwegian variants.

However, one learner who began with very native-like Norwegian phonology became alienated from the target culture during the study, dramatically altering her social network. Her negative experiences with her Norwegian in-laws as well as other Norwegians in a range of social situations led her to believe that Norwegians were not likely to provide her with the supportive relationships she needed. She experienced a negative change in her self-described sociocultural identity and attitude toward the target culture. Over the same period of time, this learner's interlanguage phonology showed a dramatic drop in native-like accuracy; she began using a more American variant of R, and global ratings of her phonology nativeness also dropped substantially.

The impact of social context on *acquisition* (and by extension to the cognitive processes underlying SLA) is also shown in Tarone and Liu (1995). These studies suggest that in addition to *attention*, we should also consider a second construct that bridges the social and the cognitive—*social role*, a construct that may also relate to *identity*.

The processes of accommodation and divergence that are set forth in Accommodation Theory seem consistent with sociocultural constructs such as scaffolding in the Zone of Proximal Development, heteroglossia, dialogism, and double voicing (see Bakhtin 1984; Lantolf 2000). In this view, we accommodate our IL forms to fit those of interlocutors with whom we identify, and we diverge from those with whom we do not; accommodation seems like something that happens in collaborative dialogue. In sociocultural theory, new IL forms originate in collaborative dialogue with supportive others and gradually get internalized in a cognitive process that has been documented by such researchers as Swain and Lapkin (1998). Bakhtin's contribution to our understanding of SLA would be that L2 forms internalized from valued others retain the social characteristics of their origins; internalizing such voices may be part of learning related social roles. An adolescent immersion student who studies abroad may find that interacting with and identifying with a TL-speaking peer allows her to internalize the 'voice' and the social role of that peer (Tarone and Swain 1995). Broner and Tarone (2001), and Tarone (2000b), show how L2 learners can call up and practice the previously internalized 'voices' of others when they engage in language play. Ohta (2001) also documents language play in an immersion classroom.

The centrality of social setting and social role in the longitudinal process of SLA is clear in the work of Guo-qiang Liu, in a study supervised by Howard Nicholas (Liu 1991; Tarone and Liu 1995).

Interlanguage variation and acquisition

Tarone and Liu (1995) report a longitudinal study of 'Bob', a 5-year-old Chinese boy learning English L2 in Australia. Liu audiotaped Bob over a period of two years in three social settings. Bob produced different levels of sentence complexity and different stages of questions in three different social settings. Social settings were defined in terms of interlocutor and the topics Bob normally talked about with each interlocutor: (1) interactions with his teacher in class, (2) interactions with his fellow students at deskwork in class, and (3) interactions at home with the researcher, who filled a role as 'Chinese uncle'—described in Liu (1991) as someone a child can play with, tease, and argue with. In Setting (3), the researcher and Bob spent a good deal of time on the floor playing with Lego and coloring; their discourse focuses on these activities.

Bob took few risks in Setting (1) with his teacher because his role as a student did not permit him to; he was most focused on being accurate in this setting. Looking at one interaction with his teacher, on 30 November 1987, we see that Bob does not initiate turns; he only responds to the teacher's initiations, and he produces simple sentences and sentence fragments with her. Note also that Bob does not initiate any negotiation of meaning with his teacher; he produces no clarification requests, for example, and he responds only minimally to his teacher's.

(6)   Session 59 (30 Nov. 1987) lines 8185–227
    T1:   Bob what can I do for you?
    BOB: *I want to publish a book.*
    T1:   You want to publish a book. OK.
    BOB: *This one. Ay. I'm now put in there.*
    T1:   Now what did you do about your story, my friend?
    BOB: *Zoo.*
    T1:   Do you want me to write it or you write it?
    BOB: *You write it.*
    T1:   You want me to write it. Now which cover would you like? Blue one or orange one? Which color?
    BOB: *Blue one.*
    T1:   What size do you want it? Do you want it this big or that big?
    BOB: *This big.*
    T1:   This big. OK. Right. So we have that size. Now do you want to write it or do you want me to write it?
    BOB: *You write it.*
    T1:   Me to write it. OK. You want to put some pictures in it too?
    BOB: *Yeah.*
    T1:   So we need some white paper and some paper for pictures. Have you got your stories?
    BOB: *Yeah. About zoo.*
    T1:   What?
    BOB: *Zoo.*

Clearly, Bob is capable of much more than this: four months earlier, on 20 July 1987, in Setting (2) here is Bob interacting with his fellow students in deskwork. He initiates turns several times. His sentences seem much more complex: 'Look he doesn't know how to draw' and 'I know how to draw stars.' Bob also assertively negotiates meaning with his peers, as we see at the end of the episode, where he energetically accuses Paul of presenting the teacher's drawing as his own.

(7)   Session 43 (20 July 1987) lines 5935–76

    MARK: You can't draw the same sorts as in everything you know. Like the original. [Pointing at Ben's work of wave lines.]

    BOB: *Yeah yeah. You can draw. Look that.* [To Ben]

    MARK: You can't can you? So I can't either.

    BOB: *Look he doesn't know how to draw.* [To Ben about Mark]

    MARK: I can draw better than both of you.

    BEN: Um can you draw peak? [Meaning mountain peak]

    MARK: Yes I can.

    BOB: *OK you draw.*

    BEN: Can you draw school?

    MARK: Yes I can.

    BEN: Can you draw the whole world?

    MARK: Yes I can.

    BEN: Ah ha no one can draw the whole world. [Paul comes to the table.]

    BEN: Can you draw the whole world?

    MARK: He would.

    BEN: You don't know because you don't know how to draw.

    MARK: I *don't* know how to draw the whole world.

    BOB: *You don't know.*

    BEN: Do you know how to draw stars?

    BOB: *No he don't know.*

    MARK: I *don't* know how to draw stars. There's no one in the world knows how to draw stars.

    BOB: *I know how to draw stars. It's it's very easy. You doesn't know.* [Some time later]

    PAUL: Ben I draw better than you.

    BOB: *No you not. It's not. It's teacher's draw.* [To Paul] *Look look he can't.* [To Ben about Paul]

    BEN: The teacher drawed that.

    BOB: *Yeah.*

    BEN: Bullshit.

    BOB: *Bullshit.*

And at about the same time Bob interacted with his teacher, he had the following exchange in Setting (3) with the researcher (his 'Chinese uncle') at home on 10 December 1987. Here Bob initiates multiple utterances and produces very complex sentences: 'I'm not tell you what I'm doing now,' 'I draw all of them, so it's complete.' In Setting (3), Bob is most relaxed, and most focused on meaning, not accuracy of form.

(8)   Session 61 (10 Dec. 1987)
        BOB: *Now I know what I can do.*
        RES: Yeah.
        BOB: *I'm not tell you what I'm doing now.*
        RES: Tell me what you're doing.
        BOB: *I'm not tell you. I draw all of them, so it's complete.*
        RES: What do you want to draw?
        BOB: *I'm not tell you.*
        RES: I know. It's nothing except colors.
        BOB: *No. I'm going to draw something. No. I'm not lie to you.*
        RES: I didn't say you were lying.
        BOB: *I'm just draw a ghost. Can't draw.*
        RES: You're drawing a ghost?
        BOB: *Yeah. I can draw all of them.*
        RES: OK. I'll see what sort of ghost you can draw.
        BOB: *I draw a lovely ghost.*

The quantitative analysis in Table 4.1 shows that Bob's shift in sentence complexity across social settings (2) and (3) is robust.

Similarly, Table 4.2 shows a quantitative measure of Bob's initiation of utterances in the three social settings. Bob initiated utterances far less with his

Context	No.	%
With peers	40	18
With researcher	177	82
Total	207	

Note: Social Context (1) is not included here because there were so few complex sentences produced in that setting.

Table 4.1 Complex structures produced by Bob in two contexts (Liu 1991: 211, Table 8.5)

Context	Initiations	Responses	Total
With teachers	74 (29%)	186 (71%)	260 (100%)
With peers	1,798 (73%)	651 (27%)	2,449 (100%)
With researcher	3,497 (61%)	2,219 (39%)	5,716 (100%)

Table 4.2 A comparison of initiations and responses in three contexts (3/3/87 to 10/12/88)

teacher than with either the researcher or his peers in deskwork. Unsurprisingly, he appears to initiate turns the most with his peers. He clearly initiates far more with the researcher than with his teacher.

Bob's stages of acquisition of English questions[8] were related to these three social settings. Almost every new stage of question first appeared at home, then at deskwork, and last with the teacher (for the exception to this pattern, see below). Thus, social setting affected rate of SLA; the rate of acquisition of L2 appeared to be fastest in the at-home setting. Indeed, Liu (1991) argues that if Bob's only social setting for English use had been in interactions with his teacher, his progress in acquiring English L2 would have been much slower. Crucially, sociolinguists refer to Bob's pattern of language change as 'change from below': development begins in the least-monitored style and spreads over time to the most-monitored style.

But even more important than its impact on *rate* was the impact of social setting on the *route* of Bob's question acquisition: *social setting affected order of acquisition*. This is a particularly startling finding in view of the claim (Meisel, Clahsen, and Pienemann 1981, and Pienemann and Johnston 1987) that question stages must always be acquired in a set order, from Stage 1 through 5. But for Bob, Stage 4 and 5 questions appeared before Stage 3 questions. Stages 4 and 5 emerged at home in Sessions 23 and 24, but Stage 3 did not appear until Session 36, in deskwork with peers. Clearly, something in these three different social settings affected Bob's cognitive processing and internalization of new L2 rules to such an extent that he acquired them out of their so-called 'universal' order.

Social role was pivotally important in this process. Social role affected even Bob's willingness to take the risk of initiating utterances at all. Bob took few risks with his teacher, choosing to perform the role of Obedient Student in interactions with her in her role as Teacher, responding minimally and with simple syntax to her initiations in conversation. He initiated far more utterances, and produced more complex utterances with the researcher, in his role of 'nephew' to the researcher's 'Chinese uncle' role. In interactions with his peers, Bob also initiated more; the boys' roles in this social context involved in a good deal of competition and jockeying for social position within the group. It seems likely that Bob was developing discourse domains (Selinker and Douglas 1985; Tarone 2000a; Douglas 2004) in his interlanguage that were tied to social context and social role: varieties of his interlanguage[9] tied to internally defined social contexts of language use. For Bob, innovation occurred first in the speech style with least attention to language form: a case of implicit SLA, or 'change from below' (see note 4 for definitions of the sociolinguistic processes of 'change from above' and 'change from below').

It is clear that Liu's study needs replication. We need more longitudinal studies of individual learners interacting in a set of social settings defined by different interlocutor–learner role relationships. This is the only research design that can explore the complex relationship between social setting and

L2 acquisition, and fully describe the social and cognitive factors that under-lie this relationship.

Theoretical and practical implications

This chapter has presented empirical evidence from variationist research showing that social setting affects both the L2 input provided to learners, and those learners' variable interlanguage use and acquisition over time. It has shown that social setting affects L2 input in three ways: whether learners get linguistically and conversationally adjusted L2 input (whether interlocutors feel it is rude to provide it); whether helpful negotiation of meaning occurs in the L2 (whether social dominance in a relationship prevents noticing and accurate identification of the cause of a communication problem); and whether learners notice corrective feedback and incorporate it into their subsequent language use (whether the social setting encourages a focus of attention on meaning as opposed to form, and whether uptake is affected by the learner's belief that the interlocutor is a model to be emulated). It has shown that social setting affects learners' interlanguage production (or use) in code-switching, in the use of linguistic variants tied to attention to form vs. meaning, and to attested sociolinguistic process of change in their appropriation of 'voices'—language varieties tied to prestigious or minority group social roles and identities.

Variationists have developed a detailed model of bilingual sociocognition that explains these findings and others in detail (for a detailed discussion, with empirical examples, see Preston 2000, 2002; Fasold and Preston 2007). This model of bilingual sociocognition generates several testable hypotheses about the relationship between specific social and linguistic variables and very specific elements of L2 learner language. In this model of the bilingual brain, there is a separate grammar for each language known, and each grammar is used in accordance with empirically established sociolinguistic principles. In using each grammar, the speaker has the capacity to systematically shift the frequency of production of specified variants of linguistic forms in response to a range of empirically identified contextual variables, both linguistic (such as formal characteristics of the input) and social (such as diverse interlocutors and topics). This model predicts that in each grammar (including the native language grammar) some styles and registers (typically those internalized ear-liest) are implicitly acquired (as in 'change from below'), while other speech styles (typically those internalized later in life, as at school) are explicitly learned (as in 'change from above'). These later-learned native language styles are not as 'deep' in cognition as those acquired earlier, meaning they are not as easily accessed, and may require more conscious attention and control when they are used. In the same way, the entire grammar of a second language can be expected to be less 'deep' in cognition than the entire native language grammar, meaning that it is not as easily accessed and may be characterized by relative uncertainty on the part of the speaker. (This view of learner language as less deeply embedded than the native language accords with the views of

Adjémian (1976) and Dewaele (2004).) Within the interlanguage grammar (just as within the native language grammar), there are different styles and registers, some earlier acquired and 'deeper,' and others later learned and less easily controlled. Other sociocognitive models described in this volume (e.g. sociocultural, interactionist) tend to restrict their explanations of SLA to explicit L2 learning (in sociolinguistic terms, 'change from above'). A sociolinguistic model of SLA is more powerful than these, because it can predict and explain *both* explicit *and* implicit second language acquisition, using a detailed computer model (Fasold and Preston 2007) containing sociolinguistic constructs based on decades of empirical evidence from studies of language use in a wide range of social contexts, including SLA contexts.

Finally, there is a very practical ethical consequence of the research and issues reviewed in this chapter. Since social context does affect cognition in SLA, then we as researchers need to expand the range of social contexts in which we carry out SLA research. To date almost all SLA data is taken from educated L2 learners in university or other educational settings. As a consequence, we know next to nothing about the processes and outcomes of second language acquisition in social contexts outside the university—for example, the SLA processes and outcomes of the vast majority of L2 learners on the planet who are low literate or illiterate adults and adolescents, and do not attend schools or universities (Bigelow and Tarone 2004; Bigelow et al. 2006). It is certainly possible that, in second language acquisition and use, as in general linguistics (cf. Everett 2005, 2009), social contexts far from universities and schools may impact cognitive processes of SLA in very distinctive and at present unknown ways. If we conclude that social context does indeed significantly affect cognitive processes of SLA, and if our goal is to understand the *human* cognitive capacity for second language acquisition, then we should study diverse types of L2 learners in a wide range of social contexts, and not just focus on a relatively narrow spectrum of educated L2 learners in academic contexts.

Appendix A

(stages from Pienemann and Johnston 1987; Meisel, Clahsen, and Pienemann 1981):

Stage 1	**Single word**
Stage 2	**SVO?** Canonical word order is maintained, and intonation indicates the question. Bob: *You like number one?* (Session **29** with researcher.)
Stage 3	**Do-front without inversion**, and **WHX-front without inversion**. The canonical SVO word order is retained, and a 'question word' is added at the front (either 'do' or unanalyzed WHX). Bob: *Why you do that?* (Session **36** with peers.)
Stage 4	**Pseudo-inversion**. Units can be moved from the center to the front of the string, but there can be no internal movement ('is' for example can be moved to the front of a string creating a Yes/No question. 'Where's' may front a question, but only as an unanalyzed unit. True WH questions, however, cannot be created, as this requires the movement of a unit from one internal position to another). Y/N inversion Bob: *Where's the monkey?* (Session **24** with researcher)

Stage 5   **Aux-2nd**, and **Suppletion**. This allows formation of true WH questions.
Bob: What are you doing? (Session **24** with researcher.)

Stage 6   **Question tag.** Allows different word orders in different clauses to express the question.
Bob: *You don't like green, are you?* (Session **49** with researcher.)

Appendix A Developmental Stages in Bob's English Question Formation

Notes

An earlier version of this chapter appeared in Tarone (2007*b*). I am very grateful to colleagues who have provided me with feedback on its contents: to George Yule, who helped me frame the argument more precisely, to Martha Bigelow and Bonnie Swierzbin, who provided additional suggestions, and to Dennis Preston. Bobbie Lafford's input on Tarone (2007*a*) also found its way into this chapter. As always, errors and mis-statements are mine alone.

1. The conference that produced this volume is one, of course, but there is also the 2004 special issue of the *International Review of Applied Linguistics* on variation in the interlanguage of advanced L2 learners (Mougeon and Dewaele 2004); a collection of papers on learning context and its effects on SLA in a special issue of *Studies in Second Language Acquisition* (Collentine and Freed, 2004); and a special issue of *Modern Language Journal* (Lafford 2007), including Tarone (2007*a*), on the impact of Firth and Wagner's 1997 call for an expanded research approach in SLA that is less focused on isolated cognitive factors, one that can accommodate situationally and individually specific variables.

2. Everett (2005, 2009) shows that specific predictions of UG (Universal Grammar) theorists (Hauser, Chomsky, and Fitch 2002) are simply not borne out in his study of Piraha, a language used in a remote Amazonian community. Everett claims that the community's cultural values affect the grammar of the language, so that, for example, recursion, a feature claimed in UG to be a universal characteristic of all human language, does not occur. UG, a purely psycholinguistic theory of language, thus fails to account for very significant effects of social and cultural variables on the grammar of Piraha.

3. Other approaches to socioognition in SLA described in this volume lack variationists' field-tested methodology for the collection and the analysis of variable sociolinguistic data using VARBRUL to do computer modeling of language use in relation to complex, changing contextual variables. Another advantage for SLA variationists is that sociolinguistics has identified key social variables that constrain variation in all languages in systematic and predictable ways, as well as pervasive sociolinguistic processes such as 'change from above' and 'change from below' that clearly affect SLA (Preston 1989: 59–62, 244; Tarone 2007*a*: 844).

4. 'Change from above' involves a (typically) conscious shift by a speaker toward more prestigious or standard language forms. 'Change from below' involves a less conscious process of change, involving adoption of non-standard language forms that are often identified with minority groups of various kinds. Both kinds of change occur in SLA (Preston 1989: 59–62, 244).

5. Carrier (1999) also shows that social status plays a role in L2 listening comprehension.

6. Though some may join with me in disagreeing with spellcheckers about standards, in such cases we are questioning the linguistic competence of the human who programmed the spellchecker.

7. While I focus here on the impact of social context on interlanguage variation, it must be acknowledged that many sociolinguistically oriented studies have documented the impact of linguistic context on IL variation as well. Among these are Geeslin (2003), Geeslin and Guijarro-Fuentes (2006), Bayley and Langman (2004), and Howard (2004).

8. Please see Appendix A for Pienemann and Johnston's (1987) developmental stages of acquisition of questions, illustrated with actual utterances produced by Bob.

9. As Rehner (2002) points out, there are two types of language variation in interlanguage: Type 1 variation (i.e. registers unique to interlanguages produced by L2 learners, i.e. 'erroneous' variation), or Type 2 variation (i.e. language variation that mirrors native speaker variation).

PART TWO

Interpersonal and intrapersonal perspectives on language learning

5

The intersection of social, cognitive, and cultural processes in language learning: a second language socialization approach

PATRICIA A. DUFF AND

MASAKI KOBAYASHI

Introduction

Second language (L2) socialization research is a relatively recent area of scholarship in applied linguistics, dating back to the early 1990s (e.g. Poole 1992; Duff 2003, 2007a, 2007b, 2008a, 2008b; Watson-Gegeo and Nielsen 2003; Watson-Gegeo 2004; Zuengler and Cole 2005; Duff and Hornberger 2008; Morita and Kobayashi 2008). L2 socialization research was inspired by work in cross-cultural first language (L1) pragmatics originally (see Ochs and Schieffelin 2008 for a historical overview) and concurrently emerging scholarship in Vygotskian sociocultural theory (e.g. Vygotsky 1978; Rogoff 1990, 1995, 1998, 2003; Wertsch 1991; Lantolf 2000; Lantolf and Thorne 2006; Duff 2007a), activity theory (Leont'ev 1978, 1981), the ethnography of communication (e.g. Hymes 1972); Bakhtinian dialogism (e.g. Bakhtin 1981, 1986), and by sociological scholarship related to practice theory (Bourdieu 1977), to name just a few influences (see Garrett and Baquedano-Lopez 2002). One of the key early areas of interest was the linguistic behaviors and interactional patterns of parents or caregivers in relation to their children (or teachers with their students) that potentially facilitate language acquisition and the manner in which learners are accommodated interactionally across different cultures.

In this chapter we describe L2 socialization as a theoretical perspective that can be applied in research on classroom-oriented L2 learning (Duff forthcoming a, b, c). Because L2 socialization research brings together an analysis of social, cultural, and cognitive dimensions of situated language learning, it is highly compatible with a *sociocognitive* perspective that considers the cognitive and the social to be intricately interwoven and mutually constitutive (e.g. Ohta 2001; Atkinson 2002; Doehler 2002; van Lier 2004; see also Bloome 1994; Hicks 1996; Dias 2000; Goldman 2008), although language socialization perhaps pays more attention to *cultural* and *group* interaction processes involved in learning and less attention to the cognitive processes and linguistic development of *individual* learners. Here, we use the term 'sociocognition' to refer to the complex and dynamic interrelationship and interaction between psychological and sociocultural processes that shape—both enable and constrain—L2 learners' engagement in a variety of activities and associated learning processes and outcomes. To contribute to a greater understanding of this mutual constitutiveness of human cognition and the social world, we take a language socialization approach. We illustrate the interplay of social, cultural, and cognitive factors in a study of how Japanese international students in Canada learn to participate in cultural practices designed to increase their L2 communicative competence, as manifested by their grammatical, discursive, and pragmatic performance, in a content-based university academic exchange program.

Examining discourse surrounding the 'social-cognitive' divide in SLA

Much L2 research conducted over the past three decades has taken account of certain social-interactional aspects of language learning, and specifically of how the negotiation of meaning by interlocutors involved in oral discourse can help them learn from one another and from their own language practice (e.g. chapters in Day 1986). However, some applied linguists still maintain that the 'social' is not yet well enough theorized and integrated in second language acquisition (SLA) research (e.g. Norton 2000*b*; Block 2003), apart from providing an interactional or task context that can then be examined discursively in terms of input, interaction, and output measures. As a result, social processes, social relationships, and personal investments in, or perceptions of, tasks and participants are minimized or backgrounded; and linguistic forms and modifications are foregrounded instead. Watson-Gegeo and Nielsen (2003: 156), for example, argue that:

The cognitive/social dichotomy widely taken for granted in SLA theory obscures the relationship between the knowledge about language that learners construct and the social, cultural, and political contexts in which acquisition takes place. Cognition *originates* in social interaction. Constructing new knowledge is therefore *both* a cognitive *and* a social process. SLA theory's need for just this sort of integrative perspective is one of the arguments for taking a language socialization approach in L2 research.

Like Watson-Gegeo and Nielsen, Atkinson (2002: 537) also calls for a greater *integration* of the social and cognitive in L2 research, with a greater emphasis on how learners become able to *participate* in situated linguistic *activities*:

[A] sociocognitive approach to SLA would take the social dimensions of language and its acquisition seriously....Second, language and its acquisition would be fully integrated into other activities, people, and things in a sociocognitive approach to SLA. They would be seen as integral parts of larger sociocognitive wholes, or, in Gee's (1992) term, *Discourses*... Third, language and its acquisition, from a sociocognitive perspective, would be seen in terms of 'action' and 'participation'—as providing an extremely powerful semiotic means of performing and participating in activity-in-the-world (Rogoff 1990, 1998; Lave and Wenger 1991). Finally, a sociocognitive perspective should not, strictly speaking, exclude. As an approach to language, it is fundamentally cognitive and fundamentally social... it argues for the profound interdependency and integration of both.

Few contributors to this book would dispute the notion that the construction of new linguistic knowledge is both a cognitive and social process, as Watson-Gegeo and Nielsen point out. Indeed, many SLA researchers, as this book illustrates so well, already integrate (micro-)social (i.e. interactional) and cognitive processes in their studies of SLA. However, authors might differ in their views on the relative *primacy* of the social versus the cognitive/linguistic or how much of the 'social' is directly relevant to their own research questions and needs to be addressed in SLA studies. Here we do not claim that any one theoretical or methodological approach is superior. Rather, we suggest that language socialization offers an interesting way of contextualizing and theorizing task- or activity-based language learning across time, tasks, participants, and communities or cultures. Some SLA researchers may have no desire to account for broader social and cultural issues and patterns of behavior, such as how issues of power, identity, cultural orientation, and cultural practice affect language learning and mediate learners' participation in particular linguistic communities, nor how students are socialized into particular identities and values through language and education. They might not be interested in L2 learners' broader or longer-term 'trajectories' of learning either, a metaphor used in 'community of practice' research (e.g. Lave and Wenger 1991; Wenger 1998). Yet learning (cognition), knowledge, socialization, and participation are different facets of the same experience—the development of the human mind (gaining knowledge, expertise) and the enablement of linguistic action in society—reflecting processes and understandings that are distributed across many co-participants or members in a community (or across multiple communities) both diachronically and synchronically. Different research traditions naturally capture aspects of this process in unique ways.

  This chapter presents an analysis of how one teacher socializes students into particular linguistic and cultural practices in the context of English for academic purposes and how the students, in turn, socialize one another to perform optimally as well. Central to our analysis is the manner in which a group of Japanese English-language students learn to perform one particular type of activity—a group oral presentation in English—using increasingly target-like language and genres as a result of their social-interactional experience.

Language socialization

Language socialization refers to the process by which novices or newcomers in a community or culture gain communicative competence, membership, and legitimacy in the group by means of social interaction and (often) overt assistance, and by participating in the activities of the group (see review chapters in Duff 2007a; Duff and Hornberger 2008). As such, language socialization examines not only language use and developmental processes, but also how those processes affect learners' participation and status in their communities and mediate their learning of other, nonlinguistic, matter. Simply put, language socialization is an interactional process in which more capable members of a community assist less linguistically, communicatively, or culturally competent individuals to become more competent members of their (new) communities. The process is mediated by language and other semiotic tools and the ultimate goal is the mastery of linguistic conventions and pragmatics, the adoption of identities, stances, ideologies, and other behaviors and knowledge associated with the target group and its normative cultural practices that allow newcomers to participate meaningfully and legitimately in that culture (e.g. Schieffelin and Ochs 1986; Garrett and Baquedano-Lopez 2002; Duff and Hornberger 2008; Ochs and Schieffelin 2008). Thus, language socialization is not concerned only with language and its acquisition and use but also the worldviews, ideologies, and other kinds of knowledge that are inculcated in activities along with language. Another aspect of language socialization research, and especially with young children, is how novices are socialized to perceive, attend to, and engage with certain stimuli (e.g. visual, auditory, or verbal forms) in their environment, which is perhaps a clearer example of cognitive processes being honed in social context.

L2 socialization research, like L1 research, contextualizes language learning within culturally developed activity systems (e.g. speech events) in which, for example, people learn to give oral presentations or participate in other tasks (activities), oral and written, as part of their learning and as part of their integration into new cultures such as academic communities (Morita 2000, 2004; Kobayashi 2006; Duff 2007b, 2008a, forthcoming a, b, c; Vickers 2007; Zappa-Hollman 2007; Morita and Kobayashi 2008; Talmy 2008). Thus, L2 socialization research explores the linkages and synergies between social, cultural, and cognitive domains across a variety of learning contexts. The research also aims to uncover the learning trajectories, participation, subjectivities, and intentionality or agency of learners in their L2-mediated communities.

Language and literacy learning typically involves both *explicit* and *implicit* socialization through linguistic and social interaction into relevant local communicative practices or ways of using language (Duff forthcoming a, b, c). Explicit socialization might take the form of prompts, directives, or corrections, such as 'Say x' or 'Don't say x.' Implicit socialization takes place through observation of others as they perform particular linguistic and cognitive operations that the learner is expected to internalize and adopt through experience. L2 socialization shares many of the same principles and objectives as L1 socialization research with young children learning their first language, but with the added complexity of dealing with children or adults who already possess a repertoire of linguistic, discursive, and cultural traditions, community affiliations, and perspectives when encountering new ones and must then negotiate two potentially competing systems; they may also encounter challenges in being accommodated sufficiently well within their new communities. Or they may themselves have misgivings or feel conflicted or ambivalent about becoming fuller members in the new L2-mediated social worlds for a variety of personal and social reasons related to the loss of their identities and former ways (Pavlenko and Lantolf 2000; Duff 2002, 2003, 2004, 2007*a*).

The study

To illustrate a language socialization approach, we present data from Kobayashi (2003, 2004) concerning the conceptualization of an assigned task within a particular culture; students' negotiation of task specifications and teacher expectations; students' preparation both in class and outside class and their metalinguistic discussions about the accuracy and appropriateness of particular forms; and ultimately students' group presentations of their projects in class. Eleven focal students participated in the study, selected from a much larger cohort. They were enrolled in sheltered credit-bearing content courses called Language Fieldwork A (semester 1) and B (semester 2) designed for students whose academic English still needed attention. The students' TOEFL scores upon entry did not meet the university minimum requirement of 580, and were often closer to 500. They took other 'sheltered' content courses (with other international students) concurrently, and in the second semester usually took content courses in other departments as well, according to their majors and interests.

The institutional context was an undergraduate academic exchange program at Western Province University (WPU, a pseudonym) in Canada. Up to a hundred Japanese students took academic credit courses during their study-abroad year at WPU. Some of the courses, particularly in their first semester, provided explicit language support for these international students and thereby integrated language and content instruction. Students were accountable for the course content as well as linguistic aspects of communication.

Data examined here were collected in students' first-semester Language Fieldwork A course on Intercultural Communication and in their second-semester Language Fieldwork B course on Research Methods. Data were obtained through ethnographic participant observation in both courses (350 hours of in-class and out-of-class observation of project-related work), in-depth, semi-structured interviews with students and teachers, audio and video recordings of their interactions, audio-journals kept by key students, e-mail interviews with students, the researcher's field notes and reflective journals, and collection of relevant documents such as course outlines, class handouts, and students' written journals, term papers, and notes (see Kobayashi 2004). Not all those sources of data are included here though.

The instructor for both courses, 'Izzat' (a pseudonym), was a highly proficient non-native speaker of English and an experienced English language teacher with expertise in content-based language teaching and educational research. She often noted her solidarity with her students as a fellow ESL learner herself, and she tolerated their use of their L1 (Japanese) in class, and sometimes used Chinese characters (from Mandarin, her L2) to clarify meanings of abstract concepts for the Japanese students. She was well regarded by both colleagues and students.

Our goal here is to illustrate how a language socialization approach can be applied to L2 classroom research to explore teaching and learning processes— that is, not only the social and cultural dimensions of learning but cognitive ones as well. The pedagogical unit of analysis or activity setting was not a *task* as it is typically operationalized in SLA studies—namely, a goal-directed collaborative activity involving the exchange of information between interlocutors to solve various kinds of problems. Such tasks are usually confined to one lesson or one short laboratory session. Instead, we focus on a larger activity context, a *project*, comprising a series of tasks performed inside and outside class over a number of days or weeks that culminate in one major project with a corresponding group/pair presentation and individual term papers (Kobayashi 2006). The project presentation and term paper constitute an oral and written genre of research synthesis and discussion valued within not only the academic exchange program at WPU but also the wider local academic context.

Project work is often used in content-based language teaching and academic, vocational, and other real-world settings because students must actively build 'a community of inquiry involving authentic communication, cooperative learning, collaboration, and problem-solving' (Stoller 2002: 107). It therefore provides a social setting in which peers are expected to develop their language, literacy, and communication skills, and their critical thinking and problem-solving, and also develop their identities, roles, and agency as group members working together to accomplish meaningful projects in English typically over a period of time, such as a semester.

These social, cognitive, and pragmatic aspects of project work were among the instructor's top priorities. For example, when coaching the students on strategies required for implementing particular research methods, Izzat cautioned the class:

let's say if you choose to interview [people at the volunteer sites], the first thing you have to do is—you have to know how to cooperate—with the people you're going to interview. You have to know how to ask them nicely. And you have to learn what to do if they say no.   (Kobayashi 2004: 125)

She was therefore priming them to plan requesting strategies to engage participants at the sites where they did their volunteer work. Such planning involves social and cultural finesse but also pragmatic sophistication, something that would need to be thought out and linguistically rehearsed in advance. Project work also entails Rogoff's (1995: 142) notions of guided participation and cognitive apprenticeship, the former defined as 'the process and systems of involvement between people as they communicate and coordinate efforts while participating in culturally valued activities'. The notion that cognition can benefit from social apprenticeship, from focusing, rehearsing, modeling, and so on, is highly relevant to the three-component approach to learning represented by language socialization (social, cultural, and cognitive, mediated by language) in this chapter. The instructor and other interlocutors must provide assistance to one another in order for the projects to be successfully completed.

The analysis below focuses on the 'life cycle' of one such project, and its organic in-class and out-of-class development, as students became co-agents of socialization, coaching one another through a variety of meetings and rehearsals and strategies, using both Japanese and English in order to ultimately deliver an effective English presentation mediated by Power-Point or by a poster. In the process, the learners also had opportunities to compare, evaluate, and internalize new linguistic forms, important cognitive processes.

In one of the courses studied (Intercultural Communication, semester 1), the instructor's goals were to have students work together in preparing a presentation about their experiences as volunteers with a variety of local community organizations, travel agencies, Japanese language classes on campus, and so on. The 'task' (project), therefore, required that students form groups, reach a collective understanding about the nature of their assignment, and then proceed with planning a 30-minute presentation reflecting on their set of experiences, followed by an individually completed term paper. This process typically took a couple of weeks. As the course outline stated:

> The oral presentation is the sharing of your volunteer experiences. You will tell the class what you did as a volunteer, what you learned, and what significance this learning will have for your future. You have 20 minutes for the presentation and 10 minutes for discussion. Your presentation has to be well-organized and interesting. You are encouraged to use audio-visual and graphic materials in your presentation and to *talk* from them. That is, do not read from your notes. There will be a model presentation to show you how oral presentations are done. You are encouraged to do this assignment in pairs (i.e., groups of two) because working with another person can result in more and better ideas.   (Kobayashi 2004: 140, emphasis original)

When the teaching assistant for the course gave a model presentation to the class, he (ibid. 148) also stressed the importance of this particular type of task, both for the English language learners and for him as a graduate student too, that it was part of the academic life and culture of the university:

We've talked a little bit about this before but - unfortunately or fortunately - *presentations are a really important part - of classes at WPU.* Uh: almost - every single class - course I've taken at WPU and my old university - required me to give presentations. So: it's one of those skills that *we* need to work on - as uh students.

The social, cultural, and cognitive elements of the presentation assignment included the following: (1) students needed to find a partner to form a pair or a small group to conduct the project; (2) they needed to jointly negotiate the nature of the task requirements and come up with a strategy for undertaking it; (3) they then needed to exchange information based on their individual volunteer experiences in order to jointly produce a coherent and effective oral report based on their experiences or research, including a PowerPoint or poster accompanying their presentation, depending on the course; and (4) they subsequently needed to submit their own written version of the report. The project specifications were meant to conform to local cultural norms for English academic presentations.

Interpersonally, finding available, compatible group members was the first challenge. One or another student in the group often emerged as the leader and exerted some authority and initiative to keep moving the project along through a series of planning stages, distributed across time and space (i.e. classroom and dormitories). But other students also exercised their own agency and shared their opinions, knowledge, and concerns. Cognitively, they needed to compare, contrast, and synthesize their joint experiences and present the findings within the assigned time frame in comprehensible oral English and using the technology and multimodality of PowerPoint. Specifically, they needed to make sense of their experiences as volunteers at the same or different Canadian institutions and compare those experiences or institutions with their counterparts in Japan or with their readings, and consider some future implications of their experiences and reflections. The students commonly used both Japanese and English to scaffold their negotiation of the task (project) and its subcomponents, but as the time grew nearer to rehearsing and presenting it, they shifted increasingly to English.

Negotiating and deconstructing the task (project)

At first the students grappled with the task itself, reading the instructions in English from the teacher, and then trying to sort out the implications of the instructions (using Japanese) for their own planning purposes. For example, they needed to come to terms with the fact that audio-visual aids were required (which they interpreted to mean PowerPoint) and that students were not allowed to read a script—and would therefore have to memorize their script, they decided—even though another group had recently read theirs. Thus, their task (project) interpretation was a necessary reconciliation of their preconceived notions about course presentations, their prior observations, and the explicit socialization and instruction by the teacher about criteria such as not reading. As Coughlan and Duff (1994) argued, the same task may be interpreted and enacted as quite different sorts of activities by different participants.

One student in this study, for example, was convinced that, based on her prior experience in sociology, academic presentations should include library research, references, and interviews and not just an analysis of their own observations and journals about their volunteering experiences. This issue therefore needed to be sorted out by her and her group. For example, her partner, Kiku, retorted:

Not the academic thing. (maybe) it's - my opinion though - reading from this (1.7) statements (xx) yeah. ((reading the course outline)) 'You will tell the class, what - what you did as a volunteer - what you learned - what significance this learning will have for your future.' (0.8) **It's sort of like your** (0.9) **hmm - from your perspective.** <Nana: hmm.> We don't have to borrow so many books from library, (0.6) (not many) references. I think so. Do you think so?   (Kobayashi 2004: 169)

That is, Kiku interpreted the task to be more experiential and opinion-based and not one based primarily on library research. In the end, they needed to consult the instructor about her expectations in that regard though.

In the following example students were negotiating in both L1 Japanese and L2 English in one of the student's dorm rooms after class about what they would present about. (Tamiko appears to want to socialize the group into English language use, in turn 2, but there is no uptake by Ringo, the leader, to switch from Japanese to English; in fact, both she and Fuyumi seem uncertain about one of the words Tamiko has used.) All three had completed a number of hours volunteering at a senior citizens' facility. In their planning, however, they needed to clarify the meaning of the English word *facility (shisetsu* in Japanese) that Tamiko used (turn 2), since it represented what she wanted to focus on in her part of the presentation and was therefore an important concept to clarify in the context of a group presentation.

1	RINGO:	*Tami-chan purezen de nani happyo suru tsumori?* [Tami-chan, what do you intend to talk about in the presentation?]
2	TAMI:	I ju- Uh: ((laughs)) can I try to speak English? I'm just thinking to like - sur- survey - like focus on the project or **facility**, of welfare.
3	RINGO:	*Fasirit'i? Shisetsu ne.* [**Facility**? It means *shisetsu* [facility], right?]
4	TAMI:	But not so big project - I'm just like uh - thinking to -
5	FUYU:	Eh - what do you mean **facility**.
6	RINGO:	*Fasirit'i tte doo iu koto - hon nara gutaiteki ni.* [What exactly do you mean by **facility**.]...

(Kobayashi 2004: 133)

In the end, however, even after additional turns (not shown), it was still not clear to the others what Tamiko meant by *facility*, which seemed to have been relevant to her volunteer experience accompanying seniors home from a seniors' facility (e.g. activity center, social institution). Tamiko and Fuyumi tried to continue in English for a few turns afterward but eventually switched to Japanese to ensure that they all understood the main themes to be included in the presentation and what she intended to say. Naturally, Japanese was also a language that allowed them to quickly establish interpersonal rapport and solidarity as classmates in addition to helping them achieve understanding of one another's intentions. Therefore, the task itself required that students' attention be focused on shared goals and meanings because there was a joint investment in, and accountability for, one another's contributions to the project and presentation.

In another example, a different group was trying to grasp what the requirements were for the assigned project presentation. This initial stage of task clarification was crucial because it determined the criteria for the final presentation and thus the steps to be taken leading to that outcome. What follows is a short version of a longer conversation this group had about the task itself and the obvious significance given to the course outline as a source of explicit direction or socialization regarding normative performance.

1   NANA: 'Encouraged to use audiovisual and graphic materials - [in your presentation.'

2   KIKU: [*Sonnan* PowerPoint *yan na:*
[Definitely PowerPoint, right?]

3   NANA: PowerPoint. PowerPoint *tsukatta hoo ga ii kedo tooku ga mein ya yo tte koto ne.*
[This means it's better to use PowerPoint, but talking is primary, right?]
'That is do not read from your notes.' *E:::::? Anki nan?*
[What? We must memorize lines?]

4   SHIN: *Demo - yonde - yondeta yan.*
[But they were reading from notes weren't they?]

5   KIKU: *Un. Yondeta zo.*
[Yeah. They were.]

(adapted from Kobayashi 2003: 348)

This group met five times (13 hours over a 5-day period) to prepare their presentation. Nana, Shingo, and Kiku used their L1, Japanese, to help scaffold their negotiation of the parameters of the project: reading the teacher's English instructions and then trying to make sense of them (in Japanese) in light of their experiences in class to date in which some students had indeed read from notes, which was disallowed. Their L1 scaffolded their task accomplishment and intersubjectivity in ways reported in other L2 research (e.g. Antón and DiCamilla 1999; Swain and Lapkin 2000). With respect to the point that in this first-semester class some of the presenters had been reading their notes (a point they all subsequently agreed they should *not* emulate), in the second semester with the same students Izzat became stricter about the requirement not to read notes and in fact explicitly warned them: 'Reading from notes is the worst way of doing a presentation. And that's the easiest way to put people to sleep...Because you are not looking at people—you are not having eye contact...' (p. 145). Her explicit directive about this point came in response to what she had observed in the first semester in their earliest stages of academic discourse socialization at WPU, when she had not enforced that rule very strictly. Thus, a combination of her explicit socialization, the students' observations of prior practice, and their negotiation in Japanese about the task requirements helped prime them for the cognitive demands and cognitive preparation of doing an unscripted (or at least 'unread') presentation together.

Performing the task (project presentation)

When it came to actually producing their presentation collaboratively, in the 'Future Implications' phase of the assignment, Nana, Kiku, and Shingo (shown in the previous example) produced a PowerPoint slide with a question and then three items below it:

> How would we be in the future?
> [In this kind of unexpected situation]
> - Creative
> - Flexibility
> - Calm down

This slide resulted in very focused negotiation, that is, the creation of inter-subjectivity or shared cognition connected to metalinguistic awareness, regarding the words *creative*, *flexibility*, and *calm down*, which not all of them agreed belonged to the same part of speech. Kiku, for example, in turn 4 below, noted that the second item, *flexibility*, needed to be changed to an adjectival form, which Shin then supplied: *flexible*. Kiku then expressed some ambivalence about the correctness of *calm down* (turn 8), but Nana felt that it was acceptable (turn 11).

1	NANA:	**Flexibility** *da yo sore wa.* [**Flexibility**.
		[That should be flexibility.
2	KIKU:	[*Akan wa - kore.*
		[This is no good.]
3	NANA:	*E-?*
		[What?]
4	KIKU:	*Keiyoo shi janai to akan, ato no ga keiyooshi yakara.*
		[It should be an adjective because the others are adjectives.]
		(0.9)
5	SHIN:	U:mm (10.3)
6	KIKU:	*So osuru to=*
		[So it's]

7   SHIN: =Flexible?
8   KIKU: *Ya na. Kore de ii ka na.*
            [Yeah it is. Does this look OK.] (3.1)
9   NANA: Calm [down? -
10 KIKU: [*Doo?* [What do you think?] (0.8) mm:
11 NANA: *Hai. Ii n ja nai kashira.* [Yeah. I think it's okay.]
(adapted from Kobayashi 2003: 350)

They had therefore been socialized by the task demands and other instructional practices into seeking consensus about linguistic forms (part of speech; use of parallel forms in the same slide). To that end, they tapped into their collective knowledge of English grammar, sometimes correctly, and sometimes not, but definitely improving on the original version. Three days later, when they made their presentation, their oral version of the revised slide was consistent with what they had negotiated and agreed upon earlier:

KIKU: Maybe - some kind of ideas like crea- **creative** ideas (0.6) or (2.0)
         so you can be **flexible** (0.6) and then you can **be calm down** even if
         you are faced to that kind of emergency (0.9) emergency.
(Kobayashi 2003: 350)

Thus, together, they came up with adjectival forms for *creative* and *flexible*, but had changed *calm down* to a somewhat more adjectival form: *be calm down* but one that also resembled an ungrammatical passive construction (in effect, it was a hybrid of two parts of speech). The convergence of shared and individual cognition and social interaction, within the larger sociocultural context of this activity, as they now understood it, is evident in their selection and editing of the phrases they chose to stress.

The same group had another extended discussion about the appropriateness of the adjectives *self-centred* vs. *selfish* in a different PowerPoint slide. They ultimately agreed to use *selfish* for the oral presentation and *self-centred* for their written paper, because they thought their classmates would understand *selfish* more easily but that Izzat would be impressed by *self-centred*. Thus, their choice of vocabulary was determined not only by their seeking consensus about accuracy within the group but also out of consideration for their wider social context: their audience of peers, their peers' level of comprehension, and how certain lexical choices might position them (in terms of expertise), especially in Izzat's evaluation of their written version. This negotiation, therefore, involved developing an awareness of lexical choices, synonyms, and appropriate contexts of use of different forms for different pragmatic purposes.

Another group, in their out-of-class presentation rehearsal shown below, also manipulated language collaboratively, using both Japanese and English, with the intention to flatter Izzat in the conclusion of their presentation. They wanted to say, with some playful irony, how much they 'appreciated' having been given 'such a good opportunity' to present about their experiences in this forum. To do so they needed to find the appropriate speech act in English to express their (mock) gratitude.

9   TOMO: *Un.* Share. Share *dekite koo iu koto o hakken deki mashi ta. Dakara* (0.6) *minna mo*share *shita ra jibun no hakken ga aru kamo shiremasen yo tte itte* = [Yeah share. We could share our experiences and make these discoveries. So (0.6) if you share your experience you may make your own discovery - you say something like this and]

10   KOYU: = *Un un un.* = [Yeah yeah yeah.]

11   TOMO: = *de - koo iu kikai o ataete kurete* Izzat *ni* (0.6) *totemo kansha shite imasu to koo itte* [and - **we are very grateful to Izzat, who gave this opportunity - say something like this and**]

12   KOYU: **Appreciate!**

13   TOMO: *Soo.* [Yeah.] **I really appreciate you give me such a good opportunity.**

14   KOYU: **Such** **a good opportunity! Great!** *Sore sugoi.* [That's great.]

15   TOMO: **And uh - ((jokingly)) thank you Izzat.**

16   KOYU: **'Such a'** - *tte - kaite oko.* ((writes it down)) ['Such a' - I will write this down.]

17   YUJI: **Such a - such a great opportunity!** (3.6) (November 22, 2000)

(Kobayashi 2004: 203)

In fact, from the outset, this group had been rather perplexed by the fact that the three of them had had volunteering experiences in completely different settings, unlike Nana, Shingo, and Kiku, who had shared similar experiences. As a result, Tomo, Koyuki, and Yuji had initially wanted to do a series of three short 10-minute presentations of their individual experiences rather than one 30-minute consolidation of themes across all three. However, Izzat had insisted that they look for common themes across their experiences and present one integrated account, a much more cognitively and discursively challenging enterprise. They therefore prepared three short presentations that they then worked very hard together at consolidating into a coherent whole (which was a great success, earning an A+, as it turned out).

In boldface font in the excerpt above (turns 11–12), we see how Tomo's suggested proposition in Japanese in turn 11 is picked up by Koyuki, in turn 12, who offers the English word *appreciate* for their planned expression of gratitude toward the teacher (Izzat). Then, Tomo (turn 13), offers the emphatic phrase *such a good opportunity*, building on both Tomo's Japanese phrase in turn 11 and the beginning of its English counterpart by Koyuki. *Such a good opportunity* is then echoed and adopted by an appreciative Koyuki and Yuji (turns 14–17). They therefore managed to pool their collective expertise, piece by piece, phrase by phrase, and speech act by speech act, about not only appropriate or effective English usage but also pragmatic strategies and humor aligning them with Izzat and their prior experiences. In doing so they also alluded indirectly to the difficulties they had had preparing the presentation, which Izzat was well aware of. Here we see the seamless integration of social, cognitive-linguistic, and cultural processes at play in the context of the presentation project.

These same negotiated forms were ultimately used when the presentation was delivered to the class the next day with the teacher present (Kobayashi 2004: 200). In turn 1 they provided the class with a brief narrative of their experience of integrating the three experiences (using the somewhat inappropriate form *embarrassed* to express their earlier feeling of resistance to doing a more synthetic presentation), but adding that it had been an important and valuable experience and then encouraging their classmates (in effect, explicitly socializing them into the same kinds of intersubjectivity of 'sharing ideas and experience'). Izzat's quick rejoinder to their advice, flattery, and smile was (in turn 3), *Forcing you to work together?* She then laughed, thereby also acknowledging that she knew it had been a complex process for them.

> 1   KOYU: Ah - at first, we were so **embarrassed**, because Izzat told us
>   to make <u>one</u> presentation (0.5) although we have completely
>   different volunteer experiences. So we tried to share and
>   discuss our ideas and experience again and again. (0.6)
>   And - after that, we got- we lear:ned (0.5) this - conclusion.
>   <Izzat: hmm.> And also we found how important - umm -
>   the importance of sharing ideas and experience - even people
>   - among people have - completely different experience. So
>   now we want - (0.6) we strongly want you to do the same
>   things as - - as we? (1.8) because we are sure you can find
>   <u>many</u> new things. (1.7) And we ((looking at Izzat)) **we
>   really appreciate Izzat giving us such a good opportunity.**
>   ((smiles))
> 2   TOMO: [Yeah.
> 3   IZZAT: [**Forcing you to work together?** ((laughs))
> 4   TOMO: Yeah.
> 5   YUJI: Yeah. (23 Nov. 2000)

The discursive work they had done to capture their initial complaint or difficulty, to narrate their process of doing the activity, and then acknowledging Izzat's role in all of this was for the sake of the oral presentation (as public performance, with Izzat and their peers as audience) and not the final written term papers they each produced. Yet each group's ways of engaging in/with the task (project presentation) and then performing it differed, as was also the case in Morita's (2000) study of TESL graduate students' presentations and Zappa-Hollman's (2007) study of applied science, arts, and neuroscience students' presentations at a Canadian university. In Kobayashi's data, variables included the students' original choices of partners and projects and volunteer settings, their negotiation of roles and responsibilities, their definition of the task itself, the intersection and interplay of orality and literacy in their Power-Point presentations which mediated their thinking in important ways (helping them to focus on and manipulate the form of certain constructions), their L1 joint scaffolding of L2 learning and use, their relative English proficiency, mechanisms of peer support, negotiation of audience needs and addressivity (using language that was not overly difficult for their peers but was impressive enough for their instructor), and then their final performance, perspectives, and outcomes. The entire composite of steps represents a cognitively, linguistically, discursively, and socially complex form of joint problem-solving that must, in the end, result in a coherent oral and written production. This same sort of intersubjectivity is commonplace in many language classrooms and occurs at the nexus of the social and the cognitive within a cultural activity domain mediated by language and literacy.

The *project* in this study did not occur and was not analyzed in isolation, either by the students and teacher or by the researchers: other projects that had come before it, in the same course or in previous ones, became highly relevant and contributed to students' linguistic and academic socialization and the way they then performed their own project presentation (see also Morita 2000; Zappa-Hollman 2007; Duff 2009). Their presentation strategies and performance were thus contingent on other experience (see also Rogoff 1998; Wortham 2005, for discussions of the contingent nature of intertextual connections across speech events). For example, in her second-semester course, Izzat referred to the project presentations in her current course by having students recall the previous semester's and then pointing out some differences (e.g. length of presentation):

The presentation is uh: going to be the presentation of your research - project. Okay? It's not something different. Just like what we did last term - you will present - what you did - for your research project... And one thing that is different this term is that - I assigned more time for the presentation. We're going to - spend forty minutes. The presentation is forty minutes each.   (Kobayashi 2004: 142)

To summarize, the students in this study had ample ongoing opportunities to be socialized both explicitly and implicitly by Izzat and by one another, both in and out of class, and from one meeting to the next, into English language forms, discursive practices related to presentations, the production of effective and accurate PowerPoint files, and the completion of term papers. They also had opportunities to internalize the values being conveyed and modeled with respect to effective public presentations, and could demonstrate their identities as students with various kinds of expertise, leadership, English proficiency, and pragmatic resources (humor). They were also expected to internalize local instructional ideologies associated with collaborative learning in conjunction with projects. Some of this socialization had certainly begun in Japan long before their sojourn, with their predeparture orientations (see Fig. 5.1), but it continued with a different focus and in a very different constellation of social, cultural, and cognitive interactions and priorities at

Students had had many years of prior Japanese/English language socialization in Japan

At their home university in Japan, students participated in a series of pre-departure orientations organized by the Program Director and assisted by their senior peers who had just finished their studies at WPU; thus, socialization by experienced members

Some students took part in academic English program at WPU in summer prior to the academic year for preparation

Teacher (Izzat) socialized students into Canadian WPU group presentation practices/norms; students observed model presentations by Izzat and TA and in other courses (ongoing in Semesters 1 and 2); course outlines, coaching, feedback all contributed

Students provided scaffolding for one another in fulfilment of requirements, based on relative expertise, in preparation, planning, and rehearsal phases; they thus also contributed to one another's language socialization

Students presented to their classmates, providing implicit models for ongoing socialization, and opportunities for the teacher to provide explicit socialization regarding English and content and presentation style/performance

Graduates made 'model' presentations back in Japan for students planning to study in Canada the following semester; socialization of their more junior peers

Figure 5.1 Iterative, longitudinal nature of language socialization for project presentations

this Canadian university and with this very effective instructor. Furthermore, those students who had enrolled in summer English for Academic Purposes preparatory classes at WPU prior to their first- and second-semester courses received additional academic discourse socialization, which then continued during their first-semester Language Fieldwork course (and other courses), and again in their second-semester courses. Modeling was provided by the instructor, by the teaching assistant (a graduate student mentor), and by their peers, with each new presentation. Similarly, scaffolding for effective argument, analysis, and synthesis of their experiences, plus appropriate English use, was provided by the individuals themselves, by their peers, and by their instructor(s) as well as with the help of other resources available to them (e.g. electronic dictionaries, word processing tools, PowerPoint).

The iterative, longitudinal nature of their language socialization described above—into the academic discourse practices of this program and university—is captured in Fig. 5.1. A culminating form of language socialization, shown in the final box, occurred after students returned to Japan and two were selected to give model presentations to the next cohort of students preparing to travel to Canada. By doing so, they were raising new students' metadiscursive awareness of the APU program and project expectations and providing some mediation (i.e. scaffolding, socialization) for them about how to approach and perform such tasks.

Conclusion

L2 socialization, a theoretical and methodological approach that has taken root over the past two decades, builds on aspects of sociocultural theory but also draws on other traditions and disciplines to show how newcomers learning another language become competent participants (members) in their new learning communities and cultures (Duff 2007a). That learning may involve understanding the subtleties of grammatical, lexical, or pragmatic items and perhaps learning to weave together three diverse experiences into one presentation with appropriate forms of evidence, perspective-taking, and cooperation. Furthermore, it may involve learning to produce and effectively use new mediating tools, such as PowerPoint slides or posters. The learning may entail the indexing of solidarity and the expression of humor to show alignment with the instructor and each other (Duff 2002, 2004). Or it may involve monitoring a group's English language use in presentations to ensure that other groups will understand them (Duff 1995). Although it may be tempting to view cognitive and social (or sociocultural) dimensions of learning as 'two parallel SLA worlds' as suggested by Zuengler and Miller's (2006) article, at every step cognition is integrally involved in these processes of understanding and internalizing social, cultural, and linguistic experience, in knowledge co-construction, and in planning and executing public discursive performances. It is unlikely, for example, that students in the course or group members would have learned the meaning of *facility* or *appreciate x giving us such a good opportunity*, or used those words or formulaic expressions in individual presentations without the mutual investment and assistance we observed as they attempted to solve particular communication problems or goals.

Cognition is deeply embedded in the local sociocultural contexts in which it takes place, framed by particular activity and participation structures and histories, and mediated by the different roles, identities, and status of interlocutors and the semiotic tools at their disposal. Cognition is also (perhaps more obviously) crucially involved in the perception, negotiation, internalization, and use of L2 forms (e.g. *flexible* instead of *flexibility*; *calm down*, and then *be calm down*, instead of *be calm*), which invoke aspects of social experience as well. There were also traces or indexes of their prior social, intellectual, and discursive work in their interactions over time, for example when narrating the difficulties their group had had trying to put three presentations into one, a phenomenon which was also reinvoked by Izzat. Of course, their social engagement in language learning and task management did not enable them to internalize correct forms for *all* the English they wanted to produce (e.g. the use of *embarrassed* instead of, say, *annoyed* or *perplexed* in the narrative/ complaint about the difficult job of presenting as a group of three). However, the act of committing to one form, heightening one's awareness of it, even if used in an awkward or inappropriate way, will likely set in motion a more nuanced understanding of the syntax, semantics, and pragmatics of that form down the road with subsequent exposure, experience, negotiation, feedback, and so on.

According to Wenger (1998: 5), learning is not just a process of perceiving, integrating, and restructuring new knowledge. It represents a larger set of social and personal possibilities:

- Learning is doing (practice).
- Learning is belonging (community).
- Learning is becoming (identity).
- Learning is experience (meaning).

Theorized in this way, and in the language socialization and related sociocultural perspectives outlined earlier (see Duff 2007*a*), learning and social experience go hand in hand and are part of a process of internalization, performance, and personal transformation through mutual engagements with others as learners become better equipped to function in society as communicatively competent members. L2 socialization could be developed even further to account for the kinds of learning that Wenger describes with the production of close, longitudinal analyses of language acquisition in particular contexts but without losing sight of the social and cultural factors at play (e.g. Ohta 2001). We have attempted to do that here with a few representative examples. More such research will help bring together concrete, evolving instances of macro- and micro-social-interactional processes and micro-linguistic developmental processes and outcomes. Like the project presentation above in which three students needed to synthesize three seemingly disparate experiences and create a coherent narrative or account of them, a greater convergence of traditional cognitive-linguistic and sociocultural SLA analysis and L2 socialization research will enrich the field of SLA, with the sum of the parts likely being greater than the whole. We therefore advocate for the documentation and theorizing of sociocognition by means of interdependent accounts of the social, cultural, and cognitive processes across a variety of contexts for L2 learning and use. Ideally, researchers committed to more integrated accounts of this sort will also attempt to track the unfolding learning trajectories, participation, subjectivities, and intentionality or agency of learners in their L2-mediated communities. To date in language socialization research collective experience has been privileged over individual experience, perhaps because of the orientation to normative local cultures and communities of practice. Conversely, in SLA research individual experience has seemingly been privileged over that of the group. However, in research such as that presented in this chapter, fine-tuned analysis of interaction may be examined over time, across speakers, and across settings and modalities (oral, written) in such a way as to show significant points of SLA, that is, of learning-as-doing, learning-as-belonging, learning-as-becoming, and learning-as-experiencing by members of a particular culture or discourse community.

6

The social and cognitive influences on the English language development of three age groups of Iraqi refugees

LYNDA YATES, HOWARD NICHOLAS, AND MICHELE DE COURCY

Introduction

In this chapter we use insights from social and cognitive approaches to the study of SLA to explore the language development of three different age groups of migrants as they settled in a small agricultural town in rural Australia. All had fled from persecution in Saddam Hussein's Iraq. We followed both females and males of primary school age, secondary school age, and adults from seven families in order to explore both the commonalities and differences in factors affecting their second language acquisition. We focus in particular on the relationships between their progress in English, their age, their sense of Iraqi and Australian identities, and their self-presentation, together with their sense of engagement with varied communities of practice.

In approaching this investigation we understand learning a language to involve internalizing and (mentally) representing features of a semiotic system used in social contexts. This means that both the factors that impact on this process and its outcomes are cognitive as well as social, because an individual not only acquires mental representations of some aspects of that language, but also learns and uses these as she participates in various communities. In order to develop a more nuanced appreciation of factors impacting on their language development, we explored the relationship between the sociocultural context of our informants' different experiences and their progress in English as an additional language (EAL).[1] To do this we have drawn on epistemologies and methodologies from both socially oriented and cognitive perspectives on SLA.

Cognitive and socially oriented approaches to language learning

Reviewing a great divide

Recent research from a social perspective has more often tended to react *against* rather than work *with* traditions seeking to explore the cognitive aspects of SLA. Arguments have tended to polarize views on the basis that the two perspectives are ontologically and therefore epistemologically and methodologically incommensurable (Firth and Wagner 1997; Gregg et al. 1997; Kasper 1997). Debates have centred (sometimes acrimoniously) around the relative explanatory power of context and setting in accounting for second language development and whether there is any possibility of identifying universal (or widely shared) features of the second language development process. The positions have frequently been presented as contrastive and the consequent value of different methodologies has usually been seen as forcing a choice, rather than as making complementary contributions to a necessarily complex and varied phenomenon (see Block 2003).

Cognitive approaches have tended to take a positivist view of language learning and have therefore focused on the patterns that can be seen in the language produced by learners without any necessary recourse to the nature of the learner or the context in which they are learning (Long and Doughty 2003). This has favoured experimental approaches and the treatment of language samples as artefacts that are separable from the context in which they were produced. Language is usually understood as an object rather than as a tool for action and the crucial focus of interest has been on either the cognitive representation or processing of linguistic information. In an effort to explore what may be common to human beings as they learn a language, this research tradition has provided evidence for the rejection of simplistic behaviourist and deterministic cultural assumptions that underpinned many transfer views of second language development, and has offered ways of relating features of language development, particularly morphosyntax, across different languages (Dulay and Burt 1974; Larsen-Freeman 1976; Pienemann, Johnston, and Brindley 1988; Robinson and Ellis 2008).

However, cognitive approaches have been criticized for decontextualizing a process in which the social is central since language cannot be sensibly divorced from the context in which it is produced (Block 2003; Watson-Gegeo 2004). Socially oriented[2] approaches have therefore highlighted the contextualized nature of language, language use, and language learning, and have argued for the inherently subjective and embedded nature of knowledge. In sociocultural theory, for example, the social is seen as interacting with dimensions of mental processes so that the innate is transformed through socially constructed processes, one consequence being that biological aspects of the mind, such as memory and attention, are seen as crucially influenced through encounters with cultural artefacts, activities, and concepts (Lantolf 2006). From a social perspective, it is through our networks and how we relate to others through language that we construct and reconstruct our identities, a process which involves taking on roles that can be recognized by others with whom we have social relations (Ivanic 2006; Dörnyei and Ushioda 2009), because recognition by others involves sharing repertoires. Thus identity is foregrounded and attention to language as an object in its own right is reduced, with the result that the focus has been very much on participation itself rather than the learning that might occur through such participation.

Consequently, studies of migrant language learning drawing on such perspectives have tended to claim rather than illustrate specific connections between sociocultural context and language development (Mackay and Wong 1996; Miller 2000; Norton 2000*a*). As Tarone (2000*a*: 186) notes,

While SLA researchers who take a sociolinguistic or co-constructionist orientation have a good deal of evidence showing that L2 learners' IL [interlanguage] USE is variably affected by identifiable features of social context, they have usually not tried to show that those social features change the process of L2 ACQUISITION—specifically, the acquisition of an IL linguistic system—in any clear way. They have assumed it, and asserted it, but not often accumulated the evidence to prove it.

While Zuengler and Miller (2006) appear to accept the view that the differences between cognitive and social approaches are 'irresolvable' and seem content to hope that the debate between them will 'stimulate rather than befuddle the field' (ibid. 46), some recent approaches to SLA have explicitly attempted to account for both sets of factors, for example, Emergentism (Larsen-Freeman 2006), Dynamic Systems Theory (de Bot, Lowie, and Verspoor 2007), and in some ways various contributors to Robinson and Ellis (2008). Our position is that it is vital to take both the social and the cognitive into account, and that these two perspectives should be regarded as complementary rather than incommensurable.

Bridging the divide

Each approach offers different data sets and different ways of illuminating them. Both perspectives put their faith in particular ontologies and epistemologies; both are playing out the rules of the particular paradigm that they are in; and both can illuminate issues in particular ways. We view the acquisition of language as the acquisition of a cognitively represented system through participation in communities, involving agency and investment, which is thus a crucial site of identity construction. Language use is therefore an 'act of identity' where identities are multiple, dynamic, and fluid. However, the factors influencing language development will be both collective and individual, social and biological. They include age, gender, ethnicity, and community membership as well as the regularities of language processing.

Social approaches to SLA offer the field perspectives on how people are positioned by the socio-historical context which inevitably shapes who they feel they can be, what discourses they can access, what opportunities they have for engagement with the language, and so on. This gives insight into the way in which individuals may experience different degrees of comfort and conflict, as well as different degrees of agency and investment related to the identities that are made available to them in a new country. That is, the new identities that become available may be 'congruent', allowing new mixed identities to emerge, or 'incongruent' resulting in identity conflict, and options to struggle and resist with consequent effects on language investment and agency. Thus, if migrants of any age are allowed only 'peripheral' participation (Lave and Wenger 1991), that is, only partial access to mainstream communities of practice, social approaches look for connections between their experiences and how their language learning suffers (Norton 2000*a*; Miller 2000).

Cognitive approaches allow investigation of the precise ways in which this engagement impacts on language learning processes and the resultant mental representations in the brain of an individual. This relationship is interactive in that the individual can draw on and build on these cognitive representations as their language skills develop and this, in turn, can influence how successful they are in engaging with expert speakers and thus their further participation in the community and so on. A learner with greater control over the language can enter into more and more prolonged and differentiated interactions, thus increasing their exposure to the target language. In our view, therefore, language learning crucially involves an interaction between the social and the cognitive, and thus cross-fertilization and cooperation between the two perspectives is sorely needed.

There have been a few classroom studies from a sociocultural perspective which have looked at the effects of specific kinds of classroom experiences on the development of selected language features (e.g. Kowal and Swain 1997). However, the foregrounding of social issues in recent explorations of language learning by immigrants has tended to leave the specifics of their language development somewhat out of focus. Norton (2000*a*), for example, has been very influential in arguing for the importance of identity and context in language learning, but claims rather than demonstrates the impact of these on actual language development.

A notable exception to this trend is Teutsch-Dwyer's (2001) exploration of the development in the marking of temporality in the speech of Karol, an immigrant to the United States. Data on the context in which he used English and samples of his language performance were collected using a combination of interviews, recordings of conversations, observations, and field notes. On the basis of these, Teutsch-Dwyer was able to build both an understanding of Karol's gendered identity in relation to his use and learning of English and the kinds of scaffolding and support available to him in his context. She was then able to support her argument, that Karol's image of masculinity impacted on his second language learning in specific ways, through a linguistic analysis of how he marked temporal relations in his narratives over time. She was therefore able to offer a specific illustration of how social factors such as discourse and power might impact on the development of cognitive representations of an aspect of a second language.

In this study, we similarly sought to explore both second language development and the contexts of second language learning of the refugees over a period of several months as they settled in a small rural town in Australia. Although our participants came from a similar ethnic, language, and religious background and settled in the same community, they were of different ages and genders and had different roles in their families and the community. Their particular social contexts of learning were therefore different. Our aim in this study was to investigate not only the relationship between these contexts and their language learning, but also to illustrate the development (or lack thereof) of their additional language, and to relate this to their experiences in the community. To do this, we drew on methodologies and analytical tools from both socially oriented and cognitive approaches to SLA, as discussed in the next section.

The study

The study was designed to investigate the relationship between progress in EAL over time and the settlement experiences of Iraqi refugees of different ages from the same family groups who had chosen to settle in 'Laketown'. Unlike many other rural towns, it had some experience of diversity. Although the population is largely of Anglo-background, some 10 per cent are indigenous Australians. Also, opportunities for seasonal employment in the agricultural sector have attracted some migration from Europe, the Middle East, and elsewhere. Community leaders in the town had made considerable and sustained efforts to welcome and accommodate the growing Iraqi refugee community, and through the local ethnic community council and the local community college proactive cultural support services were established. These included: subsidized English language classes for adults, regardless of their visa status, separate language classes for females, driving lessons for women, interpreting and translating courses, and a volunteer home tutor scheme.

Most of the participants in this study were Shia Muslims. The four exceptions to this came from one family (S, see Table 6.2) who were Sabean Assyrian.[3] All were selected with the help of a research assistant from the community who was active in the multicultural committee in the town. Most had recently arrived. Some had Permanent Resident visas, while others had been released from detention centres and allowed to stay on Temporary Protection Visas—a special visa category created for those who had not arrived in Australia via formal channels. This allowed them to stay in the community for a specific period with restricted rights. Our informants came from a variety of social backgrounds and had often spent many years in other countries such as Iran, Syria, or Jordan. Most arrived with horrific stories of terror, brutality, and family tragedy. In Laketown, the participants were part of a mutually supportive, Arabic-speaking community in which family and other community members were very important.

We interviewed and gathered other data from participants on two occasions separated by several months and recorded a total of 39 participants. However, we selected for analysis only data from those for whom we had samples of English at Time 1 and Time 2, and who had at a least one other family member for whom we also had data at both times. This left us with a total of 26 participants who we classified as either adult, secondary age, or primary age. A summary is given in Table 6.1.

Age	G
7 Adult	F
4 Adult	M
5 Teen	F
3 Teen	M
2 Prim.	F
5 Prim.	M

Table 6.1 Summary of participants

The Shia Muslim participants closely observed traditional religious and cultural practices. This made them very visible in the rural community, not only because females over the age of 9 wore the *hijab* (covering the hair and neck but not the face), but also because their values and attitudes differed in visible ways from others in the community. For example, many families would not allow their daughters to attend secondary schools since these were co-educational, and many sought permission to withdraw their children from primary music classes because of their belief that music is an unwelcome distraction from God.

The Assyrian family had previously lived for an extended period in a major city in another state. The children had had prior experience learning English in Intensive Language Centres in that city and they did not share religious practices with the dominant group. Nevertheless, they were identified to us as 'Iraqi' by the Shia community and were perceived as such by schools and students, even if for some at least the distinction between 'Iraqi' and 'Muslim' may not have been clear.[4]

The family members differed not only in age, gender, and family role, but also in their prior educational experiences and the educational and interactional opportunities available to them in Australia. Even where the individuals in this study were members of the same family, their opportunities to use English, access education, and interact with the various communities differed widely. As noted above, the female Shia teens in this study did not attend high school as their brothers did, but rather attended special females-only ESL classes arranged at the local TAFE[5] (similar to an adult community college) along with their mothers and grandmothers.[6] Other adult females also attended these classes, while adult males joined regular TAFE ESL classes, and primary-aged children attended mainstream primary school supplemented by in-school ESL support.

Thus age and gender allowed different opportunities and affordances in the community. We wanted to see how this impacted on English language development. We were particularly interested to see whether the peripheral participation in mainstream teen culture allowed to secondary age females who did not attend school impacted negatively on their English language development.

Study design

The study was conducted over a three-year period. Since access to such a traditional, tight-knit community needed to be made sensitively, links were developed with the community gradually via professional and personal contacts. Through site visits and interviews with key members, we deepened our understanding of the community, in particular, the exact demographics, the educational opportunities open to members, links with other communities, and the perceptions of professionals who worked within them.

We engaged participants in in-depth interviews on their experiences, cultural attitudes, and language development at two points between 14 and 26 weeks apart, according to when we were able to negotiate access. These interviews were conducted partly in English and partly with the assistance of an interpreter, either at school, at college, or in their homes. In English we had 'free' conversations based on an interview protocol and also elicited language data using specific tasks (vocabulary/picture prompt, grammar, pronunciation, pragmatics). Through the interpreter (if necessary), we discussed attitudes, daily lives, feelings, language learning experiences, hopes, and needs. We also probed attitudes to Australia and the local culture by talking through an attitudinal questionnaire with the participants adapted from Waxman (2000) and Kim (1989) (see Appendix 6.1).

The interview data were then transcribed in full and major themes were analysed.[7] Some of these themes were decided a priori, while others emerged from the data. In order to have some sort of measure of language development, we rated comparable stretches of talk at Time 1 and Time 2 for proficiency using the ESL Bandscales assessment framework (McKay 1994*a*, *b*). One of the researchers provided the other two team members with anonymous, randomized samples of language use taken from the 'free conversation' and 'picture tasks' sections of the interviews with the teenagers. The other two researchers rated the samples independently, and then met to discuss and resolve any discrepancies. We then calculated an index of progress to reflect the difference between the Bandscale ratings at Times 1 and 2 after taking into account the number of weeks between the two recordings. We used the following formula:

$$\text{Rate of progress} = \frac{\text{Band at } T_2 - \text{Band at } T_1}{\text{wks between } T_1 \ \& \ T_2}$$

The Bandscales were selected as the appropriate measure of proficiency for this group because they were designed to incorporate a wide range of social and academic uses of English, had a solid basis in SLA theory, had been thoroughly piloted and trialled with learners of different ages, and allowed assessment across different age groups using a comparable measure. Based on a theoretical framework drawn from Campbell, Barnett, and McMeniman (1984), Pienemann (1991), and Bachman and Palmer (1993), they were initially drafted by a research team as a means of monitoring and reporting on ESL learners' ability in using English in a range of contexts in which they learn at their phase of schooling, and were then trialled and refined in school-based studies (McKay 1994*a*, *b*).

The scales include assessment of both errors and positives and allow for *Descriptors* from junior primary learners to upper secondary learners. Secondary Speaking levels 1–5 were used to assess the teenagers and adults and Middle and Upper Primary Speaking levels 1–4 (MP/UP S 1–4) for the primary school children. For the relevant scale, the participants were rated for morphosyntactic accuracy, fluency, independent production, range of vocabulary, and appropriateness for context.

Results of language progress data

The results for progress in English over the period between T1 and T2 for each of the 26 participants are presented below in Table 6.2 in rank order. This table also includes details of family, gender, visa status (permanent or temporary), and type of class each was attending.

ID	Fam	Age	Class	G	Visa	T1	T2	Prog	R
AB	B	T	Female class TAFE	F	T	0	2.5	11.36	1
AnS	S	T	High School	M	P	2	4	11.11	2
AS	Z	T	Female class TAFE	F	T	1.5	3	10.71	3
DQ	Q	P	Primary School	F	P	1	3	8.00	4
NM	G	T	Female TAFE	F	P	1.5	2.5	7.14	5
JR	R	T	High School	M	T	2	3.5	6.82	6
ZB	B	T	Female class TAFE	F	T	1	2.5	6.82	6
HS	S	T	High School	F	P	3	4	6.67	8
FQ	Q	A	Interpreter class TAFE	F	P	4	5	6.67	8
AaS	S	A	Community College	F	P	1	2	5.88	10
MM	M	T	High School	M	P	1.5	3	5.77	11
YS	Z	P	Primary School	F	T	1.5	2	3.57	12
IM	R	A	Regular TAFE class	F	T	2	2.5	3.33	13
AzS	S	P	Primary School	M	P	4	4.5	2.27	14
AM	N	A	Regular TAFE class	M	T	3.5	4	2.17	15
TM	M	P	Primary School	M	P	2	2.5	2.08	16
AhR	R	P	Primary School	M	T	3	3	0.00	17
MN	N	P	Primary School	M	T	1	1	0.00	17
KB	M	A	Female class TAFE	F	P	2	2	0.00	17
HuM*	M	A	High School/TAFE	M	P	2	1.5	−1.92	20
AIR	R	P	Primary School	M	T	3	2.5	−2.08	21
JM	G	A	Female TAFE class	F	P	2.5	2	−3.33	22
NQ	Q	A	Regular TAFE class	M	P	3	2	−3.85	23
HaM	M	A	Regular TAFE class	M	P	2.5	1.5	−4.35	24
LZ*	Z	A	Female TAFE class	F	T	—	—	—	
MG*	G	A	Female TAFE class	F	P	2	—	—	

* HuM originally started in High School but because of his age was required to leave. Despite encouragement, LZ and MG were not able to produce sufficient sustained stretches of English at T2.

Table 6.2 Participants' progress over time

In the table, 'ID' is the abbreviated identifier for each informant, 'Fam', the family to which they belong, so that everyone with the same letter in the second column is a member of the same immediate family. Age is recorded as either primary (P), teenage (T), or adult (A). 'Class' refers to the location of their formal ESL instruction. Classes for the adults were either 'Regular TAFE', that is classes open to all students at the relevant level, for males, 'Female TAFE class' for Shia female teens and adults, 'Interpreter' for female FQ training to be an interpreter, or 'Community College' for the Sabean adult female. This class was similar to a 'Regular' class but held at a smaller, local location rather than in the main TAFE campus. The next column identifies gender (M, F), followed by whether their visa is permanent (P) or temporary (T). The figures in the columns labelled 'T1' and 'T2' are the placement ratings of the individual on the relevant Bandscale, either clearly within a band (whole number) or on the border between bands (.5). The progress of each participant was calculated as described above, (the difference between the rating at T2 and the rating at T1 divided by the number of weeks between the two times) and can be found in the column labelled 'Prog'. Participants were then ranked according to this index in the final column.

As can be seen from Table 6.2, there was movement on the Bandscales over time for many but not all of the participants. The rate of progress does not seem to relate to level of proficiency at Time 1. Although AB, with a beginning score of 0, made the most progress over time, the second highest score in the ranking is ANs, whose starting point was 2. Neither does there seem to be any particular pattern relating to whether participants have temporary or permanent visa status, although this emerged as a major concern for some of the informants in discussions. While there is no clear result for gender and age, females generally did better than males, and teenage females cluster at the top of the table. Indeed, counter to our expectations, the teen girls in the special female TAFE class appear in the top six ranks for progress. It seems, therefore, that our concerns that their English language development might have suffered as a consequence of their peripheral participation in mainstream schooling were unfounded: these young women have generally made *more* rapid rather than slower progress than both the males and other females.

The five female teens were all among the top nine in terms of progress in English. Two teen females from the TAFE class, AB and AS, seemed to make particularly rapid progress, and while the only teen female at high school, HS, did well, she did not do better than her peers—if anything she did not make as much progress (ranking the lowest of the teen girls). While this may be related to a plateau effect, in that she started at a higher level than the others as she had been in Australia for much longer, it was noticeable that, in contrast, her brother, AnS, who had been in Australia for the same length of time and attended the same school, noticeably outperformed his male teen peers. (Compare his index of 11.11 with that of the next highest ranked teen male JR, with 6.82). At T1, AnS had been rated as at a lower level than his sister (band 3 compared to band 4), but by the end he had improved by two bands, while HS had only improved by one—even though there was space on the scale for her to have progressed further.

While there was no specific pattern for family, the females in family Q outperformed their same-age peers. With an index of 8.00, DQ progressed much more rapidly than the next highest ranking primary-aged child, the other primary female YS with 3.57. Similarly, her mother FQ had an index of 6.67 and progressed more than other adults, male or female, despite the fact that she had started at a much higher level. While the numbers here are very small and unequal in the different groupings, they do suggest a general tendency for females to do better than males overall and for female teens to outperform other family members. The primary-aged children tended to group in the middle of the ranking and adults generally showed less progress overall.

Progress in language proficiency and sociocultural data

The SLA literature on age and gender suggests that our findings may be related in some way to these gross categories. Broadly speaking, adults make the slowest progress, while adolescents make rapid initial progress on vocabulary and morphosyntax. However, in the longer term younger beginners overtake both teenagers and adults in terms of overall approximation to the target variety, including for pronunciation (Hyltenstam and Abrahamsson 2003). As far as gender is concerned, Erlich (1997: 425) notes that the claim that females are better than males in language learning is generally based on studies of early first language acquisition, where females have been found to have faster rates of acquisition than males. In her review of studies of gender and second language acquisition, she concludes that it was difficult to maintain this generalization in relation to second language and that 'the social practices and activities that often enter into the construction of gender within particular communities can have profound effects on acquisition outcomes' (ibid. 441).

The qualitative data, viewed in terms of agency and identity, offer some interesting illuminations on these generalizations. Our preconceived notion on starting the study had been that, by being confined to a female-only class with others from their community, the female teens were being denied participation in an important peer and mainstream community and that this would negatively impact on their agency, identity, and investment in English-speaking communities, and therefore also their language learning. Our assumption had been that they would be unable to make friends from the wider community and 'appropriate' the language of their peers or participate fully in teen life, and that their English language learning would suffer as a consequence. In Lave and Wenger's (1991) terms, our assumption was that they would remain peripheral and fail to gain access to the linguistic capital on which to build their new lives in Australia.

As we saw in the previous section, however, these young women actually performed better than their peers in mainstream school. While it could be argued that the specific language content of their TAFE class might have helped here, the kind of spoken English we took as samples are not typically well developed in formal language classes.[8] It should be remembered that the adult females also attended this class but did not do so well. It seems, rather, that there may be other factors at play. The picture of life in mainstream schooling that emerged from the data suggests that life at school may not always have offered the rich opportunities likely to promote full participation in either English medium communication or English language learning. There is, we think, scope to refine the notion of participation to differentiate between participation in social practices and participation in language learning experiences. Xu (1997) reported for classroom-based learners of Chinese as a foreign language how the most progress was made by the (female) learner who seemed least active in her participation in the class. The converse applied to the female learner who was most active in classroom participation.

The teens at school had to struggle with the uncertainties of mainstream teen culture of (middle) Australia and the 'racialized' life of schools. They spoke of fights and bullying and playgrounds that were self-segregated into quite sophisticated racial groupings reminiscent of Miller (2003). AnS, for example, told us how he and other members of his family had moved from one school to another within Laketown because of experiences of bullying: '... just er the students don't like him and hit him' (T1), which in turn led to a view of how protection could be provided where there were larger numbers of students who had also come from Iraq (and other countries in the Middle East).

> R:[9]   about Arabic speaking. Could you also say that because there
>   were more Arabic speaking kids, if there was any trouble people
>   wouldn't make a fight because there's more of you? Do you know
>   what I mean?
> AnS: Yeh, like more Arabic people, they can't fight with us because we
>   are more.
>
> (AnS T2)

HS described her schoolyard as being divided into non-antagonistic territories in which Islamic girls sat together, but were subdivided according to nationality to distinguish Iraqis from Kuwaitis. Close to them were located the Muslim boys (both Arabic- and Turkish-speaking). Each of these groups appeared to remain in a fairly constant location while Anglo Australians and Koories (Indigenous students with heritage in south-eastern Australia) roamed across the whole school area, though seeming to have staked out ownership of the oval and the area next to the canteen. Thus there is a quite overt representation of national/ethnic identity in the daily lives of learners, and the youngsters were confronted with this reality on a daily basis. Although the nature of the groupings was explained at length by HS, it seemed to be a feature of school experienced by all the children. It is easy to see how such playground patterning might impact on opportunities for participation in Anglo communities of practice and engagement with English.

HS and particularly AnS from family S, however, appeared to cope with this racialization relatively well, perhaps because as Assyrian Sabeans their religious traditions did not include as many points of stark difference from Anglo culture as those of the Shia. The females do not wear a *hijab*, for example, and Sabeans do not disapprove of musical activities at school or co-education or special requirements for sports clothing, and so on. HS did, however, report dealing with racial conflict at school, suggesting the need to raise awareness of the issues of mainstream education. AnS had become actively engaged in a drama group that confronted and processed the life stories and issues around the refugee experience and performed them at schools around the area. In this he seemed to have found his own voice and a sense of agency, and was proactively engaged with identity work in the community. Perhaps these activities help to explain why, contrary to the general tendency for females to do better than males, he progressed faster than his sister and made by far the most progress of any male (ranking 2nd overall with an index of 11.11). The next highest ranking males, were primary-aged JR, ranked 6th with an index of 6.82, who had an active involvement in a local soccer team, and then teen MM (ranked 11th with an index of 5.77), who had health problems which had led to him being less active in sport.

The Shia teen females led a life that was much more sheltered in several ways. They reported leisure activities such as playing with younger brothers and sisters, reading and helping their mothers with family chores. Their social networks were very much within the family and the Shia community, and outings appeared to be for shopping and family visits. This should not be taken to imply that they were 'cloistered'. Rather, their active lives involved frequent excursions to outdoor settings and community events, but these were undertaken as part of a family, and they seemed to understand their life through the perspective of these family activities—things that could be done together. Thus the range of identities available to female teens in the Shia community seemed focused heavily on domestic life and the family. They did not appear to find this lifestyle overly restrictive in the way that their locally born peers might, or complain about the fact that they could not join their peers in the wider community, although they did regret the fact that they were not able to study subjects across the curriculum but were only able to have classes in English.

AB, the female teen who made the most progress over time, had a friend who attended school. AB was positive about the thought of going to school at some point and making friends in Australia, but she did not seem to have been aware that making friends might not be as easy as she imagined:

R: Would you like to go to school?
AB: Yeh, I would like to go to school when I improve my English language, because I would like to give some, to make some friends with Australian friends.

R: Mhmm. OK. Does your friend in school have Australian friends?
AB: Mm. No.
(AB T2)

Only one participant, AS, reported any dissatisfaction with aspects of her life in Laketown, and this was because she missed the wider family and social networks that she had grown up with, and because the town was not large enough to offer female-only activities (such as female-only swimming at the local pool).

The sense of satisfaction with life in Laketown was shared by the other women we interviewed. The adult females were generally very positive towards the Laketown community because of the opportunities they saw there to escape the savage uncertainties of life in Iraq or in refugee settlements in the Middle East. They saw opportunities for their children to gain an education and for their family to acquire, at long last, a(n Australian) passport and the freedom to travel legitimately that it would give them.

These older women also made active use of the home tutor scheme, a means by which they could receive one-on-one English conversational tuition in their own homes as part of the general on-arrival English teaching programme available to adults in Australia. Many, however, seemed to have little time or energy for learning English, and this may have contributed to their generally low rate of progress overall. Another factor might be that they appeared particularly invested in their children:

KB: But sometimes, if I sit down with the, with the language, try to, to read or to write anything, but suddenly I have to leave everything and to do my housework. Especial when my children come back from the school.
(KB T2)

MG *(intp):*   *Sorry em, was going but eh really because two days a week is not enough.*
R: Ah, OK. Why were you only going two days a week?
MG: Very busy.
R: And what kind of things do you do then, that keep you so busy?
MG: I have five children. Washing, cleaning, cooking.
(MG T2)

They generally did not report that they expected to do very well, perhaps because they felt a priori that their age would count against them (see, for example, age-related presuppositions about language learning reported by Iraqi refugees in Yates and Williams 2003). An exception was FQ, who, it will be remembered, was the highest-ranking adult for progress, even though she had started at a higher level and, like the other adult females, had family responsibilities. She displayed a very high level of engagement and leadership within the Shia community and also within the Anglo community in

Laketown. She had been highly educated in Iraq and had already acquired a reasonably high level of English before her arrival. She had worked as a microbiologist teaching at a college in Iraq, and enthusiastically embraced the opportunities she saw opening up for her as a community member. She maintained relationships with Anglo-Australians, pursuing contacts she made through her visibility in the town and through her home tutor, and she trained as an interpreter during the period of the study. She also saw Australia as offering many educational and professional opportunities for her daughter and expressed a willingness to move (at a later date) to a larger city in order to assist her daughter to obtain tertiary education.

FQ: Not about the religion, not about the Arabic culture. Now for example for me, I have maybe now three or four friends Australian. Australian womens.

R: Right.

FQ: Yes, not a problem for me. They are come from my home, they are eating with me. I go [her] home.

(FQ T1)

There may also be family factors that influenced her success because, as shown in Table 6.2, her daughter, DQ, ranked 4th for progress overall and was by far the best-performing primary-aged participant with an index of 8.00 that was more than twice that of the next ranked primary child (YS with 3.57). While she reported that her little brother (not part of the study) did not like school and feigned sickness so that he would not have to attend, DQ reported that she enjoyed school, was liked by her Australian friends, and was looking forward to going to high school. Although she appeared to be very well aware that there were cultural differences between her community, and the broader community in Laketown, these differences did not seem to faze her:

R: When you look around at Australia and look at the way your Australian friends live or other people live and you think ? mm, do you think, I would like to be like that?

DQ: No.

R: No? Why not?

DQ: Because [inaudible murmur], I would like to be myself.

(DQ T2)

The father of the family NQ, however, ranked 23rd and his English appeared to have gone backwards in the time between the two data collections. He had also been highly educated in Iraq as a pharmacist and had had a high-status role there, but, like some of the other adult males, in Laketown he became frustrated with English as he failed to make progress quickly and saw the success of his wife and child. During his T2 interview he was asked whether he still liked living in the town, to which he immediately replied 'No'. The small town was not able to offer him the employment opportunities he was seeking and he was becoming disaffected. While his wife retrained, found work as a translator, and was thus centrally involved in the life of the community, NQ was unable to go back to his position as a pharmacist, or even find any work that would help him regain the traditional role as breadwinner for the family. His participation in the life of Laketown was peripheral. Neither did he appear to be active in the Shia community.

Similarly, another adult male, AM, started very positive about this language learning at T1:

AM: But we have some people some people Australian people or England, we speak with them, get a friend with them, that's good. That's best way and very fast. We can speak English very well.
R: Can you think of how you can do that?
AM: Yeh?
R: How can you do that?
AM: Me?
R: Yes.
AM: One hundred per cent I can do that.
R: You can do that?
AM: Yeh.

But had a different view by T2:

AM: Maybe I want, I can eh learn English language [in another country], but I can't learn English in Australia.
R: Mm. Because you don't feel comfortable?
AM: No.

From a social perspective, the adult males appeared to be suffering perhaps more than their wives from an identity crisis, and this may have impacted on their sense of agency in Laketown and their consequent progress in English.

If identity conflict impacts negatively on progress in the language of the host community, then it may be that the relative isolation of the teen girls attending the TAFE class protected them from some of these damaging conflicts, at least in the short term. Because they did not have to negotiate their identities on a daily basis in the maelstrom of the teen peer group at secondary school, the roles and identities available to the teen Shia girls involved less conflict than those available to the youngsters who attended school. Moreover, the conditions in the camps or other refugee locations where many had spent their early years had often permitted these young females only limited access to education outside the home. Consequently, English classes such as the TAFE, however limited in scope and clientele, represented for some a means to achieve a life-long goal—a beginning to their education. They finally felt that they were able to attend class, and because their expectations within the community had always been of female-only classes, English provision at the TAFE perhaps did not seem so strange. Moreover, they found learning English easier than did their mothers and grandmothers, and this meant they could take on the role of 'expert' in English within their female/family communities (see Kanno 2000).

Indeed, although there were certainly comments about particular teachers who appeared less successful than others in engaging the whole class, the teens were generally satisfied with their classes. While there was some occasional frustration at learning alongside older, slower learners, this did not appear to be a major source of friction, and many spoke affectionately of their teachers, as did, for example, AB:

R:	Mm. Right. OK. Tell me about your teachers.
AB:	My teacher is beautiful and eh teach me is very good.
R:	Mhmm.
AB:	And.
R:	What does she do that's good?
AB:	She is beautiful and teach me is very good and [Interpreter to interviewer].
AB *(intp)*:	*Her teaching is very good.*
(AB T2)	

Thus their expectation of the roles and the identities they were playing out seemed largely congruent/compatible (Benet-Martinez and Haritatos 2005), and they were largely insulated from negotiating the identity conflicts emerging between the traditional religious and cultural values of their homes and those of mainstream Australian teens in the marketplace of the Australian secondary school. It is likely that they therefore felt less conflicted themselves and also suffered less from the racialized tensions that seemed to characterize relations among their peers.

At school, in contrast, there are many opportunities to be constructed as the 'other', as we have noted in the discussion of the racialized patterning of the playground territory. The comments from the teenagers, and particularly AB and AnS, who made the most rapid progress in their English, suggest that if there is a pattern to be found in the relationship between identity comfort and the acquisition of English as a second language, then it is to be found in the very local sense of support for their identity that is not simply bound up with age, or gender, or education, but instead in a complex interaction between these factors that results in a sense of felt cultural security.

Conclusion

What we may be seeing reflected in these results is both the same as and different from the kind of peripheral participation that Zuengler and Miller (2006) suggest may be detrimental to language learning. Many of those attending school may have learned to 'take a less empowered position in a community of practice because of the kinds of participation made available to them' (ibid. 41), and as Toohey (1999: 135) suggests, might not be so much 'marginalized' as very 'integrated' into particular communities of practice at school, but in positions that maintain the peripheral nature of their participation in that community. Thus the teens in the schools may have been participating centrally in the social life of the school, but only peripherally in English language learning, while the teens in the female-only classes were perhaps more able to maximize any adolescent advantage in the acquisition of EAL because their participation in the language learning experience was more central. In their case, central participation and more rapid second language development of the teens in the female-only classes came as a direct consequence of being (at that time in their lives) only peripheral participants in the wider English-speaking community. Thus the differential rates of progress of the learners in this study relate to both cognitive and social factors which complement each other in complex ways and thus illustrate the importance of including both perspectives in any consideration of language learning. Clearly, language learning happens in a social context which both makes available and constrains opportunities for individuals to participate in language events and thus acquire and use language. To consider language development or proficiency without reference to the social conditions in which it occurs can only yield partial accounts. By the same token, the claims of socially oriented perspectives on language learning need to be analysed and explored in ways that explicitly link social conditions to some aspect of individual performance and change. As we have sought to illustrate, these links can be counter-intuitive and so the theorization of the relationship needs to be complex. Combining insights from both perspectives deepens our understanding of what is involved in language acquisition and the factors that impact on it as an individual experience occurring in a social context.

Appendix 6.1   Basis of questions on attitudinal questionnaire

Participants were asked to indicate on the following scale their response to questions 1–4.

Never	Rarely	Once a month	Once a fortnight	Once a week	Twice a week	3 times a week	4 times a week	Almost every day

1. How often do you read English newspapers?
2. How often do you listen to English language news programmes on radio or TV?
3. How often do you read an Arabic language newspaper?
4. How often do you listen to Arabic language news programmes on radio or TV?
5. Are refugees from your former home country among your closest friends in Laketown?
   Yes ❑   No ❑
6. How often do you contact your closest friends?

Daily	Twice weekly	Weekly	Twice monthly	Monthly

7. How many of your friends or close friends are from your former home country?

Less than 25%	25% to 49%	50% to 74%	75% to 100%

Participants were asked to indicate their responses to questions 8–17 on the following scale:

Strongly agree	Agree	Disagree	Strongly disagree	Don't know

8. 'I feel awkward and out of place in Australia.'
9. 'It is easy for me to make Australian friends.'
10. 'The future looks very bright for me in Australia.'
11. 'Many things my parents taught me in my home country are not useful in Australia.'
12. 'As an individual, I can contribute something to Australian society.'
13. 'It is difficult for me to understand the Australian way of life.'
14. 'I feel like I belong in Australian society.'
15. 'There is little I can do to improve my life in this country.'
16. 'I feel that the Australians that I know like me.'
17. 'I feel all alone in Australia.'

Acknowledgement

The authors would like to acknowledge that the research reported on in this chapter was supported by a La Trobe University research grant.

Notes

1. We use this term to make it explicit that, for many, English may be a third, fourth, or even fifth language.
2. We use this as an umbrella term which does not privilege a particular theory.
3. An ancient Christian religion that pre-dated Islam in Assyria.
4. At the times when we conducted the interviews for this research, the distinctions between different branches of Islam were far less transparent to wider members of the Australian community than they have since become.
5. College of Technical and Further Education.
6. FQ did not attend this class, but a special one for interpreters.
7. Using the QSR NUDIST software.
8. We interviewed the TAFE ESL teachers and also asked the participants about their classes. From these data we conclude that they included the usual range of activities. The youngsters attending school also attended ESL support classes.
9. R refers to researcher. Participants are identified using their letter IDs. Where a contribution from a participant has been given in Arabic and translated into English by the interpreter, this is given in italics and additionally labelled (intp).

7

'Talking-it-through': languaging as a source of learning

MERRILL SWAIN

Introduction

I have one major purpose in writing this chapter: to consider two areas of research which have been conducted in isolation, one from the other. Why? To understand what they have in common, and what remains distinct. Each area of research has its own history, and the beliefs and practices of those involved are different, yet the similarity of results across these two areas is compelling. In both cases, the research is primarily located in the discipline of psychology, but one branch sees the learner as a solitary being and the source of its own learning (cognitive theories), whereas the other branch sees the learner as a social being whose interactions with its social/cultural contexts serve as sources of learning (sociocognitive theories). In this chapter, I refer to the first branch as cognitive psychology and the second as sociocultural theory of mind (SCT). In spite of the intriguing similarity in the sets of research findings, researchers associated with the two branches appear to have interacted little with each other.

What are these similar research findings about? They are about the role of verbalization in learning. The findings are straightforward: they suggest that certain types of verbalizing—what I call languaging (Swain 2006a)—are part of the process of learning.

Languaging

I will start with an example from a murder mystery book, *Death and Judgment* (1995). The author is Donna Leon who sets her mysteries in Venice. The main character of Leon's mysteries is Commissaro Brunetti. In the excerpt, Commissaro Brunetti and Commissaro della Corte are interviewing a waiter who works at a high-end restaurant about a couple the waiter had served several times in recent months.

In the face of the silence of the two policemen, he (the waiter) continued, speaking slowly, thinking this out for the first time. 'It was about halfway through the meal, when she was looking at the papers. She glanced up from them and gave him a look.'

'What kind of look?' della Corte finally asked after a long silence.

'I don't know. It wasn't angry or anything like that. She just looked at him like he was in a zoo or something, like she'd never seen anything like him. You know, like he was of a different species or had stepped out of a spaceship. I don't know if I'm making the idea clear', he said, letting his voice trail off inconclusively.

'Did it seem like the look was threatening in any way?'

'Oh, no, not at all,' he shook his head in an effort to convince them. 'That's what was so strange about it, that there was no anger in it. There was just nothing in it.' He stuffed his hands in his pockets and gave an awkward grin. 'I'm sorry. I'm not explaining this well.'

'Did he notice it?' Brunetti asked.

'No, he was pouring some more wine. But I saw it.'

'What about the other times?' Brunetti asked. 'Did they get on well?'

'Oh, yes. They always got on well. I don't mean to suggest that they didn't get on well that night, either. They were always very friendly but in a sort of semi-formal way.'

'Were there any papers the other times?'

'No, nothing like that. They seemed like friends, no, like business associates having a meal together. That's what it was like, the way two men who have to meet for business meet. Maybe that's why I always found it so strange, such an attractive woman, and he was a handsome man, but there was none of that tension that you like to see between a man and a woman, none of that at all. Yes, now that I think about it, that's what was so strange.' He smiled now, having finally figured it out.

Thus, with just a few minor probes from the police, the waiter talked himself into understanding a vague, unarticulated feeling he had about the couple. He talked this vague idea into existence; he gave it form and meaning. As Vygotsky (1986: 218) said 'Thought is not merely expressed in words; *it comes into existence through them*' (italics mine). Through talking-it-through, the waiter came to know something he did not know before; that is, he went through a learning experience. And the waiter now had a concrete piece of knowledge which allowed him to make coherent his past knowledge of this couple with what became of them (which I cannot tell you as it would spoil your reading of this novel).

Among the data that we have collected over the last few years, we find comparable examples—not in the context of murder and mayhem (!), but rather in the context of learning a second language (e.g. Swain and Lapkin 1998, 2002, 2008; Swain 2000, 2005*b*, 2006*a*). Here is an example from a study of second language learning by a French immersion student (see Swain and Lapkin 2007 for the full study).

Neil,[1] a grade 7 French immersion student, has written a story based on a set of drawings. In the story a girl hears her alarm clock ring, wakes up, but then goes back to sleep. When Neil wrote the story, he used the phrase *elle continue à s'endormir*, which literally means 'she continues to fall asleep'. In providing written feedback to Neil, we changed the verb phrase *continue à s'endormir* to *se rendort*, meaning 'goes back to sleep'. When Neil compared his version with the reformulated version, he noticed differences between them. While doing so, he said softly to himself *continue à s'endormir,* a clear example of private speech (see Ohta 2001). Then, in his normal voice, but slowly, he read the two versions: *Elle se rendort…et elle continue à s'endormir* (She goes back to sleep…and she continues to fall asleep). By saying these out loud, Neil was able to contrast the meaning and form of these two verbs.

Two days later, Neil was shown a snippet from a videotape which showed this precise moment, the moment when he was engaging in this cognitive act of comparison, and he was asked by the researcher, 'So what's the difference there?' The researcher was, in effect, asking Neil if he could explain what the difference is between *Elle se rendort* and *elle continue à s'endormir.* Neil responded:

41	N.	Well, *elle se rendort* means she…goes back to sleep. And I wrote she continues to sleep.
42	R.	Um-hum.
43	N.	But that's not right because she was awake, so it doesn't really make much sense there. Yeah.
44	R.	Um-hum. *Se rendort* make more sense.
45	N.	Yeah, *se rendort* makes a lot more sense.

Here we see how the researcher's question and subsequent agreement ('um-hum' in turns 42 and 44) led Neil to explain the different meanings of the two verbs, and to explain why the meaning of the verb he had used did not make sense in the context: the girl at this point in time was awake, so she could not be continuing to sleep.

Through Neil's talking-it-through, that is, through languaging, he came to understand that the meaning he had expressed was logically inconsistent. His 'Yeah' at the end of turn 43 provides evidence of his agreement with the conclusions he has reached; agreement with himself. During a post-test four days later, Neil was given the opportunity to rewrite his original story: Neil made use of the appropriate verb, *se rendort.*

Another example comes from a study we have recently completed (Swain et al. 2009). In this case, the languaging of our students occurred over a longer period of time. I cannot show all the languaging that occurred, but I hope to be able to give you a sense of it by focusing later in this chapter on one particular participant, Heidi. At this point, however, I need to make two digressions: (1) to provide the central research question, and (2) to describe the design of the study and to explain why we designed it as we did.

Central research question

Our central research question is: Is languaging a *source* of learning? Specifically, we set out to look for a relationship between the quantity and quality of languaging our participants engaged in, and their performance on several immediate and delayed post-tests (Swain et al. 2009). Because our domain of interest is second language learning, we wanted our participants, who were taking a university course for intermediate learners of French, to learn a fundamental grammatical concept about their second language (Negueruela and Lantolf 2006) that would be useful to them. After debate among the research team and input from several instructors of the course, we settled on teaching the students about the concept of 'voice' in French. This concept covers active, passive, and middle voice sentences. Although our participants were studying French as a second language (FSL) in university, most had surprisingly little knowledge about the concept of voice (as demonstrated by one of our pre-tests).

Our hypothesis was that by having to read aloud each sentence of an explanatory text we developed about the concept of voice in French, and say what their understanding of it was, our students would learn what active, passive, and middle voice sentences were, and be able to identify and use them. That is, by languaging, by using language to mediate the cognitively complex task of understanding the concept of voice, the students would come to understand the concept of voice, and be able to apply what they had learned.

Background

Self-explanation studies

The research we conducted was modelled after a study reported in an article called 'Eliciting self-explanations improves understanding' written by Chi and her colleagues (Leeuw, Chiu, and Lavancher) which appeared in the journal *Cognitive Science* in 1994. One of the reasons I read Chi et al.'s (1994) article was because the title caught my eye: it was already clear to me that one aspect of languaging was explaining to oneself, or to others, that which is cognitively complex for the speaker (Swain 2006a), as did the waiter; as did Neil. In other words, the act of using language to mediate cognition—to bring thinking into existence—is what I refer to as languaging. Languaging can then mediate further elaboration and shaping of the now realized idea.

In the Chi et al. (1994) study, the domain of interest was biology, in particular, how the human circulatory system works. The students were in grade 8. The research task involved reading a text that was 101 sentences long and was about how the circulatory system works. The students were to read the sentences, one at a time, out loud, and as each sentence was read, they were to explain what the sentence meant. This was referred to as 'self-explaining', or 'generating explanations to oneself'. The researchers found that those who self-explained displayed a deeper understanding of the human circulatory system than those in a comparison group who were required to silently read the text twice. Furthermore, high explainers displayed greater understanding than low explainers.

As it turns out, self-explaining has been the object of empirical inquiry in cognitive psychology for almost twenty years (thus providing a twenty-year history of empirical evidence of the positive impact of languaging on learning). Since self-explaining was repeatedly shown to be positively related to learning, interest developed in finding ways to promote it. Thus, from the cognitive psychology literature we learn the following concerning the effects of self-explaining in non-L2 knowledge domains.

First, successful students generate more self-explaining statements than unsuccessful students (e.g. Chi et al. 1989).[2] Self-explaining includes making inferences, monitoring comprehension, justifying one's actions, and connecting new knowledge to prior knowledge. Summarizing and paraphrasing are also aspects of self-explaining (Chi et al. 1989).

Second, successful students' self-explaining statements are qualitatively different from those produced by unsuccessful students (e.g. Chi et al. 1989; Rittle-Johnson 2006). For example, 'good' self-explainers are more likely to make inferences than poor self-explainers.

Third, self-explaining statements can be facilitated by changing the research materials. For example, Butcher (2006) conducted a study where one group studied a biology text (about the heart) with no accompanying diagrams, while the other two groups studied the text with simplified or more detailed diagrams. The students were undergraduates. Those who studied the text with diagrams produced more inferences and fewer other types of self-explanation such as paraphrasing and monitoring than did the text-only group. Self-explanation with simplified diagrams was generally better than self-explanation with complex diagrams. In our study, we used text and simple diagrams.

Changing the type of prompts used also appears to be relevant. In general there are two types of prompts used in self-explanation studies: *direct* and *generic*. Direct prompts are used to elicit self-explanations. Examples of direct prompts are 'could you explain the concept or the idea discussed in this sentence?'; 'could you connect what you just read with what you have read before?'; 'what happens next?' Generic prompts (e.g. 'what are you thinking?') have also been used in self-explanation studies. Davis (2003) was interested in the differential effects of direct and generic prompts on science learning. The text was about thermodynamics and light, and the students were in grade 8. She found that generic prompts were more facilitative to science learning than direct prompts. Typically, though, self-explanation studies have combined both direct and generic prompts. In our study, we used generic prompts, based on a list of 'content-free' prompts found in Chi et al. (2001).

Fourthly, only a few studies have reported no self-explaining effects (e.g. Mwangi and Sweller 1998). (See Suzuki 2009: 50–8 for a review of self-explaining studies.)

Study design

Our study, as stated above, was modelled after Chi et al.'s (1994) research. The overall design is shown in Table 7.1. (For full details of the stages of the study, see Swain et al. 2009.) In this chapter, only the shaded parts of Table 7.1 are discussed.

Warm-up stage	Pre-test stage	Languaging stage	Break	Immediate post-test stage	Interview stage	Delayed post-test stage (one week later)
Participants explain aloud a short text containing several bolded determiners	**Pre-test A:** Participants talk about the form and meaning of the bolded verbs in the *Sophie Mercier* (Part 1) text	Participants engage in languaging activity, card by card (we provide an advance organizer and use content-free prompts as necessary)		**Post-test A:** Participants talk about the form and meaning of the bolded verbs in the *Sophie Mercier* (Part 1) text	Participants talk about their backgrounds and perceptions of the activities	**Delayed post-test B:** Participants define the concept of voice
	Pre-test B: Participants define the concept of voice (using metalinguistic terms we provide)*			**Post-test B:** Participants define the concept of voice (using metalinguistic terms we provide)*		**Delayed post-test A:** Participants complete a cloze test using the *Sophie Mercier* (Part 2) text
						Stimulated recall: Participants do a stimulated recall on the cloze test (we push for metalinguistic terms)

⟵——— 50–75 minutes ———⟶ 10 minutes ⟵——— 15–30 minutes ———⟶ 20 minutes

Session 1: The first data collection session lasts about 90 minutes, including the break

Session 2: Scheduled 1 week after session 1

* The metalinguistic terms are active/passive/middle/agent/patient.

Table 7.1 Study design

Grammatical

G1	Sentences have grammatical categories (subject/verb/object)
G8	The initial noun phrase is the subject
G11	Passive allows the direct object to occupy the subject position
G15	Passive involves inserting the auxiliary *être*
G16	The auxiliary takes the tense of the main verb of the active sentence
G17	The auxiliary is followed by the past participle of the main verb
G20	In middle voice sentences we do not insert the auxiliary *être*
G21	In middle voice sentences we use a pronominal verb

Semantic

S2	Subjects and objects have semantic roles
S3	Subjects may be agents/doers
S4	Objects may be patients/undergoers
S6	Active sentences have agents, verbs, and patients
S10	Passive voice allows emphasis on the patient
S12	In the passive, agents appear optionally in the agent phrase *par*...
S13	Passive voice allows for an unspecified agent (i.e. when one doesn't know who did the action)
S18	Another way of expressing passive meaning is through the middle voice
S19	The agent (doer) is not expressed in middle voice sentences
S22	Middle voice sentences are often translated into English passives (e.g. skirts are worn short this year [*les jupes se portent courtes cette année*])
S25	Where English uses the passive in sentences like 'Salmon is eaten cold', French prefers the middle voice (*Le saumon se mange froid.*)
S29	The other three are reflexives (*je m'habille*/I get dressed)
S30	Reciprocals (*nous nous parlons chaque soir*/we talk [to each other] each evening)
S31	Inherently pronominal verbs that never appear without the pronoun *se* (*je m'évanouis*/I faint)

Mixed: Grammatical and Semantic

M5	Most sentences are in active voice
M9	The patient is the grammatical object
M14	Passive is formed by moving the object (patient) to the subject position
M23	The grammatical object (the patient) is highlighted or emphasized
M24	The grammatical object/patient becomes the subject
M26	Both passive and middle voice sentences allow us to place emphasis on the element of the sentence we want to highlight by putting it in the subject position
M27	Not all pronominal verbs in French are used in middle voice sentences
M28	One type of pronominal verb is the type in middle voice sentences

Table 7.2 Conceptual units in the explanatory text

We developed an explanatory text of the concept of voice in French. This explanatory text consisted of an explanation of voice (active, passive, and middle), illustrative examples of sentences in each voice, and two diagrams. The explanatory text of the concept of voice is provided in Appendix A. For full details of the development of the explanatory text, see Lapkin, Swain, and Knouzi (2008).

We presented our explanatory text on the concept of voice 'meaning-chunk' by 'meaning-chunk'. Each meaning-chunk was presented on a separate card. In Appendix A, each meaning-chunk is indicated by a bolded number. There are 36 meaning-chunks. We worked with participants one at a time. Each participant read aloud the contents of a card and then explained it, one card at a time. We refer to this phase of the study as the 'languaging stage'. The cards contained 31 conceptual units (determined by the researchers at the time of data analysis) and are provided in Table 7.2.

Before the students engaged in the languaging stage, we asked them to read Part 1 of a story about *Sophie Mercier* in which 13 verbs were bolded. The participants were asked to say what they could about the bolded verbs (pre-test A). After the languaging stage, we again gave the students Part 1 of the story about *Sophie Mercier*, and asked them to explain the voice of the sentences containing the 13 bolded verbs (immediate post-test A). Approximately a week later, we asked participants to complete a cloze test in which 11 verbs of Part 2 of the *Sophie Mercier* story had been removed (delayed post-test A (written)), followed immediately by a stimulated recall in which we asked them what they were thinking as they filled out each blank.

Analyses and some results

In order to test our hypothesis quantitatively, we divided our participants into high and low languagers. We did this by categorizing what the students said with respect to the conceptual units (see Table 7.2). For each statement that a student made about a conceptual unit, we coded it in one of five ways: as a rereading, as a self-assessment, as a paraphrase, as an inference, or as an analysis, of the conceptual unit. These five codes represented five different types of languaging. Thus, adding these coded utterances together told us the number of languaging units each student produced in response to the explanatory text. We then divided our sample of nine students into three groups: high languagers, middle languagers, and low languagers according to the number of languaging units produced (see Swain et al. 2009 for details). For this chapter, I have selected the two highest languagers, Heidi and Holly, and the two lowest languagers, Lisa and Lucy.[3] Table 7.3 provides background information about these four participants.

Participant pseudonym	Birthplace	Language background	Programme background
Lisa	Canada	English and Cantonese spoken at home; considers herself English-dominant	Core French until grade 10; extended French till end of secondary school
Lucy	Hong Kong; moved to Canada at age 4	Speaks Cantonese, English, and French; considers herself English-dominant	Core French from grade 1
Heidi	Canada	English monolingual	Mid-immersion from grade 4–12
Holly	Canada	Speaks Korean and English; English-dominant	French immersion from grade 5

Table 7.3 Participant characteristics

Table 7.4 shows that on the one hand, Heidi and Holly produced 135 and 116 languaging units respectively during the languaging stage; on the other hand, Lisa and Lucy produced only 37 and 42 languaging units respectively during the languaging stage.

Prior to engaging in the languaging stage during pre-test A, although students were able to provide information about the meaning and form of the bolded verbs in the *Sophie Mercier* (Part 1) story, none mentioned anything about active, passive, or middle voices. However, as shown in Table 7.4, after the languaging stage the students were able correctly to identify the voice of a number of sentences in the *Sophie Mercier* (Part 1) story. Table 7.4 shows two measures for the immediate post-test A: (1) how many times each participant correctly identified the voice of a sentence in the context of the *Sophie Mercier* story (maximum = 13); and (2) how many languaging units the participant used to explain her response. This number was added to the number of correct identifications. As Table 7.4 (columns 3 and 4) indicates, Heidi and Holly's scores are higher than Lisa and Lucy's.

Table 7.4 also shows the results of the delayed post-test A, administered about a week after the immediate post-test A. The fifth column shows how many times each participant was able to write the correct form required by the voice of the sentence in Part 2 of the *Sophie Mercier* story. The participants were provided the infinitive of the verb to be used. The maximum score possible was 11. Immediately after having completed the written delayed post-test A, the student was asked to do a stimulated recall about what they were thinking while completing each test item. The sixth column represents the number of times the student named (orally) the correct voice, while the seventh column represents the number of languaging units each student used to justify her answer. On all delayed post-test measures, Heidi and Holly did better than Lisa and Lucy, thus confirming our hypothesis that those who language most, learn the most.

Examples of languaging

In this section, I provide some examples of languaging from the study I have just described. The excerpts come from Heidi's transcript, and represent only a small portion of the data we gathered from her. These excerpts should provide the reader with an idea of what languaging, from a high languager, looks like in this context. I have selected her responses to Cards 15 and 16, and part of her responses to Cards 18 and 25. Why these? Because they relate to Heidi's developing concept of the middle voice in French, of which she had no understanding at the beginning of the study. In the excerpts below, quotation marks have been put around what Heidi reads from the card.

CARD 15: Another way of expressing a passive-like meaning without using the type of structure illustrated in diagram A is through what is known as the middle voice.[4]

| Participant | No. of languaging units during languaging explanation stage | Immediate post-test | | Delayed post-test | | |
		Immediate post-test A score (Correct identification of voice; out of 13)*	Immediate post-test A score plus no. of languaging units used to justify responses; 13 test items)	Delayed post-test A score (written) (max = 11)†	Stimulated recall (no. of correct oral items)‡	Stimulated recall (no. of languaging units used to justify answers)
Lisa	37	10	31	5	3	3
Lucy	42	10	22	6	3	3
Heidi	135	13	42	9	10	14
Holly	116	12	46	8	6	15

* This score is based on the ability to identify the voice of the sentences containing each bolded verb.
† This score is based on the ability to write the correct form of the verb required by the voice of each sentence.
‡ This may or may not be identical to the number of correct forms produced in the written delayed post-test.

Table 7.4 Overview of post-test results

HEIDI: 'Another way of expressing a passive-like meaning without using
the type of structure illustrated in diagram A is through what is
known as the middle voice.' Okay so uh, I don't take much from
this card. I just take that I'm going to learn about the middle
voice now. It's ba- it's not teaching me anything. It's not showing
me like uh, it's not, it's not showing me anything, it's not saying,
it's not referring to an example or explaining what the middle
voice is but I guess it just tells me to get out of the mind frame
of the passive voice now because we're moving on...because
it's saying 'Another way of expressing a passive-**like** meaning
without using the type of structure illustrated in diagram A is
through what is known as the middle voice.' So I suppose I take,
well, I get the sense that the middle voice will be similar to the
passive voice? So you might assume that the patient will take on
the role of the direct object [*sic*, should be subject] in the middle
voice as well because that's similar to what the passive voice
does? But it just says passive-like meaning so I'll, for now I don't
take any, I don't really take too much from this but I can assume
we'll go on to middle voice [laughs].

In this excerpt, we see Heidi assessing her understanding of the purpose of
the sentence, and in doing so, putting herself in the frame of mind to 'move
on' from learning about the passive into learning about something 'passive-
like'. She rereads the sentence to deepen her understanding of it, and then,
with some uncertainty, paraphrases it: 'I get the sense that the middle voice
will be similar to the passive voice?' Although the next languaging unit is
actually wrong (she says she assumes the patient will take on the role of direct
object rather than subject in the middle voice), Heidi infers what the similarity between the passive and middle voices might be, but concludes that she
should wait and see what is coming, certain that it will be about the middle
voice.

CARD 16: *Even though the agent is not expressed, we understand that an agent is the doer of the action.*

HEIDI: 'Even though the agent is not expressed, we understand that an
agent is the doer of the action.' So assuming it's talking about
the middle voice uh...it's same, it's the same as the passive
voice except you take from it that the agent is **not** expressed at
all whereas in the passive voice the agent is optional so it can be
expressed.

As we saw from the previous excerpt, Heidi set herself up to expect this
card to be about the middle voice, and, assuming that, she draws on her
recently learned knowledge about the passive voice where 'the agent is
optional so it can be expressed' and contrasts it with some of the information presented to her in this conceptual unit: in the middle voice, 'the agent
is **not** expressed at all'.

CARD 18: Sentence 6 is in the active voice; sentence 7 has a passive meaning, expressed in the middle voice, using a pronominal verb.

HEIDI: 'Sentence 6 is in the active voice; sentence 7 has a passive meaning.' Okay so sentence 6 '*Les filles portent des jupes courtes cette année.*'[5] Uh...7, '*Les jupes se portent courtes cette année.*'[6] 'Sentence 7 has a passive meaning, expressed in the middle voice, using a pronominal verb.' Okay, so...what I ta-, what I take from this is...mm...this is an interesting one. Uh so sentence 6 is in the active voice and then it shows you the middle voice and after doing the activities with the passive [earlier in the text], you uh...I, I can, I, I understand what they mean by passive meaning because

R: Yeah

HEIDI: Yeah. Uh you, you use, you see that *les jupes*, you see that how the, the patient is now becoming the subject but they totally eliminated the a-, they, yeah, they totally eliminated the, the agent and there isn't...there isn't really a space to put it in like it, this, the phrase like '*Les jupes se portent courtes cette année.*' Well you could say *par les filles* but I guess it's kind of implied because guys don't really wear skirts.

In this excerpt, we see Heidi puzzling about the two example sentences given, the first one being in the active voice, and the second in the middle voice. She thinks she understands what is meant by 'passive meaning' without it actually being in the passive form. With the encouragement of the researcher, she provides an analysis of what the difference is between the two sentences: 'the patient is now becoming the subject but they totally eliminated the agent'. Midway in her talking out loud, Heidi indicates that she knows she is on the right track, agreeing with her own analysis: 'yeah, they totally eliminated the agent'. She continues her analysis, trying to decide if there is 'space' for an agent, and then decides that one does not have to fit in an agent because we know who wears skirts and who does not (!). Here we see Heidi's reasoning about why there is no agent in the example using the middle voice, but it is a personal, localized justification. In the next excerpt, however, we see her go beyond the example sentence and come to the understanding that the middle voice can be used to make general statements.

CARD 25: For 9,[7] English uses the passive: Salmon is eaten cold.

HEIDI: 'For 9, English uses the passive: Salmon is eaten cold.' So again this is helpful for me. What I take from it is what it [it = *Le saumon se mange froid*] means, because I think that for English speakers it's a bit confusing when they say *Le saumon se mange froid* because you're thinking that the salmon, you, you think in your head that the salmon might be eating something? Instead of uh, the, the salmon is eaten cold. I knew that because we're doing these exercises and we're **changing** them but I can see that if I was really tired and reading this, I might easily be confused and thinking that the salmon was eating something cold so when I see the **English**, it uh just reaffirms for me that okay, so I, I know what's going on. I was right with what I thought about that and now I can see the practical use of it because normally I would just see that and I would say why would anybody say that in, in French, but then you see, salmon is eaten cold. Oh well okay if that's what it means in English, then I can understand why someone might want to say *Le saumon se mange froid* because it's really, it's nice and simple. And I think reading it in English and then reading it in French gets an idea of how you can use this tense yourself when you're speaking, not just understanding it. Uh, when you're reading other people's work because at least where I am in French, I still mainly have to translate stuff in my head before I say it so I think that that's really helpful and I just get from this a practical use of this phrase instead of just oh, this is, this changed into middle. It's like oh this is why it's changed into middle because they're just making a general statement about salmon. Doesn't, no, no, no one necessarily has to be eating it cold, just in general.

This excerpt is a fine example of languaging. In it, Heidi moves from a personal, sentence-specific understanding of the middle voice sentence *Le saumon se mange froid* to a broader understanding of its use, which is that it represents 'a general statement about salmon'. In other words, Heidi moves from what Vygotsky (1987) would call 'everyday concepts' to 'scientific concepts', from specific, experiential knowledge to abstract, reasoned knowledge.[8] In doing this, Heidi goes beyond the information she has been given, and creates knowledge that is new for her.

Theoretical accounts

It appears that self-explanation and languaging are similar, if not equivalent, phenomena. The cognitive psychological literature offers as categories of self-explanation inferencing, monitoring comprehension, justifying one's actions, connecting new knowledge to prior knowledge, summarizing, and paraphrasing. In the limited sociocultural literature, the categories that have been used for types of languaging are inferencing, self-assessment (overlaps with monitoring comprehension, justifying one's actions), analysing, rereading, and paraphrasing. Thus, what I will do next is describe the accounts given for *why* self-explanation and languaging are related to learning from the perspectives of cognitive psychology theory and sociocultural theory respectively.

From a cognitive psychological perspective, Chi (2000) suggests two possible cognitive processes which might underlie the self-explaining effect: (1) generating inferences and (2) repairing mental models. Initially, Chi et al. (1994) proposed the 'generating inferences hypothesis'. When students explain to-be-learned material to themselves, they are likely to generate inferences beyond information contained in the material and/or fill gaps in the material presented. According to the generating inferences hypothesis, self-explaining encourages students to infer new information that is missing from the material. The new information is encoded into memory and is available to facilitate later performance.

Subsequently, Chi (2000) proposed a 'repairing-mental-model hypothesis' (see also Leeuw and Chi 2003) which considers self-explaining as the process of revising one's existing mental model of the to-be-learned material. In this view, self-explaining can facilitate students' monitoring so that they notice a gap between the information in the material and their prior knowledge, leading them to repair their mental models. Through self-explaining, students' attention may focus on the material that is not consistent with prior knowledge. Self-explaining is also the process that reflects their attempt to integrate the new knowledge into existing knowledge and enables them to encode this new knowledge into memory.

And finally, a third hypothesis is that the beneficial effects of self-explanation may be attributed to time-on-task. To avoid this time-on-task issue, Renkl (1997) asked all participants to generate self-explanations while working on probability calculations individually. The outcome measures were not correlated with time-on-task but were positively correlated with the quality of self-explanations (e.g. principle-based self-explanations[9] or anticipative reasoning[10]). Based upon this finding, this time-on-task issue is unlikely to be a tenable account for the self-explanation effect (see also Aleven and Koedinger 2002; Ainsworth and Loizou 2003).

Thus, overall, cognitive psychologists have provided a set of hypotheses that suggests that the role of language is to facilitate thinking, that is, to facilitate the cognitive processes (e.g. inferencing) involved in learning. Ericsson and Simon (1998: 183) argue that requirements for verbalized explanations (e.g. the need to unpack complex thoughts into a coherent series of ideas, the need to develop a referential system for ideas and objects, the need to monitor speech for comprehensibility, and the need to 'make corrections and further explications of their thoughts') 'bias participants to adopt more orderly and rigorous strategies' for communicating coherently how they solved problems. Doing so might alter the sequence of thoughts, but doing so *does not alter the thoughts themselves*. In other words, language imposes certain requirements on the expression of our thoughts, but language per se does not change those thoughts. Change occurs as cognitive processes operate on information stored in memory, which is then 'made public' through language.

From a sociocultural perspective, however, language (a sociocultural artefact) is central to the genesis of cognition and cognitive processing (see e.g. Lantolf 2005, 2006; Lantolf and Thorne 2006). This centrality of language to the development and functioning of our higher mental processes is what differentiates cognitive and sociocultural theories. Let me explain.

Developmentally, children's behaviour is initially controlled, that is, regulated or mediated, by individuals and artefacts in their external, social world. Much that occurs in the activities of children as they interact with others is mediated by language. In the activities in which children participate, language mediates the process of making meaning and shaping knowledge and experience. The intermental functions language serves (e.g. questioning, reasoning, attending, remembering) as children participate, are internalized. Arievitch (2003: 287) defines the process of internalization as 'the transformation of certain (material) forms of an individual's external activity into other (mental) forms of that same external activity'. For children, as they develop, this means that these originally social (intermental) functions of language are transformed into intramental activities. Vygotsky (1978, 1987) demonstrated that these social functions of language are transformed into speech for the self,[11] speech which goes 'underground' and comes to regulate the child's own social and cognitive behaviour.

We see this speech for the self re-emerge as private speech when children or adults are faced with a complex cognitive task, and they begin to talk aloud in an attempt to regain control over their cognitive processes, their thinking (Lantolf 2003; Centeno-Cortés and Jiménez-Jiménez 2004). And we also see this speech for the self emerge in what appears to be social speech as in the case of Heidi, Neil, and the waiter. In these cases, although others were present to encourage the speakers on, their speech served to transform the unknown to the known by mediating their cognitive activity. In other words, their speaking, their languaging, created ideas that were new for them (Smagorinsky 1998; Swain 2006b). Language is not thought stated out loud, or even thought shaped by the structure and requirements imposed by a linguistic system as Ericsson and Simon (1998) claim, but thought that is brought into existence by the very process of languaging.

Thus, in the end, it is the theoretical accounts which have kept these two branches of psychology apart. The empirical findings strongly support the same claim that verbalization/languaging enhances learning/internalization. However, the cognitive psychology perspective as presented here assigns no particular theoretical role to the act of using language, whereas a sociocultural theory of mind sees languaging as mediating higher mental functioning. This position is based on an understanding of the genesis of language use as it comes to mediate psychological behaviour. The origin of human mental functioning is based on the relationships between persons, and persons and the artefacts, of their world: the social becomes and transforms cognition.

Appendix A: Explanatory text

Note: Each 'chunk' is numbered in bold so that the reader will know what appeared on each card.

The following activity is designed to teach you something about the concept of voice in French. There is research to suggest that explaining grammatical *concepts* rather than focusing on 'rules of thumb' leads to a deeper understanding of the grammar of the second language. This process is more effective when learners get a chance to 'think aloud' about the concept. So the attached sheets present information about the concept of voice in 'chunks', allowing you time to think about each piece of information and explain it out loud.

The concept of voice in French

1 Most sentences in French consist of a subject, a verb and an object; these are grammatical categories. 2 The subject and object also have semantic roles (i.e. they contribute to the meaning of the sentence). 3 So in (1) below, *le joueur de baseball* is the grammatical subject of the sentence and its semantic role is that of agent, the 'doer' of the action. 4 The noun *la balle* is the grammatical object; its semantic role is that of patient, the 'undergoer' of the action of throwing.

5 In French, most of the sentences we write or the utterances we speak are in the active voice, like examples (1) and (2).

    1. Le joueur de baseball lance la balle.
    2. Le chat a mangé toutes les souris.[a]

6 In the case of sentences like (1) and (2), there is an agent (the 'doer' of the action) that serves as the grammatical subject, a verb, and a 'patient' that is the grammatical object. 7 The initial noun or noun phrase is the subject; the main verb follows; and the patient (the 'undergoer' of the action) is the grammatical object.

8 Using the passive voice enables us to put the emphasis on the patient, in order to focus on it, as illustrated in diagram A [Fig. 7.1].

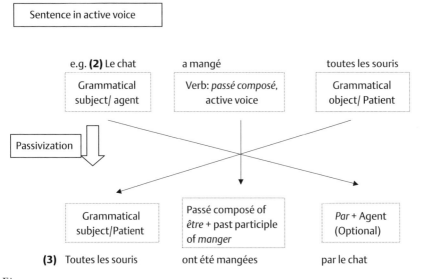

Figure 7.1

<hr />

[a] The first prompt is inserted here:
    * *Can you tell me about sentence (2) in terms of semantic roles?*
      If participant does not understand the question, or gives a brief (or wrong) answer, prompt further.
    * *Can you tell me about sentence (2) in terms of object, subject, agent, patient?*

9   Another way of explaining sentences like (3) is that the passive allows the direct object, i.e. the patient (*toutes les souris*), to occupy the subject position; the subject (*le chat*) appears optionally in the agent phrase (*par* + agent). 10 That is, in (3) the phrase *par le chat* could have been omitted. 11 In other words, the passive voice does not require the agent to be mentioned: in (4) we assume that members of parliament voted in a particular law; but the agent is not specified.[b]

12   In (5), the person who stole the bicycle is unknown and therefore not specified.

4. La loi a été votée.
5. Sa bicyclette a été volée (on ne sait pas par qui).

13   We obtain the passive by moving the object (patient) to the subject position and inserting the auxiliary *être*. 14 The auxiliary takes the tense of the main verb of the active sentence, followed by the past participle of that verb.[c]

15   Another way of expressing a passive-like meaning without using the type of structure illustrated in diagram A [Fig. 7.1] is through what is known as the middle voice. 16 Even though the agent is not expressed, we understand that an agent is the doer of the action. 17 In the middle voice, we do not insert the auxiliary *être*, but the meaning is passive-like. 18 Sentence (6) below is in the active voice; sentence (7) has a passive meaning, expressed in the middle voice, using a pronominal verb.

6. Les filles portent des jupes courtes (cette année).
7. Les jupes se portent courtes cette année.

19   In middle-voice sentence (7), the pronominal verb *se porter* would be translated into English as 'are worn': Skirts are worn short this year. 20 Again, the agent is not expressed. 21 Rather, the grammatical object (the patient) '*les jupes*' is highlighted or emphasized and becomes the subject. 22 This is illustrated in Diagram B [Fig. 7.2].

23   Consider examples (8) and (9).

8. *On mange le saumon froid.*
9. *Le saumon se mange froid.*

24   Sentence (8) is in the active voice; sentence (9) is in the middle voice, which gives the sentence a passive-like meaning.[d]

---

[b] The second prompt occurs at this point:
   * *Can you tell me about sentence (2) in terms of semantic roles?*
      If participant does not understand the question, or gives a brief (or wrong) answer, prompt further.
   * *Can you tell me about sentence (2) in terms of object, subject, agent, patient?*
[c] The third prompt is inserted here:
   * *Can you change sentence (1) into the passive voice?*
      If participant does not understand the question, or gives a brief (or wrong) answer, prompt further.
   * *You can refer back to diagram A if you want.*
[d] The fourth prompt occurs here:
   * *Please explain sentence (9).*
      If participant does not understand the question, or gives a brief (or wrong) answer, prompt further.
   * *Is there an agent, patient in sentence (9)? What is it?*

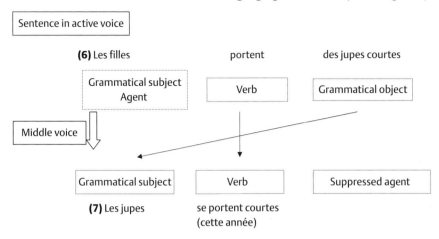

Figure 7.2

25 For (9), English uses the passive: Salmon is eaten cold. 26 Some grammars refer to this as the agent-less passive. 27 French prefers the middle voice in sentences like (9).

28 Sentence (10) may be seen as a passive counterpart of active voice sentences (11) and (12). 29 In the case of passive AND middle voice sentences, it is important to remember that they allow us to place emphasis on the element of the sentence that we want to highlight by putting it in the subject position.

> 10. *Les tomates se sont bien vendues cette année.* [Tomatoes sold well this year.]
> 11. *La vente de tomates a été bonne cette année.*
> 12. *On a bien vendu les tomates cette année.*

30 It is important to note that not all pronominal verbs in French are used in middle voice sentences. 31 There are four main types of pronominal verbs. 32 One is the type we have been discussing, those used to form sentences in the middle voice. 33 Here are the three others:

34 (a) reflexive pronominal verbs such as *s'habiller* ('to dress oneself' or 'to get dressed'), *se laver, se peigner*. Example: *Je me lave les mains.*

35 (b) reciprocal pronominal verbs such as *se rencontrer* ('to meet each other' or simply 'to meet'), *se parler*. Example: *Nous nous parlons chaque soir.*

36 (c) inherently or intrinsically pronominal verbs that never appear without the pronoun *se*, for example *s'évanouir, se souvenir*. Example: *Il se souvient fréquemment de son premier voyage à Paris.*

Acknowledgement

Designing the study reported in this chapter, working out the procedures of analyses, and interpreting the outcomes are products from 'languaging-them-through' with colleagues and students. In particular, I would like to thank the project team: Lindsay Brooks, Ibtissem Knouzi, Sharon Lapkin, and Wataru Suzuki for their collaborative dialogue. Additionally, Penny Kinnear, Helen Moore, and Linda Steinman have languaged with me on these and related issues for close to a decade. I would also like to thank Paul Quinn for his helpful comments on an earlier draft. A Social Sciences and Humanities Research Council of Canada grant (research grant 410-04-2099) gave us these opportunities, for which I am very grateful.

Notes

1. All names used in this chapter are pseudonyms.
2. The non-L2 domain in this study was physics.
3. For a detailed analysis of Heidi and Lisa, see Knouzi et al. (forthcoming).
4. Examples of the middle voice in English are: The car drives well. The wine glass shattered. The store closes at 6 p.m. The book sells well.
5. Translation: Girls are wearing their skirts short this year.
6. Translation: Skirts are being worn short this year.
7. Example 9 is: *Le saumon se mange froid.*
8. For a detailed demonstration of how languaging mediates the links between scientific and everyday concepts, see Brooks et al. (forthcoming).
9. That is, self-explanations that are related to domain-based principles.
10. Anticipative reasoning is similar to what we call inferencing.
11. Egocentric speech, which then becomes inner speech, once internalized.

8

Minding your hands: the function of gesture in L2 learning

JAMES P. LANTOLF

Introduction

More than three decades ago, the renowned kinesiologist, Ray Birdwhistell (1970), suggested that to exclude kinesthetic behavior from the analysis of communication is to incorrectly assume that this activity contributes next to nothing in the making of meaning. Unfortunately, within mainstream linguistics Birdwhistell's admonition has, for the most part, gone unheeded as theories of language continue to focus on traditional areas of morphosyntax, phonology, and the lexicon. Even theoretical stances that concern themselves with language use, including discourse analytic approaches, sociolinguistics, and pragmatics, have shied away from incorporating meaning-making behaviors that do not 'look and smell' like the traditional linguistic rose. Recently, however, at least two important approaches to language analysis have recognized the contribution of the human body to our meaning-making prowess and have taken this capacity into account in constructing their theoretical edifices.

Roy Harris (2003: 67), the founder of integrational linguistics, comments that 'human beings do *not* [italics in original] live in a communicational world that is neatly and permanently compartmentalized into language and non-language'. According to Harris (ibid. 45) 'linguistic communication is a continuum of interaction which can be manifested both verbally and non-verbally' and therefore includes phenomena either ignored or marginalized in general linguistics. These areas include such phenomena as silences, pauses, grunts, tone of voice, facial expressions, eye gaze, haptic behavior, gestures, and movement of the entire body. For its part, cognitive linguistics likewise understands the importance of the body not only in communicating but also in giving rise to specific types of metaphorical and metonymic concepts that guide our thinking (see Lakoff and Johnson 1980; Gibbs 1994; Kövecses 2006). Kövecses (2006: 212), for example, argues that our 'conceptual system is structured by image-schemas' predicated on our 'embodied spatial experience'.

Some approaches to psychology have always recognized the fact that the human body is implicated in the making of meaning and therefore in the thinking process itself (see Mead 1934; Fogel 1993). Vygotsky (1987) was especially interested in gesture as a means of mediating social relations between parents and children. More recently, David McNeill (1992, 2005) and his colleagues (e.g. Goldin-Meadow et al. 2001; Goldin-Meadow and Singer 2003) have featured the dialectical unity formed by gesture and speech during the thinking for speaking (see Slobin 1996, 2003) process.

It is McNeill's approach to the gesture–speech interface that informs the research discussed in this chapter. Specifically, I present a case study of an L2 learner who uses gesture integrated with speech to think her way into an understanding of how to use aspect in a French narrative. While L2 researchers have begun to pay increasing attention to the function of gesture in L2 communication and even in L2 pedagogy, to my knowledge the present study is the first to consider the self-generated use of gesture to think through and resolve an L2 language problem. One of the significant implications of the analysis is that, contrary to Long's (1997) assumption that language learning is an internal process, the argument I make is that cognition, including learning, is not exclusively an internal (i.e. inside-the-head) process. This is because, in line with Vygotsky's proposal, the mind is not coterminus with the brain but is instead a functional system that includes, of course, the brain, but also incorporates the body as well as cultural artifacts (see Wertsch 1998). McCafferty (2004: 149) argues that there is a close connection between speech and gesture that goes beyond social communication. Gesture, he suggests, can contribute to the development of thinking, and as such can 'function as a separate, spatio-motoric mode of thinking' (ibid.).

The dialectics of speech and gesture

According to Vygotsky (1987), thinking and speaking form a dialectical unity that results in the reshaping of thinking as it is externalized in (social or private) speech (or writing). As such, thinking is neither independent of, nor identical with, speaking. Each process adheres to its own set of principles and constraints, but at the same time each exerts an influence on the other during the communicative process. In the mind the whole thought is present as once, but in speech it has to be developed successively (ibid. 251). As thought transitions to speech (or writing), what is originally unpartitioned and synthetic meaning becomes partitioned and analytic. This transition, according to Vygotsky, results in the reshaping of thought as it is externalized in speech. However, for Vygotsky the influence of speech on thought is not necessarily a one-way street, as there are times when thinking exerts an influence over language and reshapes it to fit the motives and intentions of the speaker. Thus psychological and linguistic processes form a dialectical unity of mutual and dynamic interaction.[1]

The contrast and interconnection between thinking and speech was the primary focus of the research that Vygotsky and his colleagues (e.g. Luria

1982) conducted on private vs. social speech. The former is assumed to be a reflection of unpartitioned thought, given that it is often abbreviated, lacking in full grammatical properties, and generally difficult to comprehend when overheard. Thus, when trying to solve a complex problem (e.g. putting a puzzle together, as Wertsch 1985 documents) speakers frequently produce utterances such as 'Ok, next'; or 'Now, white', etc. Such utterances, according to Vygotsky, are saturated with meaning for the person who produces them but for no one else, and therefore there is no need to unpack the meaning by encoding it into a fully expanded utterance.

Although Vygotsky recognized that gesture plays an important role in the early communicative interactions between children and adults, to my knowledge, he did not consider the potential function of gesture in mature thinking and communication once spoken language fully developed. David McNeill (1992, 2005), influenced by Vygotsky's theory on the integration of thinking and speech, has uncovered an important relationship between gesture and speech. According to McNeill's hypothesis, gesture and speech form a dialectical unity that parallels the connection Vygotsky proposed between thinking and speech. McNeill and Duncan (2000: 155) suggest that gestures are '*material carriers* of thinking' and therefore provide 'an enhanced window into mental processes' (p. 144). McNeill's (2005) argument is that speech, as in Vygotsky's theory, not only segments thought, but because it relies on signs to build up meaning, it represents thought; gesture, however, because of its spatial medium and imagistic quality, preserves the synthetic nature of thought and does not represent, but depicts thought. Thus, gesture, as a depiction of unpartitioned thought and speech, as a representation of partitioned thought, form a dialectical unity, which McNeill calls 'Growth Point' (GP) and is formed by the combination of 'two distinct semiotic architectures', one verbal and one imagistic (McNeill and Duncan 2000: 144). More specifically, the GP emerges, and becomes directly observable, at the point where the stroke, or central motion, of a gesture synchronizes with a particular verbal element during the production of an utterance. The GP indicates that aspect of meaning that the speaker considers salient, and therefore, as McNeill (2005) notes, is the psychological predicate of an utterance (explained below).

Gesture

Gesture researchers distinguish between gestures that occur independently of speech and those that co-occur with, and partially depend upon, speech for their full meaning to emerge. Those gestures that are independent of speech are, according to McNeill's (1992) system, known as emblems and include such behaviors as joining the tips of the thumb and index figure so as to make a circle in order to indicate OK in English. Gestures that synchronize with speech, on the other hand, depict part of the meaning through gesture but rely on speech to complete the meaning. The relationship also functions the other way around so that speech relies on gesture to complete its meaning, as will be illustrated later.

McNeill (1992) has identified four types of gestures that co-occur with speech: iconics, metaphorics, beats, and deictics.[2] Iconic gestures are most often, though not always, hand gestures (at times the entire body can be involved, as when indicating the bumpy nature of a bike moving over cobblestones) that represent physical objects or actions, such as containers, balls, drainpipes, and the like. They occur in conversations when a speaker describes an object or event, and they impart information encoded partially or not at all in speech (ibid.). Thus, a speaker might produce a verbal utterance such as 'The bird flew out of the nest' but might indicate the direction of flight through hand movements in an upward or downward trajectory. Metaphoric gestures are similar to iconics except that their referent is an abstract concept rather than a concrete object or event, as for instance when a speaker holds both hands out in front of the body separated by about a foot with palms facing each other and says 'I feel completely closed in.' The distance between the hands and the tension expressed in their movement may indicate, and perhaps more effectively than in speech, how intensely the speaker experiences the condition. Beats, which resemble someone beating musical time, entail hand movements which can be rather obvious or quite subtle involving no more than a 'flick of the hand or fingers up and down, or back and forth' (ibid. 15). Their relevance is in their 'semiotic value' as markers of the significance of the stretches of speech with which they synchronize, as for instance when a speaker introduces a new topic into a conversation or a new character into a story (ibid.). McCafferty (1998: 83) reports that one L2 speaker in his study produced a beat on each word of an utterance, as if monitoring their production: *'they might, they might have steal, stole, they might have steal, stole'* (italics in original. According to McCafferty, the beats indicate embodied attempts to maintain focus on the form of the utterance (i.e. regulate) as the speaker externally worked out the appropriate verb form to convey his intended meaning. The final category, deictics, function, as the term implies, to point to an entity or event. The object of the deictic may or may not be present in time and/or space. Thus, a speaker might point to a bus while uttering 'Here it comes,' or might point to a place or event being talked about that occurred in a distant location and at a time far removed from the time of speaking. McNeill (2003), for example, reports on a study of two speakers who were discussing the time when one of them moved from Iowa to Chicago to attend university and they both used deictics in imagined space to point to the two locations and then later in the conversation used the same imagined space to refer to two different universities in Chicago.

As I mentioned earlier, the crucial phase of a gesture is its stroke. McNeill (1992) segments gestures into four phases: rest, preparation, stroke, and retraction, or return to rest phase. In producing gestures, speakers position their hands (and often arms) from the rest position to the point where they prepare for the movement, or stroke, phase. At the stroke phase, speakers execute the part of the gesture that carries its meaning. The stroke synchronizes with a specific segment or sequence of segments in speech that co-express, or complement, the meaning expressed through gesture. Once the stroke is executed it may be held for a brief period or it may immediately return to the rest position. The stroke–speech synchronization expresses the GP, or psychological predicate, of the utterance.

To appreciate how gesture and speech intertwine to create meaning, consider the following examples taken from McNeill's research, where participants are asked to narrate an episode from a Tweety Bird animated cartoon. In the episode, Sylvester is intent on capturing Tweety Bird, who is located in a top-floor apartment. In one attempt to reach Tweety, the cat climbs up the inside of a drainpipe. While he is moving upward, Tweety drops a bowling ball down the drainpipe. Sylvester swallows the ball, which pushes him out of the drainpipe and he proceeds to roll down the street and into a bowling alley. In describing the final portion of the event, one of the participants produces the utterance given in (1), where the brackets delineate the onset and offset of the gesture phrase and the boldface indicates the stroke of the gesture and the double underline indicates that the motion is held while the hands move in a downward trajectory typical of English manner–path conflated gestures.

(1) The cat [**rolls** <u>down</u> the street] and into the bowling alley.
Both hands rotate around each other in a rolling motion while simultaneously moving in a downward trajectory: manner + path information.

In (1) the speaker describes the movement of Sylvester, but with the GP (i.e. psychological predicate) on the manner in which the cat moved down the street. In (2), however, we observe an utterance with the same linguistic segments but with a different synchronized gesture that brings forth a different GP and therefore a different meaning. The speaker's focus in (2) is on the path of the cat's motion and the manner is clearly backgrounded since it is encoded in speech only.

(2) The cat rolls [**down** the street] and into the bowling alley.
RH (right hand) is extended in a position in the middle of the body and moves diagonally downward and to the right: path information only.

Earlier I pointed out that psychological grammar may override linguistic grammar when a speaker wishes to externalize a particular GP, even if it violates the constraints of the linguistic grammar. The example given in (3) discussed by McNeill (2005) illustrates a GP which combines two linguistic segments to create a constituent that is not sanctioned in the grammar of English.

(3) Tweety Bird runs and gets a bowling ball and [drops **it down** the drainpipe]

Both hands are open with fingers slightly extended and palms facing each other with a slightly downward tilt. The hands then plunge downward: path information only.

According to McNeill's analysis, the stroke of the gesture coincides with the uttering of 'it down', which indicates a GP that combines the direct object of the verb (i.e. bowling ball) and a locative preposition into a single unit—a unit that has no status in English grammar. The unit, however, has cognitive status (i.e. serves as the psychological predicate) in the speaker's thinking. The speaker's attention is centered on the downward trajectory of the bowling and not on the fact that some entity dropped it or that the ground against which it moves is the drainpipe.

Gesture and pedagogy

While most of the general and L2 research on gesture has focused on the function of gesture in the communicative process, in particular within the framework of Slobin's (1996, 2003) thinking for speaking hypothesis, an increasing amount of research has investigated the facilitative role of gesture in classroom pedagogy. Given that the communicative function of gesture is not directly relevant to my concern in this chapter and that this literature has been extensively reviewed in a series of recent publications (Lantolf 2006; Lantolf and Thorne 2006; McCafferty and Stam 2008), I will limit my review of the literature to several studies dealing with the pedagogical function of gesture.

Goldin-Meadow and her colleagues conducted a series of studies on the effect of gesture on math learning in elementary-school classrooms. In Goldin-Meadow, Alibali, and Breckinridge Church (1993) the researchers investigated the strategies that children used in solving math problems of the following type: 4 + 5 + 3 = ___ + 3. The children produced three different types of strategy: gesture exclusive, speech + gesture, speech exclusive. In a gesture-exclusive strategy, children using their index and middle fingers held in a V-shape pointed to the 4 and the 5 and then to the blank indicating that they had added the first two numbers and inserted the sum into the blank. In the gesture + speech strategy, the children used the same gesture but this time accompanied by speech, as in 'I added the 4 and the 5'. In the speech only mode, the children produced utterances such as the one just given but failed to use co-expressive gestures. The researchers then examined the number of speech–gesture mismatches produced by the children when solving the problems. Those children who produced a high number of mismatches exhibited a larger gesture-exclusive repertoire than children who produced a low number of mismatches. Importantly, the high and low mismatchers did not show a significant difference in their speech + gesture or speech-exclusive strategies. According to the researchers this meant that the additional strategies used by the mismatchers occurred only in their gesture-based strategies. Thus, the researchers concluded that in order for teachers to fully understand what students know about solving math problems it is necessary not only to listen to them but to look at them as well.

In a series of additional studies, summarized in Goldin-Meadow (2005), the research team discovered that mismatchers frequently manifested appropriate strategies for solving math problems in gestures even if their speech exhibited incorrect strategies. Furthermore, those children who showed mismatches between speech and gesture responded more positively to instruction than children who did not show mismatches in their solutions to math problems. Thus, when solving problems such as the one given above, children who produced an incorrect solution, but who pointed to the 4 and the 5 and not the 3 on the left side of the equation (and even if they included the 3 in their speech) were more likely to benefit from instruction than those children who pointed at and co-expressed the three numbers in speech. According to Goldin-Meadow (ibid. 252), the reason the mismatchers responded to instruction to a greater degree than did the matchers is because even though the mismatchers were unable to articulate the solution to the problem 'they have the pieces in place to make progress' and instruction serves to help them pull things together. Those children with fewer mismatches do not have the same level of substantive knowledge and therefore require longer and more intensive instruction.

In a related study with adults, Alibali et al. (1999) gave participants a series of verbal math problems of the following type: 'A bookcase has six shelves; the number of books on each successive shelf increases by a constant number. If there are 15 books on the top shelf and 45 on the bottom, how many books total are there'? According to the researchers the problem can be solved either by adding discrete units or a continuous rate of books. When asked which strategy they would use to solve the problem, the participants frequently matched their verbal accounts with their gestures. That is, those that said they would use the discrete strategy deployed short, choppy, step-like gestures in their description of the solution and those that said they would use the continuous strategy accompanied their verbal descriptions with long, flowing and curving gestures. Some of the participants, however, displayed a mismatch between their gesture and speech, stating either that they would use the discrete strategy accompanied by continuous gestures or vice versa. It turns out that when the speech and gestures matched, it could be predicted with considerable certainty that they would then use the stated strategy to actually solve the problem and when there was a mismatch it was much more difficult to predict which of the two strategies would be deployed. When there was a mismatch (i.e. conflicting approaches to the problem), the solution to the problem generally unfolded in a confusing and uneven process as opposed to when there was a match between speech and gesture.

In a later study, Goldin-Meadow et al. (2001) investigated the impact of gesture on memory. In this study the researchers combined elements of the original math research with a verbal memory task. They asked children and adults to solve algebraic problems that were appropriate for their age while at the same time attempting to remember verbal information. Following each math problem the children were given a list of words and the adults a list of letters to memorize. The participants then had to explain how they solved the math problems, while at the same time remembering the requisite words or letters. Once the explanation was completed, the participants had to recall the respective lists. The explanations were carried out under two different conditions: one where gestures were permitted and one where the participants had to keep their hands in place on a tabletop. In the no-gesture condition both groups recalled fewer words than in the gesture condition. The researchers considered two possible accounts for the effect observed in both groups, which, by the way, was not a function of accuracy of the solutions offered for the math problems. On one account, gesture serves to lessen the cognitive load on verbal memory by transferring part of the load to imagistic memory during the math task, thus freeing up memory that could be used to remember the words or letters. On another account, being compelled to avoid gesture, as in the second condition, forced the participants to engage in a third task—remembering not to gesture, which then increased the cognitive load on the memory task rather than decreasing the load through gesture use as in the first hypothesis. As it turned out, several of the children and adults did not gesture when solving some of the math problems, even when the first condition permitted them to do so. The analysis shows that when the lists of words or letters was long, when the participants did gesture, their recall of the verbal items was significantly better than when they voluntarily failed to gesture or when they were instructed not to gesture. The researchers conclude that gesture clearly has an impact on processing capacity, although they are uncertain on the specifics of how this functions. It could be that gesture lightens the cognitive load on verbal working memory, or it could be that gesture shifts the load from this memory system to other cognitive systems—for example from verbal to spatial memory, given that gesture is a spatial system of thinking. As Goldin-Meadow (2005: 254) observes with regard to the study, 'gesturing may not only reflect a speaker's cognitive state but, in reducing cognitive load, it may also play a role in shaping that state'.

In another study, Wang, Bernas, and Eberhard (2004) report on the effect of gesture-based instruction on learning among children with ADHD (Attention Deficit/Hyperactivity Disorder). As in the Goldin-Meadow research, focus was on elementary-school children (mean age = 7.5 years), although in this case, the children had been independently diagnosed with one of three types of ADHD: inattentive, hyperactive, and impulsive, or a combination of these. A large percentage (76%) of the children had also been diagnosed with an additional disorder (e.g. conduct disorder, learning disability, etc.). The children (N=45) were divided into groups and each group was assigned to one of five different teachers. The task was for the teachers to help the children solve a series of puzzles. The teachers interacted with the children in three modalities: speech only, gesture only, and speech-gesture combined. The results showed that the children responded more frequently to the gesture-only and gesture-speech modalities than to the speech-only modality and their success rate in solving the puzzles was higher as a consequence of instruction through the first two modalities, and in particular when the gestures used were deictic or iconic. The researchers suggest that the reason for the positive pedagogical effect of gesture-linked modalities is that they attracted and held the students' attention for longer periods of time and thus provided 'more complete information' than was possible through speech alone (ibid. 226). Thus, when a teacher wished to inform the students that to solve a particular puzzle it was necessary to bring two pieces together, a combination of a deictic gesture (e.g. pointing to the relevant pieces) and an iconic gesture (e.g. bringing the fists into contact) 'provides more concrete, visual, vivid, dynamic and easy-to-follow information for a child than the teacher's verbal message alone' (ibid.).

Gesture and L2 pedagogy

Allen (1995) reports a positive effect for teachers' use of emblems (i.e. gestures unaccompanied by speech) on learner uptake of fixed expressions in a French as a foreign language classroom. In a later study (Allen 2000) found that emblems along with iconics and deictics generated strongly positive reactions from students in a US high-school Spanish class. The gestures apparently enhanced student comprehension of the meaning of the teacher's speech more than speech alone. In terms of SLA theory, this finding suggests that the gestures provided the students with enhanced comprehensible input (ibid. 169).

Lazaraton conducted a study on the use of gestures by two ESL instructors at a North American university, although in her published work (2004) she reports on only one of the teachers—a Japanese MA ESL graduate student with a total of six years of teaching experience (i.e. five years in Japan and 1 year in the US). The researcher examined gesture use during unplanned vocabulary explanation over the course of three lessons. The majority of the gestures were used to explain the meaning of verbs (e.g. argue, swear, weave, etc.), although in some cases (e.g. quit, give up, draw) gestures were not used. Importantly, according to Lazaraton, the gestures did not appear to have a compensatory function; rather they seemed to occur as a natural part of explanatory talk, adding to the depth and efficiency of communication. This is precisely what McNeill (2005) intends by the co-expressivity of the gesture–speech interface. Unfortunately, Lazaraton did not investigate the effects of the teacher's use of gesture on student learning. This important research remains to be carried out.

The present study

The present study examines the use of gesture by an advanced student of French as a foreign language. Although the study differs from the previously surveyed pedagogical use of gestures by teachers, I nevertheless believe that it is appropriate to situate the study within the pedagogical literature since the student's use of gesture has a clear pedagogical goal—to think through how verbal aspect functions in French narratives.

The data is taken from the video appendix of the recent teacher's guide on dynamic assessment produced by Lantolf and Poehner (2007). The appendix presents several examples of how a mediator can scaffold the performance of L2 learners in order to maximally promote development. In one of the examples, the participant under consideration here, given the pseudonym Donna, is narrating a scene from the Hollywood movie *Nine Months*. In the scene the two principal characters, Rebecca and Sam, are driving to a party, when Rebecca informs Sam that she is pregnant. Sam is shocked at the news and questions Rebecca as to why she failed to use appropriate birth control to prevent the pregnancy. As Donna is relating Sam's emotional state, she vacillates between use of the imperfective and perfective aspect in French, a feature of the language that is notoriously difficult for speakers of English. The mediator reacts to Donna's uncertainty and asks her which is the appropriate aspect to use in this case. Donna responds by saying that the imperfect is the appropriate form because Sam was shocked at the news. The mediator interrupts Donna's line of thinking by repeating Donna's use of an imperfect construction. Donna then begins to explain her reasoning, at which point she begins to realize that perhaps the imperfect is not the appropriate form to use in this case. The initial interaction between Donna and the mediator is given in (4), with the relevant verb form indicated in upper case letters in Donna's first turn in the exchange:

(4)

DONNA:	*...et Samuel ÉTAIT* [imperfect] *tres choqué A ÉTÉ* [perfect] *choqué ÉTAIT choqué et...ah c'est...okay* (laughs) 'And Samuel was very shocked was shocked, was shocked, and...ah this is...OK'
MEDIATOR:	*était, a été ?* 'was [imperfect], was [perfect]'
DONNA:	*c'était un choque á lui cette nouvelle. Donc il était choqué...et ça et juste aprés ça ah* 'It was a shock for him this news. Therefore he was shocked...and this and just after this ah'
DONNA:	*ils...ils ont ah ...* [mediator interrupts] 'they...they have ah...'
MEDIATOR:	*so...il...il était choqué* 'so...he...he was shocked'
DONNA:	*il était choqué a cause de cette nouvelle* 'he was shocked because of this news'
MEDIATOR:	okay, using imparfait because...
DONNA:	using imparfait.

Following the exchange, Donna begins to work out for herself which of the two verb forms appropriately expresses Sam's reaction to the news. As she does this, two innovations are introduced into her discourse: she switches to

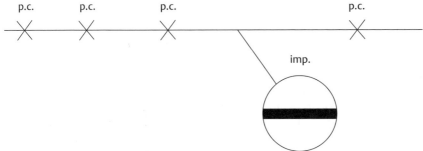

Figure 8.1 Pedagogical diagram explaining use of imperfect and perfect aspect in French

English and she begins to use a specific sequence of gestures. The switch to English occurs not because Donna lacks proficiency in French, but because English, her L1, serves as her tool for thinking. It has more cognitive meaning for her than does French at this point in her language-learning history (see Lantolf and Thorne 2006 for a full discussion of use of the L1 as a tool for thought). The specific types of gesture that Donna makes throughout her externalized thinking process are, in my view, connected to the pedagogical diagram given in Figure 8.1. The diagram, which had been given to students four months earlier in an enrichment tutorial as part of their advanced grammar class, graphically illustrates the difference between imperfect and perfect aspect in French.

In the diagram, the extended horizontal line represents the passage of time. The Xs are intended to capture the notion that at specific points on the timeline where events or states begin and/or end the perfect aspect (i.e. *passé composé*) is typically used. The segment indicated by the magnified portion of the timeline represents the notion that if a user wishes to refer to events and/ or states without making salient their beginning or end, imperfect aspect (i.e. *imparfait*) is normally used.[3]

Gesture–speech analysis

As a reminder to the reader, the GP occurs where a particular speech segment synchronizes with the stroke of the gesture. The transcription convention used to indicate this is bold upper case font. The segment with a single underline indicates that the gesture is held through the next segment(s) of speech before the hands are retracted to the rest position. The abbreviations given in braces following the transcribed portion of speech, indicate the speaker's eye gaze (EG). The > signals direction of movement of EG, @ indicates the focus of the EG. DL = down and to the left, LH = left hand, RH = right hand, UR = upper right, UL = upper left. The gesture–speech analysis was carried out using *Final Cut Express* software for MAC. The software enables video segments to be run in slow motion without audio distortion, thus allowing greater precision in determining the synchronization of gesture and speech.

Donna is seated next to a table located to her left facing the mediator, who is not visible in the video. Her left arm is often in contact with the table. On the table is a yellow notepad and pen that was made available by the mediator in case Donna wanted to take notes on the events depicted in the film. She did not, however, take notes at any point while watching the clip.

In the excerpt given in (5) Donna makes the switch to English and begins to use gestures that reference the diagram in Figure 8.1, although she makes no specific mention of this in her speech.

(5)

    a. *parce que il était choqué* ... he was he was shocked
    b. *parce que* [*il était cho*QUE]
      Beat: LH rises, palm turned inward with fingers extended and pointing to the right but tilted slightly downward with thumb extended. HAND PUMPS SLIGHTLY AWAY FROM BODY
    c. [he was ... he was SHOCK ed] {EG > DL@ LH}
      Beat: LH in same shape as in (5b) moves to L over notepad. Fingers pointing downward hand moves forward horizontally over notepad with slight beats for 'he' and 'was' and then her hand while MOVING FORWARD A THIRD TIME THRUSTS DOWNWARD UNTIL FINGERTIPS TOUCH TABLETOP

In (5a) Donna repeats the critical problematic utterance. She uses an inappropriate imperfect construction and then repeats the utterance in its English version. In (5b) she repeats the utterance in French and again uses imperfect aspect. She seems to be using repetition as a strategy to resolve the problem. In (5b) she begins to use gesture as part of her thinking process. Donna's focus is on the verb *choqué* 'shocked' as signaled by the stroke of the gesture whereby her left hand moves sharply away from her upper body. The horizontal movement in this case could well indicate that she is focusing on the movement of time intended by the magnified portion of the line in Figure 8.1. Moreover, the stroke of the gesture occurs on the past participle form of the verb rather than on the problematic segment, which carries imperfect aspect morphology, *était*. In (5c) Donna code-switches to English. English does not make a morphological distinction between perfect and imperfect aspect: 'was shocked' can impart either perfect or imperfect meaning. In French, using the imperfect with the past participle, as Donna does in (5a) and (5b), imparts a sense that the construction is more adjectival than verbal. That is, *choqué* used with the imperfect form *était* functions as an adjective, describing Sam's state, and not as a verb indicating that he became shocked as a result of the news related by Rebecca. However, Donna's gesture in (5c) is distinctly different from the gesture she produced in (5b). The gesture combines forward movement, typical of imperfect aspect, with a downward thrust, depicting a point on the timeline, indicative of perfective meaning. Thus, Donna's gesture can be interpreted as the imagistic version of her uncertainty as to the appropriate aspect with which to relate Sam's reaction.

In (6) Donna's uncertainty is even more clearly marked in both gesture and in speech.

(6)

    a. [he STARTed to be shocked] {EG > DL@LH}
       Iconic: palm facing inward fingers extended downward touching the table in front of notepad; hand rises slightly off the table and then back down into contact with the table MOVING BACK AND FORTH WHILE FINGERS REMAIN IN CONTACT WITH THE TABLE
    b. and [then con TIN ued to be shocked] {EG > M} by this news {EG > DL@ LH}
       Iconic: palm turned inward, fingers extended with tips touching table. ARM SUDDENLY THRUSTS FORWARD HORIZONTALLY ALONG THE TABLE MOVING AWAY FROM THE NOTEPAD. Hand then retracts to original position.

In (6a) Donna uses the verb 'start', which clearly indicates that Sam entered into a state of shock as a result of hearing the news from Rebecca of her pregnancy. Donna depicts this through her gesture whereby her left hand, in contact with the table, representing the timeline in the diagram in Figure 8.1, moves back and forth. This movement, fixed upon by her eye gaze is an iconic image of the Xs in the original diagram. In (6b), however, Donna generates a GP with an imperfective meaning. Her arm moves forward along the imagined timeline with the stroke synchronized with the second syllable of the verb 'continued'. She holds the gesture through the final syllable and the following segment 'to be shocked'. In this case, however, her eye gaze shifts to the mediator, as if seeking his approval. The mediator did not produce a verbal response, but since he was not videotaped, I am unable to say anything about a possible non-verbal response. Donna then shifts her gaze back to her slightly extended left arm.

In (7a) Donna states, inaccurately, that she first used the *passé composé*, when in fact she had first used the imperfect. She does not complete the utterance, instead she repeats 'I think' and simultaneously moves her eye gaze to the upper right, a typical movement when people engage in the thinking process. Upon uttering the word 'first' she produces a beat gesture in which her left hand, fingers pointed downward, moves slightly toward the table. In (7c) she synchronizes an iconic gesture whereby her left hand moves back and forth vertically across the table, and most likely, the imagined timeline in Figure 8.1. Her eye gaze then shifts from the upper right downward to her left hand. In (7d and e) she repeats the beat gesture produced in (7b). Donna's gestures throughout the utterances presented in (7) depict a point along the imagined timeline where the perfect aspect (*passé composé*) is normally used, in this case, to indicate the onset of Sam's shock. Unlike in (6) Donna's co-expressive speech no longer reflects the actual French (or English translation thereof) utterance she produced in her narrative; instead, she begins to think through her choice of aspect. Even though her speech in (7) does not fully reveal that perfect is the appropriate aspect, her gestures do. This is reminiscent of the mismatchers in Goldin-Meadows research surveyed above. Recall that the mismatchers generally produced the appropriate strategy for solving math problems through gestures even though through speech they did not.

(7)

    a. but I think I first chose *passé composé* to note that
    b. but I think {EG > UR} I [FIRST]
       Beat: hand points downward fingers extended but not touching table
           makes a SLIGHT DOWNWARD THRUST
    c. [CHOSE] {EG > DL@LH} *passé composé* {EG > DL –@LH}
       Iconic: hand points downward fingers extended but not touching
            table, hand makes a SLIGHT BACK AND FORTH MOTION
    d. to [NOTE] {EG >DL@LH}
       Beat: hand pointed downward with diagonal tilt THRUSTS DOWNWARD
           BRUSHING TABLE
    e. [THAT] {EG@LH}
       Beat: hand pointed downward with slight diagonal tilt THRUSTS
           DOWNWARD

In (8) Donna finally works out and commits to her choice of aspect. In (8a) and (8b) she initiates a series of exaggerated gestures, which she follows with her eye gaze. Each of the gestures again depicts a point on the timeline where perfect aspect is called for. Her co-expressive speech is the temporal preposition 'at', indicating the point at which Sam's state of shock began. In my view, Donna has, at this point in her reasoning, made a definite commitment to perfect aspect, as she now turns her gaze away from her left hand and onto the mediator. In (8c–f) she explains to him the reason for her decision in gesture and co-expressive speech. The fact that Donna continues to produce gestures that depict points on the timeline where perfect aspect is called for could serve to reinforce her decision for herself as well as to explain her decision to the mediator. Thus, Donna's discourse in (8) may well have a dual, communicative and cognitive, function (see Wells 1999 for a discussion of the dual function of speech).

(8)

    a. He [A // __] {EG@LH}
       Beat: palm facing toward body and fingers extended in a position parallel to but above the desk HAND THRUSTS DOWNWARD AND RECOVERS
           UPWARD
    b. [AT /] {EG > FOLLOWS LH > DL}

    Beat: palm facing toward body and fingers extended in a position parallel to but above the desk HAND THRUSTS DOWNWARD AND RECOVERS UPWARD

  c. [a VERY DISTINCT] {EG > M}
    Beat: palm facing toward body and fingers extended in a position parallel to but above the desk HAND THRUSTS DOWNWARD AND RECOVERS UPWARD

  d. [POINT] {EG@M}
    Beat: palm facing toward and fingers extended in a position parallel to but above the desk HAND THRUSTS DOWNWARD AND RECOVERS UPWARD

  e. [he /// {EG@M]
    Beat: palm facing toward and fingers extended in a position parallel to but above the desk HAND THRUSTS DOWNWARD AND RECOVERS UPWARD

  f. [STARTed] to become shocked {EG@M}
    Beat: palm facing toward body and fingers extended in a position parallel to but above the desk HAND THRUSTS DOWNWARD AND RECOVERS UPWARD.

In (9a) the mediator asks Donna a leading question, to which Donna responds in (9b) by announcing her decision to use perfect aspect, which again is formulated in speech and co-expressive gesture. The segment of speech that synchronizes with her perfective imaging gesture 'so' is often an indication that someone either is about to undertake (e.g. 'So, let's see what I can do here') or has completed a thought or action process ('So, here is what I've decided'). In this case, it most likely indicates the completion of the process. Donna's eye gaze is directed at her interlocutor. Finally, in (9d) she produces the appropriate French utterance using perfective aspect to indicate that Sam went into a state of shock at the news of Rebecca's pregnancy. As she produces the initial portion of the utterance, *il a*, 'he has', Donna's eye gaze moves from the mediator, to no one, to upper right and finally to upper left, as she works out the morphosyntax of the utterance. Once she has completed the utterance, her gaze shifts back to the mediator, an indication that she is satisfied with what she has produced. In (9c) Donna no longer produces timeline gestures; which is understandable, given that she has reached a decision with regard to aspect and that all she needs to work out is the morphosyntax.

(9)

  a. MEDIATOR: so emphasizing that ?
  b. DONNA: [yeah so] maybe what I want to say is {EG@M}
    Beat: palm facing toward body and fingers extended in a position parallel to, but above, the desk HAND THRUSTS DOWNWARD AND RECOVERS UPWARD

c. DONNA: il a {EG@M > AHEAD > UR > UL} *IL A ETE CHOQUE* {EG > M
             'He has   he has was shocked' = 'He
             went into a state of shock'

Discussion and conclusion

In this chapter, I have considered data from what I believe to be a new area of L2 research: the use of gesture–speech synchronization in order to think through a linguistic problem in the second language. The theoretical framework that informed the analysis, and which holds considerable promise for future L2 research, is provided by McNeill's concept of Growth Point. As I mentioned at the outset of the chapter, this framework has already been implemented quite productively by researchers investigating the thinking for speaking process of L2 users; however, to my knowledge it has not been used to investigate how learners themselves can use gesture–speech interface to mediate their own learning.

There are at least two important implications of this research. The first is that acquisition itself is not necessarily an internal process hidden from the observation of researchers. This is because the mind and cognition are not restricted to an inside-the-head domain. Certainly the brain is a necessary component of thinking, but it is not the exclusive site of thought. As others in linguistics and psychology, including Vygotsky nearly a century ago, have argued, and as I have tried to show in the case of L2 learning, cognition incorporates features of the human body (as well as human artifacts). I have argued in a separate study (Lantolf 2007) that it is quite likely that research that takes a narrow view of language as a process that is purely verbal and of cognition as a process that unfolds exclusively inside of the head will miss a great deal of information regarding its object of study.

The second implication relates to the pedagogical significance of gesture. As I discussed earlier, the general education research has already uncovered positive effects for gesture use by instructors in classroom settings and it has shown that gesture-based thinking of students often reveals appropriate solutions to math problems even when speech does not. General education and some L2 research have also pointed to promising outcomes of teachers' use of gesture to impart information to learners about the object of study. However, given the results of the present analysis, a very attractive possibility is to undertake a program whereby students are instructed to use gestures in systematic way in order to mediate their own learning much in the way Donna spontaneously used gestures to work out the aspect problem in her French narrative.

The research of Negueruela (2003) and others (see Lantolf and Poehner 2008) has shown that providing learners with systematically organized information on specific grammatical concepts, including aspect, mood, voice, deontic modality, and genre, in a new language can positively impact learning, if the concepts can be effectively schematized so that learners can rely on verbal as well as imagistic information. The principle, as proposed in the pedagogical theory of Vygotsky's student, Piotr Gal'perin (see Haenen 1996; Talyzina 1981), is that succinct imagistic information, such as that depicted in Figure 8.1, is a crucial component of the learning process whereby learners proceed to internalization of the concept through this type of information more readily than they do through purely verbal explications of a given concept. Donna's gestures which, as I have argued, are an imagistic depiction of the aspect schema provided by her instructor, provide considerable support for Gal'perin's proposal. Given this, it should be possible through instruction to help students develop not only an awareness of gestures for regulating their own learning, but also a way to use gestures to effectively enhance the learning process itself. In light of the research reported by Goldin-Meadow, Wang, and their colleagues, learners might also be taught to use gestures to compensate for problems with their working memory capacity for dealing with verbal input. Only future research can confirm this extremely interesting possibility.

Notes

1. While the present volume addresses 'sociocognitive' processes in L2 learning, it is important to appreciate that Vygotsky's central argument is that human mental functioning is mediated by social activity. From this perspective it is understood that cognitive processes are social in origin and it is therefore redundant to speak of sociocognition. Indeed, Vygotsky frequently refers to psychological development as the cultural, social, or sociocultural development of the person.
2. Although McNeill differentiates between gestures (i.e. those movements that impart meaning independently of speech) and gesticulations (i.e. those movements that co-occur with the co-depend on speech), for present purposes, I will use 'gesture' to refer to the latter type of imagistic signaling as well.
3. In fact, things are a bit more complicated than what is illustrated in the diagram. However, since a full understanding of French aspect is not relevant for the present analysis, I will forego further discussion of this feature of the language.

PART THREE

Sociocognitive perspectives on classroom second language learning

9

Cognitive, social, and psychological dimensions of corrective feedback

ROD ELLIS

Introduction

Corrective feedback takes the form of responses to learner utterances containing an error. The responses are other-initiated repairs[1] and can consist of (1) an indication that an error has been committed, (2) provision of the correct target language form, or (3) metalinguistic information about the nature of the error, or any combination of these (Ellis, Loewen, and Erlam 2006). Corrective feedback (CF) episodes are comprised of a trigger, the feedback move, and (optionally) uptake, as in this example of a simple CF episode from Ellis and Sheen (2006):

(1)   T: When were you in school?
        L: Yes. I <u>stand</u> in the first row? (trigger)
        T: You <u>stood</u> in the first row. (corrective move)
        L: Yes, in the first row, and sit, ah, sat the first row. (uptake)

CF episodes can also be complex involving a number of corrective moves and further triggering moves.

Interest in CF in both language pedagogy and second language acquisition (SLA) has been and still is acute. Language educators are concerned with whether or not to correct learners' errors and, if correction is viewed as desirable, when and how to do it. SLA researchers are concerned with whether corrective feedback has any effect on learners' interlanguage development and, for those who argue it does, what type of CF is most effective. There is ongoing controversy among teacher educators about whether CF is desirable and even less agreement about how it should be undertaken. Similarly, SLA theorists cannot agree about the role that CF plays in L2 acquisition, and, if they do agree it is beneficial, disagree about what type works best.

In this chapter, I will examine dimensions of corrective feedback: the cognitive dimension, the social dimension, and the psychological dimension. Research on corrective feedback (CF) and its effects on second language (L2) acquisition has been conducted largely within a cognitive framework based on a computational model of learning. That is, it seeks to account for how learners process the information provided by CF for acquisition by examining the interactions between input, output, and the learner's internal mechanisms. The theories that have been developed to account for these interactions are universalistic—they assume a set of processes common to all learners irrespective of the context in which CF takes place or individual differences among the participants (the learners and the teacher). The social dimension acknowledges that both the practice of CF and learners' capacity to benefit from it will be influenced by the social context in which it is enacted and by the social background of the participants. The psychological dimension concerns how individual difference factors such as beliefs about learning and personality impact on both the teacher's choice of CF strategies and learners' responses to them. Both the social and the psychological dimensions view CF and language learning as variable phenomena. My basic claim is that a full account of corrective feedback requires a sociocognitive orientation that combines the cognitive, social, and psychological dimensions. I will first discuss these three dimensions in some detail.

The cognitive dimension

Whereas nativist theories of acquisition reject any role for CF on the grounds that Universal Grammar operates only with positive evidence and thus cannot adapt to the negative evidence provided through CF,[2] a cognitive account of CF incorporates a number of interrelated theoretical perspectives to explain how CF is used by learners to restructure their interlanguages. It is directed at identifying the general conditions under which CF will be effective in promoting acquisition. The main theoretical perspectives are the Interaction Hypothesis, the Output Hypothesis, and the Noticing Hypothesis. These come together in what Long (1991) has termed 'focus on form', in which CF has a central place. These Hypotheses are well known and have been the subject of extensive discussion in the SLA literature. Thus rather than revisit them here, I will instead present a general cognitive model of how CF fosters acquisition.

CF works for acquisition when:

- participants are focused primarily on meaning in the context of producing and understanding messages in communication;
- they produce errors;
- the receive feedback that they recognize as corrective;
- the feedback causes them to notice the errors they have committed;
- they compare their own production and the feedback (i.e. the CF affords them an opportunity for 'noticing the gap');
- as a result they construct a form-function mapping for the problematic form;
- they modify their original utterance by correcting the error (a discourse process known as 'uptake') and thereby rehearse and consolidate the form-function mapping;
- they subsequently incorporate the corrected form into their interlanguages.

I will now illustrate this model with a number of examples of CF episodes taken from classroom data.[3] The first example comes from a communicative classroom where the teacher had asked the students to construct imaginary alibis for a crime.

(1) s: I have an ali[bi]
     T: you have what?
     s: an ali[bi]
     T: an alib-? (.2.) An alib[ay]
     s: ali [bay]
     T: okay, listen, listen, alibi
     s: alibi

The student begins by volunteering an alibi but mispronounces the word (i.e. ali[bi]). The teacher responds with a clarification request (i.e. an output-prompting CF move), either because she did not understand the student or simply because she wanted to encourage the student to self-correct. The student responds by repeating the same pronunciation error. The teacher then attempts to elicit the correct pronunciation ('an alib-?') but after a pause supplies the correct form ('an alib[ay]'). However, the student still fails to pronounce the word correctly (i.e. 'ali [bay]'). At this point the teacher breaks out of the communicative activity to model the correct pronunciation for all the students who then repeat the model chorally. In this episode, then, the participants are focused entirely on meaning (at least initially), an error is committed, the teacher responds with a CF move which causes the student to notice his error. However, the learner experiences difficulty in noticing the gap between his own production and the teacher's feedback and thus is unsuccessful in repairing it. It is of course possible that he did acquire it as a result of the choral practice but there is no evidence to show this.

In the second example, a student is talking about a fishing expedition:

(2) s: We <don't> catch, we can't
     T: we didn't
     s: didn't
     T: we didn't catch it, we didn't keep it, we threw it back, Ah very good, so you didn't eat it?

The student tries to explain that they threw the fish they caught back into the water. In his initial utterance he produced two errors—a past tense error ('don't') and a lexical error ('catch'). The teacher's partial recast focuses on the past tense error. The student corrects this error. The teacher then models the whole sentence ('We didn't catch it') before moving on to address the lexical error ('we didn't keep it, we threw it back'). The learner has no opportunity to uptake this, however, as the teacher proceeds immediately with a discourse continuing move ('... so you didn't eat it?'). In this episode then we see evidence of a focus on meaning, the learner perceiving the feedback as corrective and the learner noticing the error. The learner is successful in noticing the gap between his own and the teacher's production as shown by his uptake of the correction ('didn't'). But we cannot be certain that the learner has constructed a form-function mapping for the problematic form (i.e. he might be simply echoing the teacher's correction). Also, we have no evidence that the learner has noticed his lexical error.

The cognitive model outlined above provides a means of interpreting how CF episodes such as (1) and (2) above provide opportunities for acquisition to take place. The model itself, however, is not without controversy and masks a number of issues that are the subject of ongoing debate:

- How essential is it that CF occurs as a response to communicative problems? Long (2007a) argues that a meaning-focused context is essential to ensure that learners link form to meaning. However, Lyster (2002) has argued that CF involving the negotiation of form (i.e. when there is no communicative problem) can be just as effective as CF involving the negotiation of meaning. R. Ellis, Basturkmen, and Lowen (2001) found that what they termed code-oriented feedback occurred twice as frequently during fluency work as meaning-oriented feedback, although uptake was more likely to occur in the latter. In fact, it is not always clear whether the CF episode entails the negotiation of meaning or form (as example (1) above illustrates).
- To what extent is it essential that learners recognize the corrective force of the feedback they receive? Carroll (2001) argued that in order for the learner's attention to switch from meaning to form, it is essential that the corrective intention is recognized and that this can only take place if the feedback is perceived as irrelevant to the ongoing discourse. However, other researchers are less adamant. In the case of recasts, for example, learners receive both positive and negative evidence. Leeman's (2003) study suggests that recasts work for acquisition because they supply the learner with positive evidence, not because they are corrective. In fact, learners may fail to recognize that recasts of the more implicit kind are corrective (Sheen 2006a). The growing evidence that CF of the more explicit kind is more effective than CF of the more implicit kind (Loewen and Philp 2006; R. Ellis, Loewen, and Erlam 2006) suggests that it is important that learners are able to identify the corrective force of the CF. Examples (1) and (2) both involve explicit CF. In (1) the teacher responds first with implicit CF but when that does not work resorts to explicit CF. In (2) the teacher opts for a relatively explicit partial recast. However, in neither case is the CF entirely effective, as shown by the learners' uptake moves.
- Do learners have to notice their errors and notice the gap between their own production and the feedback? In example (1) above, the learner clearly identifies the error he has made but is unable to carry out the cognitive comparison required for noticing the gap. In example (2), however, both noticing and noticing the gap are evident. Carroll (2001) argued that learners must not only notice the error but also must be able to decide whether

pronunciation, morphology, syntax, or semantics is causing the problem. Mackey, Gass, and McDonough (2000) reported that the learners they investigated noticed phonological and lexical corrections but generally failed to notice morphological corrections. To date, there is not much evidence to link noticing with acquisition. Reinders and Ellis (2009) found no relationship between intake (an indication of noticing) measured by performance on the instructional task and acquisition of the target structure (subject–verb inversion following negative adverbs like 'rarely') measured by means of grammaticality judgement tests. Mackey (2006a) found a relationship between high levels of noticing of corrections for one grammatical structure (question forms) but no relationship for two others (plurals and past tense), reflecting the fact that the salience of the corrected forms varies, possibly as a product of their linguistic form (i.e. word order features are inherently more salient than morphological features).

- How important is uptake? Long (2007a) argues that it plays no significant role in acquisition and emphasizes the importance of input-providing CF (e.g. recasts). Lyster (2004), however, draws on skill-building theory (another cognitive model that has informed thinking about CF) to claim that output-prompting CF is more effective and provided evidence to suggest that it is. Loewen's (2005) study suggests that uptake is related to acquisition. Episodes (1) and (2) show that uptake often occurs following CF but do not constitute evidence that acquisition has taken place. To show this it would be necessary to establish that these learners were subsequently able to avoid the errors that were corrected. Loewen administered tailor-made tests to his learners to investigate this.

These issues are unlikely to be resolved in the short term and some possibly not in the long term either, given the difficulty of investigating such phenomena as noticing and noticing the gap.

Given the uncertainty that surrounds these issues it is perhaps surprising that some cognitively oriented researchers have felt able to specify the conditions that make CF effective. Based on her longitudinal study of a small number of learners, Han (2002) proposed four conditions to account for the effectiveness of CF (in this case intensive recasts): (1) individualized attention, (2) a consistent focus on a single grammatical feature, (3) the developmental readiness of the learners, and (4) the intensity (CF was provided over a period of 8 weeks). However, the feasibility of teachers achieving all four conditions in the context of real classrooms with large numbers of students must remain in doubt. Kim (2004) argued that the key is ensuring that the feedback can be recognized without ambiguity and suggested that this can be achieved in three ways: (1) by making the corrective force of the feedback clear to the learner, (2) by focusing on a specific feature, and (3) by allowing learners time to detect input–output mismatches. These conditions are perhaps more achievable but there remains the problem of ensuring that the CF is matched to the learners' stage of development and this is just as problematic for CF as it is for form-focused instruction in general (Lightbown 1985).

The idea that it is possible to identify an approach to CF that will be effective for all learners—the aim of a cognitive theory of CF—is an attractive one. We all want to know what 'method' works best. But researchers are a long way from agreeing what that approach should be. Furthermore it may be fundamentally mistaken to look for one single approach given the social and individual learner factors that must be taken into account if CF is to be made to work for all learners.

The social dimension

Commenting on research into written CF, Goldstein (2001: 77) noted that it 'has largely been non-contextual and non-social, focused largely on texts and conducted within a linear model of teacher respond and student revise'. Goldstein (2004) identified a number of contextual factors that can impact on writing, which included programme philosophies about feedback.

A similar comment could be made about research on oral CF in SLA— namely, that it has focused on the generic feedback strategies used by teachers with little or no account taken of the social background of the learners or the teacher, or the classroom context in which the feedback takes place, or the specific activity in which learners are engaged. Both written and oral CF research have been driven by what Block (2003) called the 'Input-Interaction-Output Model' and reflect Tarone's (2000a: 182) stricture of SLA in general—'too much SLA research focuses on psycholinguistic processes in the abstract and does not consider the social context of L2 learning'. But what evidence is there that social factors impinge on how CF is conducted and the effect it has on learning?

There is, in fact, clear evidence that CF varies from one context to another, whether context is defined narrowly or more broadly. Chaudron (1988) reviewed studies that showed that the extent to which errors are corrected is dependent on whether the setting is a second or a foreign language one and on the pedagogical focus (i.e. correction is more intensive in grammar-based than in communication-based instruction). Seedhouse (2004) also noted differences in the way CF was conducted in form and accuracy contexts. He found that teachers viewed trouble with linguistic form as problematic and face-threatening but procedural problems as non-problematic and non-face-threatening, preferring indirect correction strategies in the former but direct in the latter.

Differences in the participatory structure of the classroom can also affect CF. Ohta (2001) carried out a longitudinal study of seven learners of L2 Japanese as a foreign language in a university in the USA. She compared the CF that took place in teacher-fronted and peer-learning settings, finding that although the former dominated, there were almost as many CF episodes in the latter (i.e. 69 and 63 respectively)—but see note 1. She also observed considerable diversity in how the learners responded to CF in the two settings; the rate of uptake was much higher in the peer-learning setting than the teacher-fronted setting. Overall, Ohta found that 'corrective feedback was most strongly characterized by its flexibility and situational adaptability' (ibid. 141).

There is also evidence of clear differences in CF practices according to the macro-setting. Sheen (2004) reported no difference in the overall types of CF found in in four teaching contexts (Canada immersion, Canada ESL, New Zealand ESL, and Korea EFL) but she noted quite marked differences in the frequency with which the different types occurred. The frequency of recasts, for example, varied significantly from one context to the next while explicit correction was rare in Canada ESL but quite common in the New Zealand ESL classes.

The social context also influences the extent to which learners respond to CF with uptake, both successful and unsuccessful. Oliver and Mackey (2003) found differences in the frequency of uptake and modified output in the specific contexts found within child ESL classrooms. Uptake and modified output were more likely to occur in explicit language contexts while feedback, uptake, and modified output were least frequent in management-related exchanges. Lyster and Mori (2006) also reported differences in uptake and repair according to instructional context, in this case two different immersion contexts—French immersion in Canada and Japanese immersion in Japan. Output-prompting CF (called 'prompts') induced higher levels of uptake and repair in Canada but recasts did so in Japan. On the basis of these findings they advanced the 'counterbalance hypothesis', which predicts that the extent to which different CF strategies lead to uptake/repair is influenced by whether the overall instruction orients learners to attend to form, as it did in Japan, or to meaning, as in immersion classes in Canada. Sheen (2004) found marked differences in both the level of uptake and repair in the four contexts she investigated. In particular, there was variation in the effectiveness of recasts in eliciting uptake and repair, which she suggested reflected differences in the pedagogical focus of these contexts, the age of the students, their L2 proficiency, and educational background. The social and educational background of learners can also influence how they respond to CF. Bigelow et al. (2005) found that the more educated and literate learners in a group of Somali learners of English were better at recalling recasts of their erroneous utterances than the less educated and literate learners.

What these studies suggest is that teachers and learners vary in how they orientate to CF depending on the institutional context in which they work, the specific pedagogic activity they are engaged in, and their social background. These factors influence both the choice of CF strategies and learner uptake. They demonstrate that CF is not a monolithic phenomenon but is as highly variable as any other type of language use. The question arises, however, as to whether these socially driven differences affect the internal processes responsible for converting input and output into acquisition. Here there is no evidence to date. Long (1998) noted that changes in the social setting have not been shown to have any effect on the way in which learners acquire an L2. Thus, while social factors may influence the extent to which the cognitive mechanisms are engaged, it can be argued that they do not alter the nature of the processes themselves. However, this should not be used as an excuse to ignore the social context in which CF takes place. At the very least, the study of CF within and across various contexts of learning will help to identify the variables that affect and impede acquisition in general while, from a pedagogic point of view, it will reinforce the need to adopt CF practices that are differentiated and sensitive to context.

The psychological dimension

Dörnyei (2005) characterizes the field of psychology as having two relatively distinct strands: the study of the general principles of the human mind and the investigation of the uniqueness of the individual mind. The former corresponds to the cognitive dimension of CF that I have already examined while the latter concerns the characteristics or traits that account for differences in individuals. In the case of CF, this involves examining how differences in such factors as attitudes, language aptitude, learning style, personality, motivation, and anxiety influence the practice and outcomes of CF. This is my focus in this section although, unfortunately, there has been little research directed at the psychological dimension of CF.

Learners certainly vary in how they respond to CF. For example, Ohta (2001) reported marked differences in the levels of uptake in the seven learners of L2 Japanese she investigated. Two learners produced no uptake at all while another demonstrated uptake at every opportunity. There was also marked variance in the number of corrective episodes that each learner participated in. One possibility is that these differences reflect differences in learners' (and teachers') attitudes towards the importance of correctness in general and to CF in particular.

However, L2 learners manifest surprising unanimity in their attitudes towards CF. Surveys of learners' attitudes to written CF (e.g. Leki 1991) show that they rate it as very important, prefer to be corrected by the teacher than a peer, and are accepting of the value of indirect feedback (Hyland and Hyland 2006) although they generally prefer more direct, explicit feedback. Cathcart and Olsen (1976) found that ESL learners like to be corrected by their teachers and want more correction than is usually available. Chun et al. (1982) reported that learners liked to be corrected not only during form-focused activities, but also when they were conversing with native speakers. However, differences do arise between learners and teachers. Thus, while Schulz (2001) found that both Colombian learners of English in Colombia and American learners of foreign languages in the USA placed great store on explicit grammar study and error correction, she also found a difference between the learners' and teachers' beliefs, the teachers in both contexts demonstrating much less confidence in the efficacy of error correction than their students.

Of course, the fact that learners want to be corrected does not mean that they will benefit from correction, as Truscott (1996) has pointed out. Truscott (1999) argued that learners are only convinced that written CF is helpful because they have been conditioned to expect CF by teachers who have corrected them and that his own correction-free approach soon changed their attitude. However, the results of a study by Sheen (2006*b*) suggest that Truscott may be wrong and that positive attitudes towards correction may be a factor in determining how effective it is. Sheen examined the relationship between learners' attitudes to grammatical correctness and error correction and the learning gains that resulted from four types of CF. She reported sizeable and statistically significant correlations between three of the CF types (oral metalinguistic, written direct correction, and written metalinguistic) and learning gains in English articles. However, there was no relationship between oral recasts and learning gains for the learners as a whole although, as discussed below, this may simply reflect individual differences in the ability to process the recasts. Sheen's study indicates that in a CF context where learners are aware they are being corrected those with more positive attitudes to CF benefit from it to a greater extent than those with less positive attitudes.

Sheen considered two other individual difference factors, with interesting results. She found that learners' language analytical abilities interacted with the four types of CF in much the same way as their attitudes towards error correction did. That is, she found strong and significant correlations between the language analysis scores and both short- and long-term learning gains for oral metalinguistic, written direct, and written metalinguistic feedback but none for oral recasts. Language anxiety worked in a very different way, however. The correlations between language anxiety and short- and long-term gain scores were much stronger for the learners who received oral CF. In other words, language anxiety had a negative effect on learners' ability to process oral CF but not written CF. In the case of the oral metalinguistic feedback group, the correlation reached statistical significance but not for the oral recasts group. However, when Sheen divided the oral recast group into low- and high-anxiety subgroups she found that the low-anxiety learners performed significantly better than the control group (which did not receive any feedback) whereas the high-anxiety group did not. Sheen's study raises the fascinating possibility that individual difference factors not only influence learners' ability to benefit from CF but that different factors (i.e. cognitive vs. affective) mediate different kinds of CF in different ways. The resulting picture is of a highly complex interaction between learner characteristics, CF types, and learning outcomes.

This raises two key questions. The first is a question for L2 writing and SLA researchers: What kind of theory is needed to explain how and for whom CF works and does not work? The second question is for teachers: How can teachers most effectively take account of individual differences in learners when providing CF? The final sections of this article will seek to address these questions.

A sociocognitive theory of CF

Any theory of CF needs to take account of all three dimensions—the cognitive, the social, and the psychological. The approach that seems best equipped at integrating these three dimensions is a sociocognitive one. The essence of such an approach is that 'linguistic phenomena can only be accounted for if the cognizing individuals' linguistic knowledge is seen as abetted by, actuated within, and broadly continuous with a rich social context' (Atkinson 2002: 530). This emphasizes the importance of 'joint cognition', which can only be achieved if there is not only a shared sense of the purpose of a social activity (i.e. social convergence), which Atkinson emphasizes, but also compatibility among the participants in terms of their individual beliefs and predispositions (i.e. psychological convergence).

What this requires—and what is central to a sociocognitive view of CF—is what Atkinson et al. (2007: 170) refer to as 'alignment'. They define this construct thus: 'Alignment is the complex means by which human beings effect coordinated interaction, and maintain that interaction in dynamically adaptive ways.' They then go on to provide a concrete example of how alignment can foster L2 acquisition in a detailed study of the interactions between Ako (a Japanese high-school student) and Tomo (her aunt) as they worked together on a grammar exercise involving the use of the present perfect tense. These interactions include what I have defined as corrective feedback. For example, when Ako establishes the adverbial 'ever' but fails to find the verb form she is searching for, Tomo provides feedback in the form of an elicitation—'Have you ever toka nantoka' ('Have you ever blank blank'). In another example, Ako attempts to produce the past participle verb form herself when she realizes that if she doesn't do so Tomo will prompt her or produce it for her. Here, then, it is the learner's awareness that she will be corrected that motivates her behaviour. Corrective feedback, then, is not just what the expert (Tomo in this case) does to assist the novice but a process of 'co-cognizing'. This co-cognizing is evident in the participants' verbal behaviour, their posture, and their response to the artefacts of the learning situation. It is reflected in a blurring of the boundaries between learner (Ako) and corrector (Tomo), between person and object (the language exercise), between social action and cognition, and between learning and use. In short, corrective feedback needs to be understood in terms of what goes on between participants in their sociocognitive worlds rather than in terms of what happens inside their heads.

Arguably, the theory best equipped to explain CF as a sociocognitive phenomenon is a sociocultural theory (SCT). SCT sees learning, including language learning, as dialogically based; that is, acquisition occurs *in* rather than *as a result of* interaction. From this perspective, then, L2 acquisition cannot be treated as a purely individual-based process but as one shared between the individual and other persons. Dialogic interaction enables an expert (such as a teacher) to create a context in which novices can participate actively in their own learning and in which the expert can fine-tune the support that the novices are given (Antón 1999). In particular, dialogic discourse demonstrates what a learner can and cannot do without assistance.

SCT sees learning arising out of affordances constructed in a particular context through the successful tailoring of interaction to the developmental level of individual learners. It acknowledges that what constitutes a facilitative interaction for one learner might not be for another, either because it is pitched at a level too far in advance of the learner or because it fails to 'stretch' the learner by posing a sufficient challenge. It also acknowledges that affordances are socially constructed in that interpersonal behaviour is ultimately internalized as self-regulated cognition. Thus SCT can be viewed as a sociocognitive theory that also recognizes the autonomy of the individual.

SCT has typically made use of the microgenetic method. According to Lavelli et al. (2004), this has four key characteristics; (1) individuals are observed through a period of change, (2) observations are conducted before, during, and after the period of change, (3) observations during the period of transition are conducted regularly during the period of change, and (4) observed behaviours are analysed intensively, using both qualitative and quantitative methods, in order to identify the processes that arise in the developmental change. A good example of how this method can be applied to the study of CF can be found in Ohta's (2001) study, referred to above. Ohta made use of the microgenetic method to examine the interplay between the cognitive, social, and individual aspects of CF in a way that would be difficult if not impossible in the experimental studies that characterize the dominant cognitive paradigm.

A key SCT construct for explaining corrective feedback is the zone of proximal development (ZPD). To understand the ZPD three levels of development need to be distinguished. Vygotsky (1978: 85) distinguished 'the actual developmental level, that is the level of development of the child's mental functions that has been established as a result of certain already completed developmental cycles' and a level of potential development as evidenced in problem-solving undertaken with the assistance of an adult (an expert) or through collaboration with peers (novices). The third level, not commonly mentioned by sociocultural theorists, is the level that lies beyond the learner, that is, the learner is unable to perform the task even if assistance is provided. The ZPD lies at the second of these levels; the level of potential development. To borrow Vygotsky's own metaphor, it is the 'bud' rather than the 'fruit' of development. CF episodes can be viewed as an arena for studying how interaction mediates learning through the construction of ZPDs.

What then are the implications of dialogic learning and the ZPD for a theory of CF? I would like to suggest the following general principles:

1 First and foremost, CF must constitute 'a collaborative endeavour' (Aljaafreh and Lantolf (1994); that is, the participants must agree on the goals of the CF.
2 CF must be contingent in the sense that it must reflect an actual need on the part of the learner (i.e. if the learner can self-correct without any feedback then the CF serves no purpose).

3 CF must be highly flexible, adapted to the individual learner and to the social/ situational context in which it occurs.

4 CF will be effective if it succeeds in enabling the participants interactively to construct a ZPD for the learner.

5 Thus, CF facilitates when the assistance is fine-tuned to the developmental level of the learner; this means it must be graduated, providing no more help than is needed to enable the learner to correct the error.

6 CF must also be performed in a way that takes account of the affective needs of the learner.

7 To this end, it is not possible to claim that one type of CF (e.g. explicit or output-prompting CF) is inherently more effective than another type (e.g. implicit or input-providing), as what is best for one learner in one context will not be best for the same learner (or another learner) in a different context. CF needs to be dynamic and situated.

8 Learner uptake involving repair of the original error is beneficial because it constitutes the first step in the learner's path toward self-regulation.

9 Ultimately, however, the decision about whether to appropriate the corrective feedback provided by an expert must be taken by the learner him/ herself.

These principles can be applied equally to oral and written CF. One key difference, however, is that oral CF allows for a more dynamic response to learners' errors, and in this respect can be hypothesized to be more effective in constructing affordances and pushing learners to self-regulate than written CF.[4]

An often-cited example of how SCT can be applied to CF can be found in Aljaafreh and Lantolf (1994). They examined the one-on-one interactions arising between three L2 learners and a tutor who provided corrective feedback on essays they had written. Aljaafreh and Lantolf developed a 'regulatory scale' to reflect the extent to which the help provided by the tutor was implicit or explicit. For example, asking learners to find and correct their own errors is considered an implicit strategy while providing examples of the correct pattern is highly explicit. An intermediate level occurs when the tutor indicates the nature of an error without identifying it for the learner. In detailed analyses of selected protocols, Aljaafreh and Lantolf show how the degree of scaffolding provided by the tutor for a particular learner diminished (i.e. the help provided became more implicit over time). This was possible because the learners assumed increased control over the L2 and, therefore, needed less assistance. Clearly, however, a teacher needs considerable skill to determine the appropriate feedback needed. In a subsequent paper, Lantolf and Aljaafreh (1995) noted that the tutor was not always successful in tuning his assistance to the learner's level of development. Sometimes he provided more assistance than was required, thereby failing to push the learner towards greater autonomy.

In a follow-up study, using the same regulatory scale as in Aljaafreh and Lantolf (1994), Nassaji and Swain (2000) examined a tutor's oral feedback on the written compositions of two Korean learners of English. This study sought to compare the effectiveness of feedback on the two learners' acquisition of articles. The assistance to one learner was provided within her ZPD (i.e. the tutor systematically worked through Aljaafreh and Lantolf's scale to negotiate the feedback she supplied) while the assistance to the other learner was random (i.e. the tutor was supplied with a random list of correcting strategies drawn from the scale). The results showed that providing feedback within the learner's ZPD was effective in (1) helping the learner to arrive at the correct form during the feedback session, (2) enabling the learner to arrive at the correct form with much less explicit assistance in subsequent sessions, and (3) enabling the learner to use the correct form unassisted in a post-test consisting of a cloze version of the compositions she had written previously. In contrast, random feedback did not always succeed in enabling the learner to identify the correct article form in the feedback sessions and was much less effective in promoting unassisted use of the correct forms in the post-test.[5]

Episode (3) illustrates the graduated approach to CF that these two studies found so effective:

(3) s: oh my God, it is too expensive, I pay only 10 dollars
     T: I pay? //
     s2: okay let's go
     T: I pay or I'LL pay? (.1.) // I will pay // I'll
     s: I'll // I'll pay only 10 dollars.

Here the learner fails to use the contracted future form 'll'. The teacher responds first by attempting to draw the learner's attention to the error by means of a repetition but another student interrupts by responding meaningfully to the first student's message. The teacher, however, continues to focus on form, using a more explicit CF strategy—an elicitation consisting of an either/or question. When this does not work she corrects directly ('I will pay') first using the full form of the modal verb and then the contracted form ('I'll'). The learner responds with uptake, first by echoing the teacher's 'I'll' and then by incorporating it into a correct version of his original sentence. This episode lasted only a few seconds but within this brief period the teacher was able to fine-tune her feedback to the learners' ZPD. In terms of SCT, it illustrates learning in interaction.

Another study, however, illustrates how CF can sometimes go wrong because teacher and learner fail to establish the intersubjectivity needed to build a ZPD. Hyland (2000) reported a study of CF in an academic writing programme by analysing the CF practices and learner responses of two teacher–student pairs. In one pair, the teacher rejected the student's use of her husband as a peer corrector, insisting that she attempt to self-correct. In the other, the teacher focused his correction on the student's vocabulary errors, advising him to use simpler vocabulary to avoid making numerous errors, while the students wished to continue to experiment with high-risk vocabulary as a learning strategy. Hyland highlights the mismatch between the teachers' and the students' goals. Whereas the teachers tended to treat the drafts as finished pieces that needed 'fixing up', the students saw feedback as a means of enhancing their learning of English. Hyland felt that the teachers tried to control the feedback process too rigidly and failed to take account of the students' own goals.

From theory to practice

All teachers base their teaching on theory but very often the theory is not an explicit, research-based theory but rather a more implicit theory derived from teachers' experience of what works and does not work in particular contexts. This is as it should be. I have argued elsewhere that the function of an explicit, research-based theory is not to supplant the teacher's own personal theory but rather to provide a basis for evaluating it, and, perhaps, amending it.

My own CF policy is:

1 Teachers should ascertain their students' attitudes towards CF, appraise them of the value of CF, and negotiate agreed goals for CF with them. The goals are likely to vary according to the social and situational context.
2 CF (both oral and written) works and so teachers should not be afraid to correct students' errors. This is true for both accuracy and fluency work so CF has a place in both.
3 Focused CF is likely to be more effective than unfocused CF so teachers should identify specific linguistic targets for correction in different lessons. This will occur naturally in accuracy-based work with a structure-of-the-day approach but can also be usefully applied in fluency work.
4 Teachers should ensure that learners know they are being corrected (i.e. they should not attempt to hide the corrective force of their CF moves from the learners).
5 Teachers need to be able to implement a variety of CF strategies and to adapt the specific strategies they use to the particular learner they are correcting. One way of doing this is to start with a relatively implicit form of correction (e.g. simply indicating that there is an error) and, if the learner is unable to self-correct moving to a more explicit form (e.g. a direct correction). This will necessitate teachers being responsive to the 'feedback' they get from learners on their own corrective feedback.
6 CF can be both immediate and delayed. Teachers need to experiment with the timing of the CF.
7 Teachers need to create space following the corrective move for learners to uptake the correction. However, whether the correction is or is not appropriated should be left to the learner (i.e. the teacher should not require the learner to produce the correct form).
8 Teachers should be prepared to vary who, when, and how they correct in accordance with the cognitive and affective needs of the individual learner. In effect this means they should be prepared to be inconsistent.

9 Teachers should be prepared to correct a specific error on several occasions to enable the learner to achieve full self-regulation.
10 Teachers should be adaptive when they see that an initial CF strategy is not working or is causing anxiety in the learner. In order to achieve 'co-cognizing' teachers need to respond to students' affective as well as cognitive needs.

This policy reflects the cognitive, social, and psychological aspects of CF discussed above; it represents a sociocognitive approach to CF.

It will be easier to implement this policy in one-on-one interactions. The practicality of such an approach to CF in interactive contexts involving large classes is questionable. However, Ohta's (2001) study suggests that it is possible. Indeed, there is plenty of evidence to show that teachers do vary the way they conduct CF with individual learners in whole-class contexts—as shown in examples (1), (2), and (3), all of which came from lessons where the participatory structure was teacher–class. Also, if, as Ohta has shown, CF is not just of value to the addressee but to auditors as well, these examples testify to the rich affordances that can be derived from skilfully managed CF for not just the learner participating in the exchange but for other learners as well.

Notes

1. Ohta (2001: 135) offers a much wider definition of corrective feedback: 'An utterance was considered to have a corrective function if it had the potential of drawing a learner's attention to his or her erroneous utterance.'
2. A strict UG-based account of L2 acquisition dismisses CF as irrelevant for acquiring grammatical competence although it acknowledges that it can contribute to the deductive learning processes involved in building 'another type of knowledge' that is distinct from competence (Schwartz 1993: 160). Also, not all nativists dismiss CF so completely. L. White (1989) acknowledges that negative evidence may be necessary to enable learners to eradicate certain types of error from their interlanguage.
3. These examples come from the data collected for the study of learner uptake reported in Ellis, Basturkmen, and Loewen (2001).
4. It is possible of course that a combination of oral and written CF will be especially effective. Bitchener, Young, and Cameron (2005) found that such a combination resulted in significant gains in accuracy in the use of past tense and the definite article.
5. It is, of course, not so surprising that random feedback did not promote learning in Nassaji and Swain's study. A more interesting comparison—one that would juxtapose cognitive and sociocultural theory—is a study that compared the effects of explicit CF (shown in a number of studies to be the most effective CF strategy) and tailored feedback on acquisition (as in Aljaafreh and Lantolf 1994).

10

Students' engagement with feedback on writing: the role of learner agency/beliefs

NEOMY STORCH AND
GILLIAN WIGGLESWORTH

Introduction

There is currently a large and growing body of research on feedback provided to second language (L2) learners on their writing. This interest in feedback is understandable given the inordinate amount of time teachers spend on providing feedback comments and the centrality of feedback in dominant theories of second language acquisition. For example, in psycholinguistic theories, feedback is seen as a means of focusing learners' attention to gaps in their knowledge (Long 1996). In sociocultural theories (Vygotsky 1986), finely tuned and graduated feedback provided by an expert interacting with a novice is perceived as the means of facilitating the novice's cognitive development. This chapter adopts a hybrid sociocognitive approach drawing on both cognitive analyses of writing through examining accuracy, complexity, and fluency in relation to uptake, or the process of incorporating the feedback provided into their linguistic knowledge, as well as through social analyses which attempt to explore the learners' thought processes as they work their way through the feedback with which they are provided. In this sense there is an interdependence between the social and cognitive in so far as uptake, which is primarily a cognitive notion, is socially and discursively co-constructed through the discussion that takes place in the dyads. In doing this we focus on learner agency—in other words the active role the learner takes through which they achieve control over their own writing, and acceptance, or not, of the feedback with which they are provided.

We focus on the corrective feedback provided on language errors that L2 learners make in their writing. This feedback can take a number of different forms, and can be distinguished in terms of directness (Ferris 2002, 2006). Direct feedback means provision of the correct language form and can be given by way of reformulating the learner's text (Thornbury 1997), where the teacher rewrites the learner's text, attending to language forms and style but preserving the original meaning as much as possible, or by writing the correct forms directly above the incorrect forms. Indirect feedback means an error is identified but not corrected. Indirect feedback can also be provided in different ways (see Guénette 2007), including signalling to the learner the location of the error with or without a code providing a cue as to the type of error committed. A crucial question which has generated much research interest is whether some forms of feedback are more effective than others in developing learners' ability to write more accurately.

Ferris (2002, 2006) suggests that students are likely to learn more if they are given indirect feedback which requires them to work out the cause of their errors, rather than being given direct feedback. Intuitively, Ferris's claim sounds convincing. Working out the cause of an error and how to amend it would presumably engage learners in deeper processing of language. Yet studies which have attempted to investigate the efficacy of different types of feedback (e.g. Lalande 1982; Robb, Ross, and Shortreed 1986; Chandler 2003; Sachs and Polio 2007) do not necessarily support this stance, and the results have been quite mixed. Thus, for example, whereas a study by Lalande (1982) found a significant effect for indirect corrections over direct corrections, Robb, Ross, and Shortreed (1986), who compared direct feedback and three types of indirect feedback, found no significant differences between the direct and indirect feedback. Chandler (2003) also compared the efficacy of direct and three types of indirect feedback: coded correction (underlining the incorrect form and using a code in the margin to identify the error type), a code in the margins but no underlining, and underlining the error only. Chandler found that direct corrective feedback was the most effective. Interestingly, the next most effective feedback was simply underlining the incorrect form. The other two indirect types of feedback, which involved using codes to describe the learners' errors, did not lead to improved accuracy. Our own research (Wigglesworth and Storch 2007) which compared the efficacy of direct (reformulations) and indirect (editing symbols and codes) feedback provided to learners working in pairs has shown that although both forms of feedback lead to improved accuracy in the short term (after 5 days), the effects of reformulations are more enduring (after 28 days). Sachs and Polio (2007), who compared the effects of two forms of direct feedback, reformulation and corrective feedback, found that learners who received corrective feedback outperformed those who received reformulations. The researchers attribute their results to the learners' familiarity with corrective feedback and its perceptual saliency (correct forms were written in purple ink directly above the incorrect forms). Thus, based on available research, it is not clear whether it is best to provide learners with direct feedback which gives learners the correct models of the target language forms or indirect feedback which requires learners to work out the correct form.

One explanation for these mixed findings is that they could be attributable to the different research designs employed by the researchers and the learners' L2 proficiency (Guénette 2007). However, another reason is that in order to determine which form of feedback is more conducive to the development of learners' writing, we need to investigate the nature of learners' engagement with the feedback provided. The nature of engagement with feedback is important in psycholinguistic and sociocultural theories of learning. From a psycholinguistic perspective, the work by Schmidt (2001) has highlighted the importance of noticing specific linguistic features for language learning. As a number of studies (e.g. Sanaoui 1984; Qi and Lapkin 2001) have shown, it is not just the noticing per se which is important for second language learning, but the quality, or depth, of that noticing. Deeper noticing of linguistic information (i.e. not only noticing but actively engaging with the feedback information) is more likely to lead to language learning.

The generally accepted claim is that input (positive as in target language forms or negative as in corrective feedback) needs to be noticed so that it can become intake for further processing and uptake. From a sociocultural theoretical perspective, Lantolf and Thorne (2006) argue that learners are intentional agents in their language learning activity who assign relevance and significance to certain events. Their claims highlight the importance of learners' goals and beliefs which may affect what they notice and, more importantly, whether they accept or reject the feedback provided.

Feedback in writing

Few studies have thus far investigated the nature of learners' engagement with the feedback provided on their writing. Those that have examined learners' processing of feedback have considered only direct forms of feedback. For example, a small-scale study by Qi and Lapkin (2001) involved two learners thinking aloud as they processed the reformulations they received on their writing. Using the learners' verbalizations, Qi and Lapkin distinguished between perfunctory noticing and substantive noticing. Perfunctory noticing was defined as noticing only, without articulating reasons for the observed reformulation; substantive noticing included articulating a reason for the reformulation and thus suggesting that the learners gained an understanding of the feedback provided. Qi and Lapkin found that the nature of the noticing was related to improvements made, with substantive noticing leading to greater improvements in writing than perfunctory noticing. The study by Sachs and Polio (2007), mentioned above, also used think-aloud protocols but with a larger cohort of students (n = 54). The study found that in their revised draft, learners were most likely to make changes to items where the feedback was noticed (i.e. verbalized) and understood (i.e. a reason was articulated) than to items where the feedback received was not noticed. However, the researchers point out that their results suggest an association rather than a cause–effect relationship between noticing and subsequent changes, admitting that 'it does not appear possible to tell definitely how deeply a correction has been processed and why it later appears in a revision' (ibid. 89). Furthermore, think aloud as a data collection tool is problematic, particularly with second language learners, because it imposes an additional cognitive load on the learners which may distort the processes investigated (Wigglesworth 2005). Indeed, Sachs and Polio report that learners who did not have to provide think alouds produced significantly more accurate revisions than those who were asked to verbalize their thoughts while processing the feedback.

Another way to collect data on how learners process feedback is to get learners to work in pairs, composing and processing the feedback they receive on their writing. According to Swain and Lapkin (2002), pair work enables learners to externalize their thoughts. Researchers who have used pair talk of learners processing feedback have shown that it is not only the depth of engagement with the feedback received (see Tocalli-Beller and Swain 2005), but also learners' attitudes and beliefs which may affect the uptake of feedback (Swain and Lapkin 2002; Watanabe 2004; Swain 2005a). This research of pair talk has shown that learners may reject teacher's feedback because it is perceived as violating their own held beliefs about language conventions or as altering the meaning of their original text. However, studies of pair talk have tended to consider feedback only in the form of reformulations rather than comparing learners' engagement with indirect feedback.

The study

This study, part of a larger research project on the efficacy of different forms of feedback, aimed to compare the nature of learners' engagement with direct (reformulations) and indirect (editing) feedback. It also sought to investigate the relationship between the nature of the engagement and the subsequent revisions made. Thus the research questions guiding this study were: (1) Do direct and indirect forms of feedback elicit different levels of engagement? (2) Does the level of engagement affect the revisions made to the subsequent draft? As mentioned above, the study investigated and compared direct and indirect forms of feedback: reformulations and editing. Reformulations involved the rewriting of the learners' text, preserving the text's meaning but making the language sound as native-like as possible. Editing included the provision of both symbols and codes, as is commonly the practice in L2 writing classes. The symbols used included underlining to locate the erroneous word, an insertion symbol to show a word has been omitted, and brackets to identify parts of a sentence that can be omitted. The codes were letters that identified the error type (e.g. F to indicate a grammatical form error—see example below). The number of editing symbols and codes was kept to a minimum and learners were presented with a clear key to the editing symbols and abbreviations used.

To maintain parity between the two forms of feedback, feedback was given only on grammatical accuracy, lexical choices, and mechanics (spelling, punctuation). No new sentences were added, nor were significant changes made to the order of existing sentences. Furthermore, both forms of feedback were provided by the same native speaker, a trained and experienced ESL teacher.

The following excerpts illustrate the two forms of feedback provided. Excerpt 1 illustrates reformulations. In this example (from the data of Pair

11), the reformulation consisted of changing the singular form 'an average rainfall' in the original to 'average rainfalls'.

Excerpt 1: Reformulations

Original:
This chart illustrates an average rainfall in each season in the year 2000.
Reformulation:
This chart illustrates average rainfalls in each season in the year 2000.
[P11]

Excerpt 2 illustrates the form of editing used in this study. In this example, an insertion symbol and two words were underlined with C written above 'amongst' denoting an error in word choice, and F written above 'season' denoting an error in word form.

Excerpt 2: Editing

Original:
The rainfall in Lagos city is 240 mm on average in summer, which the
      highest amongst the other season.
Edited version:
The rainfall in Lagos city is 240 mm on average in summer, which ∧ the
             C   F
highest <u>amongst</u> the other <u>season</u>. [P34]

Participants

The participants were students at a large university in Australia. Students were recruited via advertisements and were paid for their involvement in the study. The students' ESL proficiency was carefully vetted. In this part of the study we invited students with advanced ESL proficiency levels (IELTS scores of 6.5 or above) to attend in self-selected pairs. Forty-eight participants (24 pairs) were recruited. The majority were from Asian language backgrounds, and came predominantly from mainland China.

Study design

Participants were required to attend on three occasions over a four-week period. On Day 1, each pair was asked to write a joint report based on a graphic prompt (see Appendix 1). They were allowed 30 minutes for this activity and their talk was recorded. Five days later (Day 5) the participants returned, again in their pairs, and received a copy of the original prompt, and feedback on the report written at Day 1. One group of learners (n = 24 i.e. 12 pairs) received feedback in the form of editing; the other group received feedback in the form of reformulations. They were given 15 minutes to discuss the feedback (processing session). The feedback was then removed, and the pairs were given the unmarked and original version of their text (written on Day 1) and asked to rewrite their report (rewriting session). They were given 30 minutes to do this, and their pair talk in both the feedback processing and rewriting sessions was recorded. Three weeks later (Day 28) the learners returned, were given the graphic prompt and 30 minutes to write the report, but this time they wrote their reports individually.

Data and data analysis

Although the entire data set consisted of data collected on three separate days (Days 1, 5, and 28) in this study we focused mainly on data collected on Day 5. Thus the main sources of data used in this study were: the feedback the participants received on their data commentary reports written on Day 1, the participants' rewritten texts (Day 5), and the audio recorded and transcribed pair talk elicited during the feedback processing session and the rewriting session.

Feedback

All forms of feedback were counted. That is, all reformulations and editing symbols were counted. For example, Excerpt 1 above was coded as containing one reformulation; and Excerpt 2 as containing three editing symbols.

Written reports

A comparison of reports written on Day 1 and rewritten on Day 5 together with the feedback comments enabled us to determine whether the feedback provided was taken up. We also noted whether the learners had made changes to the rewritten version that were unsolicited, and the extent of these changes (i.e. whether at word level, clause or phrase level, or sentence level).

Figure 10.1 illustrates the analysis of uptake employed in this study. The reformulated version contains two reformulations: the word 'apparently' was reformulated to 'clearly' and the phrase 'experiences variations' was rewritten as 'varies'. The rewritten version (Day 5) shows that one reformulation was accepted (varies), one was ignored or perhaps rejected (clearly), and there was an unsolicited change at the word level (insertion of the word 'average').

Original (Day 1)	Feedback: Reformulation	Rewritten version (Day 5)
Apparently the rainfall level amongst seasons experience variations.	**Clearly** the rainfall level amongst seasons **varies**.	**It is apparent that** the **average** rainfall amongst seasons **varies**. [1 accept (1 ignore/reject and 1 unsolicited word)]

Figure 10.1 Analysis of uptake

Pair talk data

The transcripts of pair talk were analysed for language related episodes (LREs) to determine the extent to which language-specific issues (as opposed to content and ideas) were discussed, whether the aspects of language discussed related to the feedback provided, and the engagement with the feedback.

The original definition of Language Related Episodes comes from the work of Swain and Lapkin (1998). In this original definition, LREs refer to episodes in which learners deliberate over items of language as they attempt to jointly construct a text. In this study, the definition was extended to capture the learners' noticing of aspects of their writing that had been reformulated or edited. Thus LREs included segments in the pair talk where the learners noticed a reformulated or edited aspect of their earlier language use.

LREs were analysed in the first instance for their focus. That is, LREs were coded for whether they focused on *form* (e.g. verb tense, articles, sentence structure), *lexis* (word choice—including choice of prepositions—and word meaning), or *mechanics* (spelling, punctuation errors) as exemplified below. LREs were then analysed for the nature of engagement. However, rather than analysing for the quality of noticing, given the difficulties noted by Sachs and Polio (2007) and discussed above, here we focused on the level of interaction. We thus distinguished between LREs consisting of a single turn, and which therefore involved only one learner, and those consisting of more than one turn, thus indicating engagement by both learners. In coding LREs, notes were also made about whether they dealt with items of language identified in the feedback and any other salient features. Finally, the outcome of the LREs was coded as either correct, incorrect, or left unresolved.

In Excerpt 3, the learners (Pair 30) are focusing on the choice of prepositions. The LRE was coded as dealing with word choice (i.e. a lexical LRE), related to the feedback provided (word choice denoted as erroneous by the symbol and code). The LRE was coded as consisting of multiple-turns and resolved correctly, regardless of the fact that there is evidence here that the learners did not know the reason for the use of 'at' rather than 'in'.

Excerpt 3: L-LRE

                                                                    C
Written version (and editing): the rainfall in winter is always <u>in</u> the lowest level

88	SOPHIE:	at the level
89	YING:	yeah at
90	SOPHIE:	really, why?
91	YING:	I don't know
92	SOPHIE:	Maybe on the level yeah at the level
93	YING:	at the level should be

[P 30]

The example in Excerpt 4 comes from the data set of learners (Pair 6) who received reformulations. The reformulations consisted of changing the plural form 'variations' to its singular 'variation' and replacing the pronoun 'those' with 'that'. There are three LREs in this excerpt (the double dashes signal the beginning of each LRE). The first, line 18, was coded as an F-LRE dealing with the choice of singular/plural forms and corresponding to the feedback provided. The second LRE (also beginning in line 18) was a lexical LRE, dealing with the choice of pronouns, and again corresponding to the reformulations provided. The third LRE (beginning in line 20) was a lexical LRE dealing with the word 'clearly', but was unsolicited. That is, it did not correspond to feedback provided. Furthermore, the first two LREs were coded as single turn LREs since it seemed that only Jay was audibly involved in the deliberations; the third LRE was a multi-turn LRE since it involved Hang (confirming the word 'clearly'). All three LREs were coded as resolved correctly.

Excerpt 4: F-LRE and L-LREs

Original:
Also, the variations in rainfall in Bucharest is less than those in other cities. Clearly...
Reformulation:
Also, the variation in rainfall in Bucharest is less than that in other cities. Clearly...
Relevant LREs:

18	JAY:	Also, the variation, without –s, //in rainfall in Bucharest is less
19		than that... That not, yeah. Because here we used variations so
20		that in other cities. //Clearly, yeah, once more, yep.
21	HANG:	Yep, it's clearly.

[P6]

Excerpt 5, from Pair 31, shows an example of an LRE dealing with punctuation and thus coded as a M-LRE. It corresponded to the symbol provided in the editing feedback and involved both participants in the resolution, and thus was coded as a multi-turn LRE. It was coded as resolved correctly.

Excerpt 5: M-LRE

x
Written version (and editing): four cities, however...

44	ST 1:	hmm and this one maybe should be the semicolon
45	ST 2:	mm hmm semicolon
46	ST 1:	yeah.

[P 31]

Findings

In reporting our findings, we begin by presenting our quantitative findings: a comparison of the amount of feedback provided via editing and via reformulations; the amount of uptake, and the number and nature of LREs. We then report on some salient characteristics noted in analysing the pair talk data. The final section presents a qualitative and detailed analysis of two case study pairs.

Feedback

Our tally of the feedback provided is summarized in Table 10.1. As can be seen, there were more reformulations than editing symbols and codes provided. The range suggests that there was also substantial variation in the students' writing proficiency.

	Total	Average	Range
Reformulations	334	27.80	8–53
Editing symbols	171	14.25	2–26

Table 10.1 Feedback

Uptake

Table 10.2 below summarizes findings about the uptake, showing the number of instances where feedback was accepted and incorporated in the rewritten version on Day 5. However, it should be noted that analysis for evidence of uptake and quantification of uptake proved quite difficult, particularly in the case of the reformulation data. Students often reformulated entire chunks of language, reorganizing or adding sentences. Also, in response to the reformulations, some pairs (e.g. Pairs 1, 4, 5) made changes mainly at the word level, whereas all other pairs rephrased clauses and sentences when incorporating the feedback received. In the case of learners who received editing, changes tended to be at the word level. Nevertheless, it is clear that there was a higher level of uptake in the case of pairs who received editing feedback (87.72%) than in the case of pairs who received reformulations (54.49%), with variations between learners as suggested by the range of instances of uptake.

	No.	Accept	Range
Reformulations	334	182 (54.49%)	3–34
Editing	171	150 (87.72%)	0–26

Table 10.2 Uptake of feedback (Day 5)

Pair talk data: LREs

Tables 10.3 and 10.4 show the number of LREs found in the pair talk data on Day 5, in the processing session, when the participants discussed the feedback received, and during the rewriting session. We have also included in these tables, in column 2, the tally of the feedback received. Table 10.3 presents findings for pairs who received reformulations; Table 10.4 presents data for pairs who received editing feedback.

As the figures in Table 10.3 suggest, there appeared to be an inverse relationship between the number of reformulations and the number of LREs generated by the feedback. That is, pairs with the highest number of LREs in the processing session (e.g. Pair 4, Pair 12) received a below-average number of reformulations, whereas pairs receiving a relatively high number of reformulations (e.g. Pair 7, Pair 9) had a low number of LREs. It may be that a high number of reformulations overwhelmed the learners and thus had a discouraging effect. It is interesting to note that once the feedback was removed and the learners asked to rewrite their text, a greater number of LREs were generated. The number of LREs during the rewriting session (n = 224) was almost double that of LREs during the processing session (n = 127).

Table 10.4 shows that in the case of learners who received editing feedback, the number of LREs during the processing session (n = 188) roughly corresponded to the number of editing symbols received (n = 171). Although there were more LREs generated during the rewriting session (n = 219), the difference was not as stark as in the case of reformulations.

As shown in Table 10.5, most LREs dealt with either grammatical form (e.g. verb tenses, articles, singular/plural nouns), or lexis (i.e. word choice

Pair	No. Reformulations	No. LREs during processing of feedback	No. LREs during rewriting
P1	41	13	18
P2	31	5	17
P3	20	2	15
P4	16	19	16
P5	14	15	n/a[i]
P6	8	16	26
P7	53	1	2
P8	49	14	61
P9	43	6	1
P10	11	13	14
P11	28	4	11
P12	20	19	43
TOTAL	334	127	224
AVERAGE	27.83	10.58	20.36

[i] Data for pair 5 had to be discarded because of the predominant use of L1.

Table 10.3 LREs generated by learners who received reformulations

Pairs	No. editing symbols	No. LREs during processing of feedback	No. LREs during rewriting
P25	4	8	7
P26	7	25	33
P27	2	4	24
P28	17	16	14
P29	15	21	9
P30	15	15	17
P31	25	20	26
P32	12	20	21
P33	26	6	—ii
P34	15	17	19
P35	24	22	13
P36	9	14	36
TOTAL	171	188	219
AVERAGE	14.25	12.5	19.91

ii The disc used to record the pair talk during this session was subsequently found to be corrupted and thus unusable.

Table 10.4 LREs generated by learners who received editing

	No. LREs	F-LREs	L-LREs	M-LREs
Reformulations				
Processing session	127	55 (43.31%)	68 (53.54%)	4 (3.15%)
Rewriting session	224	92 (41.07%)	103 (45.98%)	29 (12.95%)
TOTAL (% of total)	351	147 (41.88%)	171 (48.72%)	33 (9.40%)
Editing				
Processing session	188	77 (40.95%)	82 (43.62%)	29 (15.43%)
Rewriting session	219	70 (31.96%)	119 (54.34%)	30 (13.70%)
TOTAL (% of total)	407	147 (36.12%)	201 (49.39%)	59 (14.50%)

Table 10.5 Focus of LREs

and particularly choice of prepositions). There was slightly greater attention paid to word choice than to grammar (i.e. more L-LREs than F-LREs) in both sessions and in both feedback conditions. There were relatively few LREs dealing with mechanics, regardless of the form of feedback received. This is perhaps not surprising since most of the feedback related to errors in grammar and expression.

Table 10.6 summarizes the results for the nature of engagement and LRE resolution. As the table shows, most LREs (over 75%) were resolved correctly. Furthermore, editing seemed to focus learners' attention on items identified by the feedback more so than did reformulations, particularly in the rewriting session when the feedback was removed. Thus, whereas 55.12 per cent of the LREs in the processing session dealt with items directly indicated by the reformulations, 66.49 per cent of the LREs generated by the editing feedback

	LREs during processing				LREs during rewriting			
	No.	No. correctly resolved	No. related to feedback	No. 1-turn LREs	No.	No. correctly resolved	No. related to feedback	No. 1-turn LREs
Reformulations	127	102 (80.31%)	70 (55.12%)	32 (25.20%)	224	174 (77.58%)	44 (19.6%)	38 (16.96%)
Editing	188	142 (75.53%)	125 (66.49%)	30 (15.96%)	219	180 (82.19%)	68 (31.05%)	14 (6.39%)

Table 10.6 Nature of LREs

related directly to the feedback received. During the rewriting session, less than 20 per cent of LREs dealt with the items identified in the reformulations; whereas 31.05 per cent of the LREs dealt with items identified by the editing.

Table 10.6 also shows that in terms of engagement, a greater proportion of LREs elicited by reformulations were single-turn LREs in both the processing (25.20%) and rewriting sessions (16.96%) compared to the LREs elicited by editing. In the data of pairs who received editing feedback, multi-turn LREs were pervasive in the processing and in the rewriting sessions.

Two points emerge from these results. First, in discussing the feedback, some learners were not clear about why certain words were reformulated, as Excerpt 6 illustrates. Such questioning perhaps explains the lack of uptake, evident in Table 10.2 above.

Excerpt 6: Rejection of feedback

8   JAY: [reading] a glance at … reveals that … Lagos had highest average rainfall level with almost in summer, yeah, compared to … Huh? Yeah, clearly not apparently. Ah, but, now, what is the difference in, yeah, what is the difference between the use of clearly and apparently? Because I I I find, yeah, we often use I often use apparently …
9   HANG: apparently
10   JAY: … yeah, in … in the … in the task one.
11   HANG: I I think that … I think that it's it's it's same … be the same, yeah. It's very similar.
12   JAY: Mmm.
[P6]

Furthermore, it became quite apparent that a number of learners who received reformulations decided to memorize the reformulated text. The data of four pairs contains evidence of learners explicitly adopting a strategy of memorization to deal with the feedback received. Similar observations have been reported by other researchers who have investigated reformulations (e.g. Sachs and Polio 2007). The following excerpt from the data of Pair 7 illustrates that the learners set out to memorize the reformulated paragraphs, dividing the text between them:

Excerpt 7: Learners memorizing the reformulations

14	HAAN:	We try to remember the mistakes. I remember the first part, you remember the second part, OK? From this sentence.
15	CHAY:	Ah, which one? The rainfall in autumn
16	HAAN:	Ah, yeah. You know
17	CHAY:	the rainfall in autumn
18	HAAN:	Yeah, you remember this. If we remember the separately, it will be much more easy.

[P7]

Thus in response to our research questions, our findings showed that editing, an indirect form of feedback, elicited more LREs, that is more engagement with the feedback provided, than the reformulations, a direct form of feedback. Furthermore, editing tended to engage both learners in searching and evaluating alternative words and grammatical structures resulting in a greater proportion of multi-turn LREs. This greater engagement may explain the higher uptake of the feedback provided. On the other hand, a number of pairs who received reformulations adopted a strategy of memorization. Others seemed more likely to question or reject the reformulations. Our findings would thus seem to support Ferris's (2002) claim that indirect feedback engages learners in deeper processing of language than direct forms of feedback and is thus more conducive to the development of learners' writing. Yet, as mentioned earlier, in a study that examined accuracy gains on Day 5 and Day 28 of the same cohort (Wigglesworth and Storch 2007), we found that both reformulations and editing led to greater accuracy on Day 5, but that the effects of reformulations were more enduring than those of editing feedback.

We were somewhat puzzled by these seemingly inconsistent findings and decided to use a qualitative case study approach in order to analyse the data of pairs who received reformulations more closely. Informed by sociocultural perspectives on language learning, our focus in this analysis was on trying to gain an understanding of the learners' goals and beliefs that shaped their engagement and uptake of feedback rather than uncovering cognitive processing. In the case studies, the data used were the pair talk in the processing and rewriting sessions as well as the texts produced on Day 5 in pairs and the texts produced on Day 28 individually.

Case studies

The two case study pairs selected were Pair 1 and Pair 8. The pairs had a number of similarities: all the learners were Indonesian, they received a high number of reformulations on the texts they produced on Day 1 (Pair 1: 41;

Pair 8: 49), and both generated an average number of LREs (Pair 1: 13, Pair 8: 14). Furthermore, the pair talk of both pairs showed evidence of an attempt to memorize the reformulations. Where they differed was in the amount of uptake: Pair 1 showed a very high level of uptake and a dramatic improvement in accuracy; Pair 8, on the other hand, showed a very low level of uptake and little or no improvement in accuracy.

Pair 1: Eko and Sherry

Eko (male) and Sherry (female) were highly proficient ESL learners. Both had an IELTS score of 7.5. The pair received a relatively large number of reformulations (41) on the text produced on Day 1 and of those, 30 were taken up in the subsequently revised text (Day 5). The changes made to the text were mainly at the word level. The other interesting detail about this pair is the dramatic improvement in their accuracy scores. For example, in terms of percentage of error-free clauses, the text produced on Day 1 had an accuracy score of 38.89 per cent, an accuracy score of 88.89 per cent on Day 5, and soared to an average of 94.99 per cent on Day 28.

The following two excerpts taken from their pair talk on Day 5 represent the pair's attitude to the reformulations received. What we see in Excerpt 8 is that Eko and Sherry thought that the reformulated text was not very different to the text they produced, and adopted a memorization strategy, dividing the paragraphs between them. They clearly succeeded in memorizing the text, because during the rewriting session (see Excerpt 9) Eko seemed concerned that they were producing an exact replica of the reformulated text. Sherry placated him, pointing out that since they were the original authors of the text, it was not simply a case of copying but of amending for errors.

Excerpt 8: Eko and Sherry processing session

607	EKO:	yeah. Not much of a difference
608	SHERRY:	Yeah. Maybe we ought to memorize, ah
609	EKO:	This
610	SHERRY:	So I memorize the first paragraph, you the second

Excerpt 9: Eko and Sherry rewriting session

| 735 | EKO: | We are copying totally from her... |
| 736 | SHERRY: | No it's not. It's ours but its wrong, so we change it. No it's Ok. |

Figure 10.2 provides an example of how the reformulations were discussed and incorporated in their text. The reformulated text contains six changes (verb form, writing the figure in words, punctuation, writing the ampersand in words, and capitalizing the name of the city). There were no relevant LREs that dealt with any of the suggested changes, perhaps not surprising since most dealt with quite superficial aspects of language use. Yet clearly the learners noticed the

Original	The graph is showing the average seasonal rainfalls in 2000 for 4 cities, Bucharest Beijing, Lagos, & mexico city
Reformulation (6)	The graph **shows** the average seasonal rainfalls in 2000 for **four** cities, Bucharest, Beijing, Lagos, **and M**exico **C**ity
Relevant LRE during processing	0
Relevant LREs during rewriting	Eko: the graph shows Sherry: the graph shows… //the average seasonal rainfall… for four cities, and then you use like double dots Eko: yeah
Rewritten version (Day 5)	The graph **shows** the average seasonal rainfalls in 2000 for **four** cities: Bucharest, Beijing, Lagos, **and M**exico City.
Writing Day 28: Eko	The graph **shows** the average seasonal rainfall in **four** cities, Bucharest, Lagos, Beijing **and M**exico city, in 2000.
Writing Day 28: Sherry	The graph **shows** the average seasonal rainfall in 2000 for **four** cities: Bucharest, Lagos, Beijing **and M**exico **C**ity.

Figure 10.2 Pair 1 dealing with reformulations

changes and remembered them. During the rewriting session, the only relevant LRE related to the feedback is the one dealing with the verb form 'shown'. The LRE dealing with punctuation is not in response to the feedback received. Both LREs were resolved correctly and show involvement by both learners. Despite the absence of LREs, the rewritten version shows uptake of all the reformulations and an additional change to the punctuation (colon inserted after four cities) not solicited by the reformulations. As can be seen in the texts written by both learners on Day 28, the reformulations were remembered. Sherry made additional changes (not all necessarily correct) to her text.

Thus, although the learners did not discuss the feedback given in the reformulation about the verb form (is showing vs. shows), or the punctuation, they clearly memorized it, and remembered it as evident in the relevant LRE during the rewriting phase. There is also evidence of uptake on Day 5 and retention of that uptake on Day 28 particularly for Sherry. The excerpt lends support to Sachs and Polio's (2007) claims that lack of verbalization does not necessarily indicate lack of noticing of feedback provided, and that learners may perhaps not perceive a need to verbalize certain reformulations that deal with mechanics (e.g. capitalization).

Figure 10.3 presents evidence of a slightly different scenario. Here the original text elicited two reformulations: capitalization of the name of the city and a rephrasing of 'merely around' to 'around a mere'. During the processing session, the learners discussed the reformulated phrase, Sherry noting and repeating it, and Eko offering an explanation that the reformulation is a more sophisticated expression of the same idea. It would seem that the learners' level of noticing, using Qi and Lapkin's (2001) study was substantive, showing evidence of understanding. During the rewriting, the learners tried

Original	The steadiest level of rainfall occurs in bucharest where it fluctuates merely around 50mm.
Reformulation (2)	The steadiest level of rainfall occurs in **B**ucharest where it fluctuates **around a mere** 50mm
Relevant LRE during processing	Sherry: Don't use merely. Oh, around a mere, oh, around a mere. Eko: A more sophisticated way of getting it.
Relevant LRE during rewriting	Sherry: Occurs in Bucharest… where it fluctuates… around… around Eko: a mere Sherry: Is that the how to put it? around a mere fifty millimetres? Eko: That's how she put it. Sherry: I don't know how to put merely there. Around a mere fifty millimetres Eko: I think merely around fifty millimetres would be, you know, it equate.
Rewritten version (Day 5)	The steadiest level of rainfall occurs in **B**ucharest where it fluctuates **around a mere** 50 mm
Writing Day 28: Eko	The rainfall in **B**ucharest fluctuates **merely around** 50 mm in all seasons.
Writing Day 28: Sherry	Concerning stability, **B**ucharest has the most constant level of rainfall across all seasons where it only fluctuates **a little** around 50 mm

Figure 10.3 Pair 1 uncertainty about reformulations

to recall the phrase. Sherry asked Eko for confirmation and Eko confirmed and the resulting rewritten version shows evidence of uptake. However, as evident in the LRE, Sherry felt uncertain about how to use this phrase, and Eko suggested that both versions were equivalent. It is perhaps this belief that explains their use of this phrase on Day 28. Eko reverted to the original phrase 'merely around', whereas Sherry changed it to 'a little around'.

Thus in the data of this pair, there was generally a high level of acceptance of the reformulations, and perhaps a successful memorization strategy employed. This explains the high level of uptake and the high accuracy scores. The texts produced on Day 5 and Day 28 replicate to a large extent the reformulated text. Changes made were largely guided by the reformulations, and there were very few other, unsolicited changes made. This is because the learners accepted the suggested changes. However, when they felt that the suggested change was unnecessary or unimportant, they exercised their volitional control, and rejected the reformulation, either reverting to their original version or changing the phrase altogether. That is, memorization in the long term (Day 28) and reproduction seems to depend on learners' beliefs about language use.

We should also note that in this case the learners are fairly advanced. As research by Qi and Lapkin (2001) showed, reformulations seem to work well, particularly with advanced language learners because of the minor errors they make in their writing. This means that the reformulations are easily noticed and remembered.

Pair 8: Gus and Jon

Gus and Jon were also Indonesian speakers, but their ESL proficiency was somewhat lower than that of Pair 1. Gus and Jon's IELTS scores were 6.5. The pair also tried to memorize the reformulations, but there was little evidence of uptake with only 8 out of the 49 suggested reformulations taken up in the rewritten text at Day 5. Instead, the rewritten text contains many unsolicited changes: many new words were added (46), including an entire sentence, and many of the original words deleted (31), again including an entire sentence. Their accuracy score showed no improvement with the percentage of error free clauses on Day 1, 66.67 per cent, dropping to 58.33 per cent on Day 5, and averaging 65.2 per cent on Day 28.

What became quite evident in the analysis of the talk of this pair was their negative attitudes to this form of feedback. Excerpts 10 and 11 from their data illustrate these attitudes. It is interesting to note, however, that in the processing session, despite these negative attitudes, the two learners decided to memorize the reformulated text. However, in the rewriting session, as shown in Excerpt 12, they decided to pursue their own goal—to improve their text in ways that they saw fit, ignoring whatever they recalled of the earlier memorization.

Excerpt 10: Gus and Jon processing session

41	GUS:	huh? I don't think this kind of feedback is good, because...
42	JON:	yeah
43	GUS:	people will tend to memorize this
44	JON:	yeah this still crap

Excerpt 11: Gus and Jon processing session

64	GUS:	yeah a feedback should not just give away the answer. Yeah that's...that's my opinion. Okay so, are we supposed to memorize this?
65	JON:	yeah, you got paragraph one and two, I got paragraph three and four
66	GUS:	okay, okay now you...you memorize paragraph three then four

Excerpt 12: Gus and Jon rewriting session

153	JON:	is it necessary that we have to write it in this style or...?
154	GUS:	no, you change it in any way you want to
155	JON:	okay
156	GUS:	any way that will make it better

Figure 10.4 illustrates how they proceeded with rewriting their text on Day 5 and writing independently on Day 28. In the reformulated text, the verb form was changed to a past tense form and the phrase 'during each season'

Original	To conclude, it seems that the rainfall in the four cities has the same pattern, during each season.
Reformulations (2)	To conclude, it seems that the rainfall in the four cities **had** the same **seasonal rainfall** pattern.
Relevant LREs during processing	*Gus:*　to conclude, it seems that the rainfall in the four cities (?) same pattern (?)… oh okay, not during each season *Jon:*　mm okay *Gus:*　same… have the same seasonal rainfall pattern… *Jon:*　mm hmm
Relevant LREs during rewriting	*Gus:*　to conclude, the rainfall… the rainfall in the four cities… has the same pattern during the… have the same pattern that… for each season *Jon:*　no, how about like this: can be divided into… two… *Gus:*　two categories? *Jon:*　can be divided to two pattern… into two patterns *Gus:*　okay, can divided into two patterns….
Rewritten version (T2)	To conclude, the rainfall rate in the four cities can be divided into two patterns. One that has a very large difference ...
Writing T3: Gus	The overall observation for this chart reveals that the rainfall patterns in this four cities can be put into two major categories…
Writing T3: Jon	Overall, trends for the four cities were quite similar with the peak rainfall happened in summer, and the lowest was in winter. We can then divide them into two groups ...

Figure 10.4 Pair 8 dealing with reformulations

rephrased to make the idea more succinct. The relevant LREs during the processing session did not deal with the verb tense form, and the rephrasing was simply read out, but there was little engagement with the reformulation. In the rewriting session, there was no evidence that the past tense form was noted and the learners proceeded with the present tense form. Furthermore, they decided to rewrite their sentence rather than following the reformulation. The rewritten version does not resemble the original text, nor the reformulated version. On Day 28, the learners wrote texts which resembled to some extent the rewritten version, but the texts contained many grammatical errors, and this explains the low accuracy score on Day 28.

Thus what these excerpts show is that although the learners attempted to memorize the reformulations, because they did not approve of this form of feedback, and their stated goal was to improve the text—they did not reproduce the reformulations.

Discussion

Research on different forms of feedback shows inconclusive and at times conflicting results; however, most researchers agree that for feedback to be useful for learning it needs to be noticed. Our original findings in response to the two research questions showed that editing, an indirect form of feedback, elicited greater attention to the feedback, represented by a larger number of LREs, and greater engagement and interaction between the learners (more multi-turn LREs) than the direct form of feedback, reformulations. These findings are perhaps not surprising as learners who received editing had to work out an appropriate alternative to the word identified as erroneous by the editing symbols. Reformulations seemed to elicit less focus on language than did editing perhaps because the 'correct answers' were provided, and thus the cognitive comparisons that reformulations encourage do not necessitate the same level of engagement as editing. There is no need to propose or consider alternatives.

However, our findings, and in particular our case studies, suggest that level of engagement may not necessarily explain which forms of feedback are more effective in developing learners' accuracy in writing. Whereas editing encouraged focus on forms and uptake, reformulations allowed learners to internalize and appropriate the correct target language. However, this internalization occurred when the feedback accorded with the learners' own goals and beliefs about language use.

As Lantolf and Thorne (2006) point out, uptake is a goal-directed activity. Feedback was taken up when it was accepted as correcting an error. Where it was seen as merely presenting an alternative, or merely a more sophisticated expression (Figure 10.2, Pair 1), or in instances where this form of feedback was not valued, the learners ignored the feedback received.

What these findings suggest is that a constellation of factors explain uptake. Traditional explanations of uptake tend to focus on noticing. What our findings suggest is that learners exercise their volitional control not only in what they notice but also in whether they accept, accommodate, or reject the feedback provided. Teachers' feedback, which might not resonate with learners' beliefs, may be rejected or transformed (Tardy 2006). These attitudes and beliefs about language conventions, preferred form of feedback, and learners' goals are encapsulated in the notion of learner agency. It is learners acting as intentional agents in their learning process who notice, memorize, and imitate. Imitation is distinct from emulating; imitation involves volitional processing (Lantolf and Thorne 2006). As Cumming, Busch, and Zhou (2002) point out, research on writing has tended to focus on the composing strategies and the resulting product (i.e. the written text), omitting to consider the participants' goals which drive the activity. The same criticism can be levelled at existing research on feedback. Thus far, most studies have considered different types of feedback and its effect on the revised written text, but have failed to consider the learners' goals when engaging with the feedback provided. Future research which uses a case study approach and considers uptake as a goal-directed activity may help us understand the interaction between memorization and agency and provide more robust explanations about which forms of feedback are more effective in developing learners' writing.

Appendix 1: Data commentary task

The graph below shows average rainfall (by season) for four cities. Write a report for a university lecturer describing the information shown below.

You should write at least 150 words.

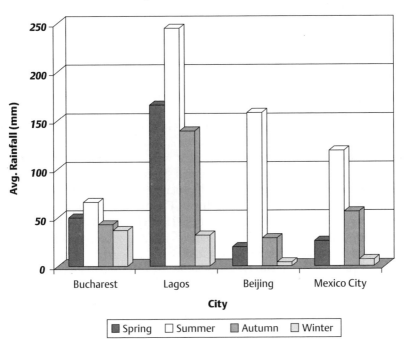

Average Seasonal Rainfall in Four Cities in 2000

11

Relevance, cohesion, and the sociocognition of form-focused, teacher-led L2 discourse

PAUL D. TOTH

Introduction

This chapter argues for the fundamental role of discourse cohesion in creating optimal sociocognitive conditions for second language (L2) acquisition during teacher-led interaction. Here, the term 'sociocognitive' refers to the parallel social and cognitive L2 theoretical strands that equally regard interaction with others as essential to development, albeit with different accounts for the process (cf. Gass 2003; Lantolf and Thorne 2006). The position taken here is that cohesion during form-focused instruction, defined as propositional connectedness among discourse turns (Widdowson 1978), yields social conditions that favor collaborative assistance among participants, as well as cognitive processes that direct attention to L2 form-meaning relationships. Based on data from two contrasting segments of teacher-led, form-focused tasks in beginning, university-level L2 Spanish classes, Sperber and Wilson's (1995, 2002; Wilson and Sperber 2004) 'theory of relevance' will be used to account for the divergent outcomes, based on the cohesion built and maintained through teacher turns.

In contexts where the L2 is not widely used outside the classroom, the quality of interactions among teachers and learners has a major impact on learning outcomes. However, despite most teachers' desire for learners to communicate freely in the L2 outside class, the nature and structure of classroom discourse necessarily differs from that of non-instructional settings in terms of the number of participants involved and the authoritative role of teachers as discourse managers and subject-matter experts (Cazden 2001; Seedhouse 2004). Hence, as in other academic areas, L2 instruction often occurs as whole-class, teacher-led discourse (TLD), which may alternate with learner interaction in pairs or small groups, but is none the less the primary way to open and close, if not also carry out, classroom tasks. Although some researchers have cited diminished learner autonomy and teacher turns that stifle rather than facilitate interaction as reasons to limit TLD (e.g. Hall 1995*b*, 2004; van Lier 1996; Donato and Brooks 2004), others have argued that when the teacher's discursive role is adequately understood, the weaknesses of TLD can be mitigated and important benefits derived from his or her L2 expertise (Antón 1999; McCormick and Donato 2000; Toth 2008).

Indeed, with an emphasis on learner-internal development, cognitive/ interactionist L2 theory maintains that L2 teachers can benefit acquisition by providing high-quality 'comprehensible input', directing attention to L2 form-meaning relationships, and creating opportunities for meaningful L2 'output' and 'negotiation' (Doughty 2003; Gass 2003; Ortega 2007*a*). Meanwhile, within sociocultural theory's focus on external developmental factors, teachers may facilitate the 'internalization' of L2 communicative practices by offering apt models for emulation, framing difficult linguistic concepts as useable support, and modulating other forms of 'mediation' within learners' 'zones of proximal development' (Vygotsky 1978, 1986; Wertsch 1985; Lantolf and Thorne 2006). Still, despite contrasts in their epistemological views of language and development (see Larsen-Freeman 2007, for a summary), both theories see L2 *assistance* as essential, and, whether framed as 'negotiation' or 'mediation', few would disagree that its feasibility rests on a shared understanding and mutual orientation toward discourse goals. Thus, given Sperber and Wilson's (1995, 2002; Wilson and Sperber 2004) account for how discourse participants perceive and align turns toward the intentions of others, their 'theory of relevance' provides a useful sociocognitive basis for understanding TLD's variable success at sustaining effective L2 assistance. Therefore, in this study, the impact of teacher turns on those of learners will be analyzed using relevance theory to assess cohesion during segments of form-focused communicative tasks in two L2 Spanish classrooms. Taking extended, silent latencies as indicators of poor cohesion, the chapter will consider the extent to which shorter latencies coincide with greater amounts of assistance. To the extent that they do, transcript analyses will identify features of teacher turns that may have played a role in building the cohesion that made such episodes possible.

A sociocognitive approach to cohesion

Since the 1970s, theoretical work on communicative competence has recognized that 'coherent', understandable discourse derives from our ability to perceive the intended meanings of utterances and logically link them together (Widdowson 1978; Canale and Swain 1980). Widdowson called this propositional connectedness 'discourse cohesion' and saw a direct relationship between ease of inferencing and comprehensibility: 'The difficulty we have in recovering propositional development is a measure of the degree of cohesion exhibited by a particular discourse' (Widdowson 1978: 26). More recently, cognitive L2 theory has sought to demonstrate how 'negotiation' facilitates L2 acquisition by ensuring comprehension and drawing attention to L2 form-meaning relationships (e.g. Long 1996, 2007*b*; Robinson 2001*b*). However, given an emphasis on learner-internal aspects of L2 development, most research has focused on the impact of lexical and morphosyntactic modifications on comprehension, with less consideration given to discourse-level factors beyond the design of instructional tasks (Skehan 1998; Robinson 2001a). Still, cognitively oriented classroom studies have shown how sensitive negotiation can be to broader contextual factors such as the orientation of curricula and established discourse routines (Nicholas, Lightbown, and Spada 2001; Lyster and Mori 2006; Lyster 2007). Thus, while discursive factors may not figure prominently in current cognitive L2 research, many such studies have shown evidence of an interdependence between the outcomes of negotiation and available contextual cues.

By contrast, sociocultural theory has viewed linguistic development as primarily contingent upon external social factors, such as supportive relationships within speech communities and the use of language to accomplish intentional goals (Vygotsky 1978, 1986; Wertsch 1985, 1998). The importance of cohesion for the 'internalization' of L2 communication is evident in the foundational belief that all mediation crucially depends on 'intersubjectivity' among participants, or a shared orientation toward activity outcomes (Rommetveit 1979; Wertsch 1985). Indeed, considerable L2 research, particularly in small-group contexts, has shown that learners often work to determine the objectives and procedures of instructional tasks as an essential precondition to engaging in them (Brooks and Donato 1994; Brooks, Donato, and McGlone 1997; Antón and DiCamilla 1999). Thus, intersubjectivity relates to cohesion in that a shared appreciation for the perspectives and motives of others makes comprehensible, productive discourse possible.

Cohesion, relevance, and teacher-led discourse

Critics of TLD have observed how purportedly 'conversational' interactions often result in disfluent exchanges characterized by minimal learner utterances and long, stony silences (e.g. Lee 2000; Hall 2004). As further evidence of the link between poor cohesion and comprehensibility, learners have at times openly expressed confusion about a teacher's line of questioning (Hall 1995b; Toth 2004). Often, a contributing factor is said to be evaluation-oriented 'IRF' sequences, where teacher questions or prompts 'initiate' an exchange, one or more learners 'respond', and teacher 'feedback' follows before another sequence begins (Sinclair and Coulthard 1975; Mehan 1979). Although some have shown that IRF sequences engage learner talk when initiations are open-ended and feedback occurs as constructive follow-ups (Wells 1996; Nassaji and Wells 2000), acute disfluencies may still result when IRFs fail to clearly reveal the discourse goal. In particular, this may happen when ostensibly conversational questions belie the intention that learners produce particular L2 forms (Brooks 1993; Toth 2004), or when initiations repeatedly consist of narrowly framed 'display' questions whose topical reference and target audience extends no further than each three-part IRF cycle (Brock 1986; Hall 1995b).

Where stony silences and disfluency are concerned, Sperber and Wilson's (1995, 2002; Wilson and Sperber 2004) relevance theory is particularly

cogent in tracing links to poor cohesion. Building on Grice's (1975) 'cooperative principle' for explaining how we understand intended meanings, Sperber
and Wilson (2002: 18–19) claim that all interlocutors assume the turns of
others to be maximally 'relevant' to a discourse goal, and that utterance interpretation occurs rapidly, even for non-literal meaning, as hearers follow a
path of least effort in selecting the one possible interpretation that best aligns
with their active assumptions. However, if the path of least effort reaches a
dead end such that no single interpretation coincides with their assumptions,
hearers, rather than dismissing the utterance, will search for new ones that
better facilitate comprehension. Depending on the degree of incongruence
with hearers' expectations, this process may literally require computational
time and effort. None the less, the belief in a maximally relevant, cooperative
interlocutor reliably overrides incompatible beliefs about discourse, such that
the former will motivate modification or abandonment of the latter.

Early work by Vuchinich (1977) on experimental participants' reactions to
discourse non-sequiturs corroborates relevance theory, as randomly inserted,
abrupt topic shifts in dyadic interaction were shown to elicit extended latencies and attempts at topic repair with 'faultless regularity' (ibid. 236). Building
on this work in an adult L2 Spanish classroom, Toth (2004) found that a
TLD lesson containing both personalized and drill-oriented questions meant
to elicit target grammar forms resulted in longer average latencies between
teacher and learner turns than a lesson where conversational questions and
follow-ups transparently built on learner responses. During a video replay
of each lesson, learner recollections of their experiences revealed that even
though many could interpret teacher intentions during the grammar-oriented
lesson, the need to process a significant gap between the literal and intended
meaning of questions extended latencies as learners tried to think up irrelevant content for their responses. This corroborated relevance theory in that,
with no other explicit cues, the path of least effort in interpreting a personalized question, such as whether or not a learner had watched television that
week, would favor an elliptical response to referential meaning (e.g., '*sí*' or
'*no*'), rather than a complete sentence that reproduces transformed L2 structures. Still, Toth concluded that grammatical objectives are not inherently
more problematic for cohesion than conversational ones, but rather that they
ought to be transparently manifest in the instructional task, so that accuracy
could be better recognized as the discourse goal (ibid. 26).

The dependence of accuracy objectives on clear, compatible discourse is
further evident from research on variability in L2 learners' self-correction
after 'recasted' feedback. For example, in immersion contexts where academic subject-matter is prioritized over accuracy, unobtrusive recasts often
fail to trigger self-correction due to misperceptions that they are mere repetitions or topic continuation moves (Lyster and Ranta 1997; Lyster 2004). In
traditional classrooms that prioritize L2 proficiency, however, higher rates
of self-correction have been found (R. Ellis, Basturkmen, and Loewen 2001;
Lyster and Mori 2006; Toth and Garritano 2008). Meanwhile, Ohta (2001)

has shown through recordings of individually miked learners' subvocal speech that when TLD adequately situates recasts within discourse goals, even those not directly involved in the exchange may attend to, process, and benefit from feedback to others. Thus, if teacher initiations could build cohesion among learner responses across multiple rounds of IRF, then learners who witness assistance to others might more directly apply this feedback to their own utterances. In this way, TLD that allows multiple relevant contributions toward a discourse goal would be transformed into a sociocognitively valid 'collaborative task', in that turns within each IRF would become cumulatively supportive reference points for subsequent contributions.

The present study

Based on this discussion, this chapter will compare descriptive quantitative and qualitative data from two beginning, university-level L2 Spanish classes where TLD targeted L2 forms in different ways within communicative tasks. In 'Class A', conversational questions were interspersed with recasted feedback designed to elicit target forms. In 'Class B', errors with target forms were more overtly identified, with the teacher consistently prompting learners for accurate reformulation. Based on relevance theory and the research procedures of Vuchinich (1977) and Toth (2004), cohesion in the two class excerpts will be assessed by measuring silent latencies between teacher initiations and learner responses. Then, episodes of assistance with L2 utterances will be counted and qualitatively compared to determine their relationship to the relative cohesion in each class.

Instructional setting and participants

The excerpts from Class A and Class B were taken from two second-semester, beginning L2 Spanish classes at the same large, public American university. The participants were adult learners between the ages of 18 and 30 who spoke English as their primary language and did not speak Spanish at home. Class A included 13 learners total, 4 male and 9 female, while Class B included 18 learners, 10 male and 8 female. As was typical of the undergraduate population at this university, learners in both classes represented a variety of racial and ethnic backgrounds. The instructor for Class A was a female native speaker of Castilian Spanish in her mid-twenties, and the instructor for Class B was a female near-native speaker in her mid-thirties who had married a native Spaniard and lived in Spain for many years.

Each class normally met five days a week for 50 minutes, with Class A running from 12:00–12:50 p.m., and Class B from 10:00–10:50 a.m. The two videotaped lessons occurred halfway through the Spring semesters in which they were held. Although data for Class A was gathered four years after that for Class B, the orientation of the curriculum remained communicative throughout, in that course goals and textbook materials emphasized oral proficiency and meaningful interaction, with more than 50 percent of learners' final grades depending on weekly evaluations of their in-class participation. Instruction in both classes regularly included a mix of whole-class and small-group activities, with TLD being most frequent.

Lesson objectives and data gathering

The researcher designed each lesson as part of two separate, larger investigations into communicative approaches to L2 grammar instruction. The teachers were briefed on guidelines for targeting L2 forms within communication activities during separate two-hour training sessions one week before their respective videotaping dates; lesson plans with all necessary materials were then distributed on the preceding day. In Class A, the teacher was to build a conversation about learners' recent leisure activities using the present perfect construction shown in Example (1). The class had engaged in accuracy-oriented practice the previous day, and with conversation now the objective for this lesson, the teacher was to make feedback on the target form unobtrusive, as recommended in the 'focus on form' literature (Long 1991; Long and Robinson 1998). Meanwhile, in Class B the teacher was to pose communicative initiations to learners, solicit multiple responses, and then give feedback on the target structure, which was the impersonal passive clitic *se* shown in Example (2), with its many English equivalents. The teacher was told that explicit error correction should focus on accuracy with *se* within the communicative objectives of each task. Thus, Class A was intended to be more conversational than Class B, with the target structure an incidental feature of discourse, while Class B was meant to induce a more overt treatment of target structure accuracy within communicative tasks.

(1)   Spanish present perfect.

Has   mirado   la televisión esta semana.
Have–2nd sing. watch–perf. television this week.
(You've watched television this week.)

(2)   Spanish impersonal passive *se*

Se   habla   español en Miami.
Anticaus. speak–3rd sing. Spanish in Miami.
(Spanish is spoken.../ One speaks Spanish.../ They speak Spanish...in Miami.)

The data to be considered come from the first set of lesson activities in each class, which in both cases consisted of three related tasks that coincidentally occupied nearly the same amount of total time (Class A = 9 min. 35 sec. Class B = 9 min. 26 sec.). The Appendix shows the section of each teacher's lesson that corresponded to these first activity sequences. In Class A, a whole-class conversation about learners' recent leisure activities was based on a set of ten laminated pictures from the previous day, placed in front of the class to suggest possibilities. The target vocabulary included *leer* (read), *mirar la televisión* (watch television), *esquiar* (ski), *tomar café* (drink coffee), *charlar* (chat), *bañarse* (take a bath), *nadar* (swim), *pintar* (paint), *tocar música* (play music), and *hacer ejercicio* (exercise). The first task asked learners to name activities in the pictures to prime potential vocabulary for the next step. Then, the teacher asked personalized questions about which activities learners had recently engaged in. Finally, the teacher had learners make comparisons between their recent activities and those of others who had previously spoken.

Meanwhile, in Class B, the teacher extemporized on the lesson plan by asking several learners at the beginning of class how they were doing and following up with comments and questions about their responses. As per her guidelines however, she repeatedly posed the same question to subsequent learners. Then, following the lesson plan, she put the names of several American cities and states on the board and used impersonal *se* to ask about products and activities for which those places are known. Finally, the teacher extended the previous task by asking learners to think of other products or activities associated with those places.

Data coding and analysis

After videotaping the two classes, each three-part task sequence was transcribed, coded, and analyzed. The length of each latency between teacher initiations and learner responses was then measured to assess cohesion. Finally, the researcher and an assistant coded the transcript independently to identify episodes of L2 assistance and count the number of learner turns involved. After comparing their results, the two parties discussed discrepancies and made adjustments to reach 100 percent agreement.

Latency gaps: Vuchinich (1977: 237) defined latency as 'the number of seconds of silence following a turn before [a] hearer's response'. Using procedures from Toth (2004), this definition was applied to the data so that gaps were measured from the first initiative question or prompt to the beginning of the responding learner's turn. Latencies thus included paraphrases or repetitions of the initiation,[1] as well as fillers before learner responses, such as 'uh' and 'um'. During assistance episodes, when feedback on a learner's turn also served as an initiation for modification or self-correction, gaps were similarly timed from the first provision of feedback to the beginning of the learner's response. However, when learners made unsolicited turns to which the teacher responded, gaps were not timed given the purpose of assessing the cohesiveness of teacher turns.[2]

Measurements were taken directly from the time stamp on the researcher's video editing software by using the accompanying sound wave profile to locate the beginning and end of each gap, and rounding to the nearest half-second.[3] Example (3) shows how this procedure was applied to data from Task 2 in Class A, with the symbol # indicating the beginning and end of latency timing, and the measurement given between teacher and learner turns. All learner names have been changed to aliases.

(3)   Class A, Task 2: What have you done this week?

a. TEACHER: *Vamos a ver. ¿Qué actividades, ah, vosotros habéis hecho esta semana?# ¿Qué actividades vosotros habéis hecho esta semana? ¿Qué actividades?... Dime, Jason.*
(Let's see. What activities, ah, have you done this week?# What activities have you done this week? What activities?... Tell me, Jason.)

9.5 sec.

b. STUDENT 1:   *#Probablemente voy a leer, o voy a mirar la televisión.*
(#I'm probably going to read or I'm going to watch television.)

c. TEACHER: Uh-huh, *¿Has mirado la televisión?#*
(Uh-huh. You've watched television?#)

0.5 sec.

d. STUDENT 1:   *#Sí.*
(#Yeah.)

e. TEACHER: *¿Esta semana?#*
(This week?#)

0.0 sec.

f. STUDENT 1:   *#Probablemente.*
(#Probably.)

g. TEACHER: *Has mirado la televisión.*
(You've watched television.)

Thus, in line (a), latency timing began after the teacher's first initiation, *¿Qué actividades vosotros habéis hecho esta semana?* and included two repetitions until Student 1 began his utterance 9.5 seconds later. Because the feedback in lines (c) and (e) appeared motivated by a lack of the target present perfect in the learner's responses, they were considered teacher prompts for modification, so that the subsequent gaps were also timed as latencies of 0.5 and 0.0 seconds.

L2 assistance: Episodes of L2 negotiation or mediation, henceforth referred to simply as 'assistance', were identified as segments that began with any inquiry into the form or meaning of a previous teacher or learner utterance and extended throughout problem-solving for that topic, regardless of how many sub-steps were involved, until another was taken up. Assistance with topical content, such as naming cities and states for the tasks in Class B, was not included in the analysis. Thus, in Example (3), the teacher's recasted feedback in line (c) began what was coded as a single assistance episode through line (g), despite the learner's failure to use the target form in his turns. Similarly, in Example (4), taken from Class B's first task, lines (c)–(j) were coded as an assistance episode that elicited other- and self-directed talk from Student 2 in lines (d) and (h), as well as turns from two others in (f) and (i). Because in line (k), Student 2 correctly responded to the teacher's elicitation at the end of (j), line (k) and the teacher's response in (l) were not coded as assistance.

(4)   Class B, Task 1: How are you?

a. TEACHER: *¿Qué pasa Pablo?#*
              (What's up, Pablo?#)

   1.0 sec.

b. STUDENT 2:   Uh, #*¿Cómo se dice,* like, 'better than yesterday', er, *más—?*
                (Uh, #How do you say, like, 'better than yesterday', er, more—?)

c. TEACHER: [to the whole class] *¿Cómo se dice,# cómo se dice? . . . ¿Cómo se dice?*
              (How do you say it,# how do you say it? . . . How do you say it?)

   4.0 sec.

d. STUDENT 2:   #*¿Yo estoy más bien?*
                (#I am more better?)

e. TEACHER: [looks for other volunteers] *Venga, Julia.#*
              (Go ahead, Julia.#)

   1.0 sec.

f. STUDENT 4:   Um, #*más mejor.*
                (Um, #more better.)

g. TEACHER: *Uy, perfecto no está, pero casi perfecto.*
              ¿'Más mejor',# 'MÁS mejor'?
              (Ooh, it's not perfect, but almost perfect.
              'More better',# 'MORE better'?)

h. STUDENT 2:   [quietly, to himself] Uh, *'bien'.*
                (Uh, 'well'.)

   3.0 sec.

i. STUDENT 5:   #It would just be *'mejor'.*

j. TEACHER: [extends hand toward Student 5] *'Mejor', exactamente, Cati. Claro, muy bien, Julia, y muy bien, Cati.* [turns to Student 2] *'Mejor'. 'Estoy mejor, que ayer'. Es verdad.* [nods head] *'Ayer es—'* [stops and looks toward Student 2] *'Ayer', ¿qué?#*
              ('Better' exactly, Cati. Right, very good, Julia, and very good, Cati. 'Better'. 'I'm better than yesterday'. That's right. 'Yesterday, I—' 'Yesterday', what?#)

   1.0 sec.

k. STUDENT 2:   #*Ayer yo . . . yo está, estuve, muy enfermo.*
                (#Yesterday, I . . . I am, I was very ill.)

l. TEACHER: *Ah, muy bien.* [looks downward with sympathetic frown] *Lo siento, Pablo.*
              (Ah, very good. I'm sorry, Pablo.)

Results

Latency gaps: Table 11.1 provides comparative statistics for latencies and assistance in the two classes, while Figure 11.1 sequentially plots the duration of each latency as it occurred on the transcript, with shading to distinguish tasks. Beginning with Table 11.1, rows (a)–(c) indicate that despite nearly equal total time, latencies took up considerably more of Class A—nearly half (44.4%) the total time—than in Class B, where they occupied less than a quarter (22.3%) of the time. Row (d) shows that average latencies were 2.9 seconds longer in Class A than in Class B, with considerably greater variation as well. Figure 11.1 vividly demonstrates this variability while further revealing Class A as one characterized by frequent extended silence. The longest gap there lasted 25.0 seconds, compared to 14.5 seconds in Class B. The dotted horizontal lines on each graph indicate 5 seconds as a point previously used by Toth (2004: 21) at which a latency might be considered 'extended', or exceptionally long.[4] Of the 54 gaps in Class A, 17 fell into this category, compared to only 5 of 69 gaps in Class B. Thus, if indeed extended latencies reflect problems with cohesion, discourse in Class A was considerably weaker than in Class B, despite its overtly conversational objectives.

Learner turns and assistance: returning to Table 11.1, rows (e) and (f) demonstrate the impact of longer latencies in Class A on interaction, with 15 fewer teacher-learner sequences than in Class B, and 31 fewer learner turns overall. In addition, by comparing rows (e) and (f) for each class, it is evident that 20 learner turns in Class B occurred as unsolicited contributions outside of IRF (cf. 69 I-R sequences vs. 89 learner turns), whereas only 4 such turns occurred in Class A (54 I-R sequences vs. 58 learner turns). When total learner turns are divided by each class's total time, Class A saw one every 9.9 seconds, while Class B had one every 6.3 seconds. Furthermore, row (g) indicates that, despite its larger size, learner talk in Class B was distributed over

Discourse descriptor	Class A	Class B
a. Total time of excerpt	575.0 sec. (9 min. 35.0 sec.)	566.0 sec. (9 min. 26.0 sec.)
b. Total latency time	255.5 sec. (4 min. 15.5 sec.)	126.0 sec (2 min. 6.0 sec.)
c. Latencies as a proportion of total time	44.4%	22.3%
d. Mean latency (Standard deviation)	4.7 sec. (6.3)	1.8 sec. (2.5)
e. No. of teacher-learner I-R sequences	54	69
f. Total learner turns	58	89
g. Turn-taking learners / total learners present	10 / 13 learners	15 / 18 learners
h. Episodes of assistance / no. of learner utterances involved	9 episodes / 15 utterances	13 episodes / 52 utterances

Table 11.1 Comparative statistics for latency gaps, learner turns, and L2 assistance episodes

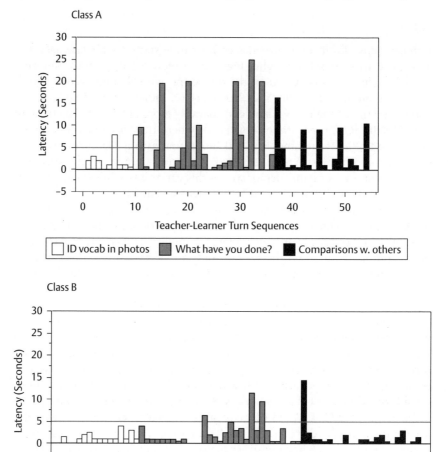

Figure 11.1 Latencies between teacher initiations and learner responses, in sequential order, shaded by task

more individuals, with fifteen learners making contributions there versus ten in Class A. Finally, line (h) shows that a greater amount of discourse in Class B was dedicated to assistance than in Class A, with 13 episodes involving 52 learner utterances (59% of the 89 total), versus 9 episodes involving just 15 utterances (25% of the 58 total). Given such overwhelming contrasts, few could argue that Class A provided a more facilitative L2 context for acquisition than Class B, despite the former's purportedly communicative lesson plan. Taken with the latency data, it indeed appears that poor cohesion negatively affected assistance and learner engagement. Hence, the qualitative data will explore the relationship between these outcomes and teacher turns.

Qualitative data: Figure 11.1 shows that in Class A more than half the latencies lasting longer than 5 seconds occurred during Task 2's conversational questions about leisure activities. The beginning of that task was given in Example (3), where a 9.5-second gap followed initial instructions in a result consistent with relevance theory, given the time needed for learners to formulate responses. Indeed, extended gaps also followed initial instructions for Task 3 in Class A (16.5 sec.), and for Tasks 2 and 3 in Class B (6.5 sec.[5] and 14.5 sec. respectively). However, the learner's continued misinterpretation of target structure time reference in Example (3), despite the teacher's initiation and two rounds of recasted feedback, clearly indicates a failure to convey key discourse goals. Thus, the learner's inferencing diverged significantly from teacher intentions in that he assumed her question to reference future plans rather than recent events. Picking up where Example (3) left off, Example (5) further suggests unraveling cohesion, as extended latencies coincided with repeated instances of misunderstanding, abrupt shifts in the teacher's line of questioning, and a narrow solicitation of turn-takers. The excerpt corresponds to gaps 14–23 on the horizontal axis of Figure 11.1.

(5)   Class A, Task 2: What have you done this week?

a. TEACHER: *Más cosas.*# [indicating the laminated pictures, and looking at Student 5]...*Luis, ¿qué has hecho esta semana?*
(Other things.# Luis, what have you done this week?)

4.5 sec.

b. STUDENT 5:   #*Repite, por favor.*
(#Repeat, please.)

c. TEACHER: *Sí, ¿qué has hecho esta semana?*# *¿Qué has hecho esta semana, Luis?* [pointing to the pictures, then checking lesson plan]...*¿No? ¿Qué has hecho esta semana? ¿Has,* uh, *has pintado? ¿Luis?* [points to a picture of someone painting] *¿Has pintado?*
(Yes, what have you done this week?# What have you done this week, Luis?...Nothing? What have you done this week? Have you, uh, have you painted? Luis? Have you painted?)

19.5 sec.

d. STUDENT 5:   #*¿Cómo se dice* 'not anymore'?
(#How do you say 'not anymore'?)

e. TEACHER: Um...'*ya no*'. #

0.0 sec.

f. STUDENT 5:   #*¿Ya no?*

g. TEACHER: *Ya no.*#

0.5 sec.

h. STUDENT 5:   *#¿Ya no pintado?*
                 (#Not anymore painted?)

i. TEACHER: *No, vale, pero no has pintado. ¿Hm?# ¿No has pintado?*
                 (No, okay, but you haven't painted. Hm?# You haven't painted?)

2.0 sec.

j. STUDENT 5:   *#No.*
                 (#No.)

k. TEACHER: *No, pero ¿esto?#* [points to skiing picture and makes skiing gesture with arms] *Shh, shh...¿No? ¿Y ésta?* [points to another picture] *¿No, no, no?*
                 (No, but this?# *Shh, shh...*No? And this one? No, nothing?)

5.0 sec.

l. STUDENT 5:   *#Yo, uh, might leo mi picture en el wanted-ero poster-o.* [a campus event]
                 (#I, uh, might read my picture on the wanted-ero poster-o.)

m. TEACHER: *¿Has, has leído tu, tu dibujo?# ¿Has, has, has, has, has, qué? Pero Luis, en ésta sí, ¿verdad?* [points to picture] *Ésta sí, ¿verdad, Luis?*
                 (You've, you've read your, your picture?# You've, you've, you've, you've, you've what? But Luis, in this one, you have, right? This one you have done, right Luis?)

n. STUDENT 5:   Uh...

o. TEACHER: *¿No?* [addressing class, pointing to a picture of an adult and a child in a gymnasium] *¿Chicos, ésta? ¿Diana? ¿Has hecho esta actividad?*
                 (No? Guys, this one? Diana? Have you done this activity?)

p. STUDENT 6:   [off camera, no verbal response]

q. TEACHER: *¿No? ¿Cuál es esta actividad, chicos?¿Cuál es esta actividad? Dime.*
                 (No? What's this activity, guys? What's this activity? Tell me.)

20.0 sec.

r. STUDENT 2:   *#El padre está ayudando su hijo.*
                 (#The father is helping his son.)

s. TEACHER: *Vale, pero ¿Qué ha hecho, qué ha hecho el padre esta semana?# ¿Qué ha hecho el padre con el hijo?*
                 (Okay, but what has he done, what has the father done this week?# What has the father done with his son?)

2.0 sec.

t. STUDENT 5:   *#¿Cuál es la actividad, uh, con President Clinton?*
                 (#What is the activity, uh, with President Clinton?)

u. TEACHER:	*¿Con Presidente Clinton?* [points to a picture of Hillary whispering into Bill Clinton's ear] *¿Cuál es la actividad de Presidente Clinton?# ¿Qué ha hecho? ¿Qué ha hecho el Presidente Clinton? ¿O qué ha hecho la mujer? ¿Qué ha hecho la mujer? Roberto.* (With President Clinton? What is Presendent Clinton's activity?# What has he done? What has President Clinton done? Or what has the woman done? What has the woman done? Roberto.)
10.0 sec.	
v. STUDENT 2:	Uh, *#¿la mujer,* uh, *ha besado Bill Clinton?* (Uh, #the woman, uh, has kissed Bill Clinton?)
w. SEVERAL STUDENTS:	[laughter]
x. TEACHER:	*No, ah. ¿Y tú?# ¿Tú has besado al Presidente Clinton alguna vez?* (No, ah. And you?# Have you ever kissed President Clinton?)
3.5 sec.	
y. STUDENT 2:	*#No.* [laughing] (#No.)
z. TEACHER:	*No.* [chuckling] *¡Por favor!* (No. Please!)

In this excerpt, then, difficulty began in line (a), as soon as the teacher called on Student 5, who had not volunteered. After his clarification request in line (b), the teacher's second initiation in (c) yielded a 19.5-second gap, during which she reframed the discourse goal from an open-ended question about the learner's activities to a more narrowly focused one about whether he had painted. The subsequent assistance in lines (d)–(j) suggests that, as in Example (3), the learner misunderstood the temporal reference of the teacher's question and failed to infer her intention to elicit target forms. After requesting vocabulary help in (d), the learner again misinterpreted the teacher's recast in (i) as referencing future plans, and after her continued attempts to elicit a desirable response in (k), Student 5's utterance in (l) suggests either an inability or unwillingness to respond in Spanish, if not resistance to the teacher herself.

In lines (m)–(q), a 20-second latency appeared when the teacher again shifted her focus to a different picture and continued prompting Student 5 for a response before turning to Student 6. Again, with no indication of having volunteered, Student 6 gave no response and the teacher finally opened the question to the whole class. Although Student 2 volunteered in line (r), his answer in the present progressive, taken with his failure to respond to recasted feedback in line (s), again suggests problems interpreting temporal reference, with conversational expectations used to infer discursive meaning instead (i.e. the more natural question, 'What *is* the person *doing* in this picture?').

The palpable frustration was finally broken in line (t) when Student 5 asked an unsolicited question about a picture where Hillary Clinton was whispering into Bill Clinton's ear. The teacher posed the question to the whole class in line (u), and after a 10-second gap, the light-hearted exchange in lines (v)–(z) finally yielded use of the present perfect.

Thus, extended latencies in this excerpt seemed related to three principal factors. First, they reliably arose when teacher initiations posed a new discourse goal to learners, as at the beginning of Task 2 (Example (3), or when the line of questioning changed. In Example (5), this included the shift in (c) from what Student 5 had done to whether he had painted; the shift in (o) from one picture to another; and the shift in (u) from what learners had done to what Bill Clinton had done. Second, large gaps also preceded the turns of learners who had not volunteered, as in lines (d), (n), and (p). Although indeed calling on non-volunteers may at times be beneficial, a third contributing factor precluded this possibility, as the teacher's attempts to frame desirable responses through feedback repeatedly failed. If we assume from the learners' conversational responses in Example (3), line (b), and Example (5), lines (d), (l), and (r), that they understood the content of teacher initiations while misconstruing her temporal reference, it follows that they must also have understood the corrective intent of her feedback without perceiving the verb form that would have led to a desirable response. Under such conditions, the extended gaps preceding non-volunteers' turns make sense, given the requirement to perform in front of peers without understanding either what was wrong with previously corrected responses or how to provide ones that better aligned with expectations. As the teacher continued managing discourse in this way, Figure 11.1 shows how this combination of anti-cohesive factors conspired to yield the longest latencies at the end of Task 2, with three lasting more than 20 seconds, and gaps in Task 3 suggesting similar disfluencies.

By contrast, extended latencies in Class B appeared to relate to topic shifts alone, rather than a narrow selection of respondents or uncertainty over discourse goals. In Figure 11.1, the four extended latencies in Task 2 corresponded to initial task instructions, followed by teacher questions that each posed a different product or activity to be matched to the places on the board. Still, the goal of making these matches remained consistent throughout, so that longer latencies came from attempts to determine correct answers rather than attempts to determine teacher intentions. For example, the 11.5-second latency (gap 37) came after the teacher asked '*¿Dónde se ven edificios altos?*' (Where are tall buildings seen?), with 'Chicago', 'New York', 'Detroit', and 'Miami' all listed as possibilities. Meanwhile, the 9.5-second gap two initiations later followed the question '*¿Dónde se cultivan manzanas?*' (Where are apples grown?). When Florida was incorrectly offered as the first response, two other learners answered with much shorter latencies before a third person correctly answered '*el estado de* Washington'.

Compared to Class A then, what is noteworthy in Class B is the absence of uncertainty over accuracy objectives within discourse, and the shorter latencies and increased assistance that resulted. Example (4) showed that accuracy was conveyed as a discourse goal even during the conversational warm-up questions in Task 1. When Student 2 inquired about saying 'better than yesterday' in line (b), the teacher immediately posed his question to the class in (c), with two peers offering solutions in (f) and (i) and the learner audibly working through the problem himself in (h). The strategy of repeatedly using feedback and initiations to direct the work of accurate communication back to the class (e.g. lines (g) and (j)) established accuracy as a clear, collective goal which, as in Ohta's (2001) research, appears to have cognitively engaged even those learners who did not initially respond. Similarly, Task 2 began with little uncertainty over discursive goals or means. In Example (6), note that unlike Class A, the teacher started with a clear statement of procedures and provided an orientation to both necessary cues (place names on the board), and the format for desirable responses (complete sentences):

(6)   Class B, Task 2: Matching places with products.

a. TEACHER: *Venga, vamos a ver. Aquí tenemos muchas ciudades y estados diferentes. Ahora, voy a decirles preguntas. Entre estas ciudades y estados, ¿dónde se producen muchos carros?# ¿Dónde se producen muchos carros? Venga, Pablo Cabral, frase completa… ¿Repito la pregunta?*
(All right, let's see. Here we have a number of different cities and states. Now, I'm going to ask you questions. Among these cities and states, where are many cars made?# Where are many cars made? Come on, Pablo Cabral, a complete sentence… Shall I repeat the question?)

6.5 sec.

b. STUDENT 2: *#Sí.*
#Yes.

c. TEACHER: *¿Dónde se pre-, dónde se producen muchos carros?#*
(Where are, where are many cars made?#)

2.0 sec.

d. STUDENT 2: Uh, *#se produce, se produzo mucho carros*—[incorrect verbal suffix]
(Uh, # much cars is made, is made—)

e. TEACHER: [facial gesture indicates the answer is not quite correct]
Bien—
(Okay—)

f. STUDENT 2: —*en Detroit.*
(—in Detroit)

g. TEACHER: *¿En dónde? En Detroit. Venga, no está perfecta la frase. ¿Cómo es?# Carla.*
(Where? In Detroit. Well, the sentence isn't quite perfect. What is it?# Carla?)

1.5 sec.
h. STUDENT 1:   #*¿Se produce?*
                   (#Is made?)
i. TEACHER: *¿Muchos carros o mucho carro?#*
                   (Many cars or much car?#)
0.5 sec.
j. STUDENT 1:   Oh. #*Se producen—*
                   (Oh. #Are made—)
k. TEACHER: [nods head]
l. STUDENT 1:   —*muchos carros en Detroit.*
                   (—many cars in Detroit. ['Many cars are made in
                   Detroit'])
m. TEACHER: *Perfecto. Muy bien.*
                   (Perfect. Very good.)

Thus, after an initial extended latency and request for clarification in line (b), the discourse went much differently than in Class A. When Student 2's inaccurate response emerged in lines (d) and (f), rather than simply recasting the desired answer and continuing, the teacher's feedback in (e) and (g) made target-structure accuracy a salient, collective endeavor by first identifying the answer as ungrammatical and then prompting others for assistance in (g). That triggered an assistance episode where, after volunteering a solution in line (h), Student 1 was pushed in (i) to reanalyze the subject of the impersonal passive in (j), with simultaneous supportive feedback occurring in (k).

Perhaps the best illustration of how L2 assistance became collective problem-solving occurred in Task 3, when the teacher asked learners to think of other products or activities associated with the places on the board. With learners now more in control over discourse than when they were responding to discrete questions, Figure 11.1 indicates that latencies declined markedly after initial task instructions in gap 47. Example (7) shows the end of this task, after a learner's comment that Spanish is spoken in Florida led others to name Miami, New York, and Hollywood as places where this was also true. Immediately prior to the excerpt, Student 8 had said, '*Se hablan español en Miami*' (Spanish is spoken in Miami), incorrectly using the plural verbal suffix *–an*, instead of singular (*–a*) to agree with *español*. The teacher's feedback then pushed learners to recognize the proper reference point for verb agreement, and frequent unsolicited learner turns show that many became engaged in problem-solving outside teacher-driven IRF, including 3 utterances whose speakers could only be identified as 'several students'.

(7)   Class B, Task 3: Other possibilities for products and places.

a. TEACHER: *Pero, 'se—' ¿qué?# Repita el verbo.*
                   (But 'se—' what?# Repeat the verb.)

2.0 sec.

b. STUDENT 8:   *#Habla.* [correct third person singular suffix]
                  (#Speak.)

c. STUDENT 6:   *Hable.* [incorrect singular suffix]

d. STUDENT 8:   *Hablen.* [third person plural suffix; incorrect]

e. TEACHER: [feigning surprise] *Ah, no.#*
                  (Ah, no.#)

0.5 sec.

f. SEVERAL
   STUDENTS: *#Habla.* [correct]

g. STUDENT 12:   *Habla.*

h. STUDENT 8:   *Habla.* But it's plural.

i. TEACHER: *¿El qué es plural?#*
                  (What's plural?#)

0.0 sec.

j. STUDENT 8:   *#Muchas personas.*
                  (#Many people.)

k. TEACHER: *Ah, entonces,* [raising four fingers for plurality]
                  'Muchas personas...'?#
                  (Ah, so then. 'Many people...'?#)

l. STUDENT 12:   Hollywood.

m. TEACHER: [to Student 8] *Venga.*
                  (Come on.)

1.5 sec.

n. STUDENT 8:   *#Hablan.* [correct third plural suffix]

o. TEACHER: *Hablan. Muchas personas hablan.*
                  (Speak. Many people speak.)

p. STUDENT 8:   *Hablan.*

q. TEACHER: *Pero, ¿con se?#*
                  (But with *se*?)

r. STUDENT 12:   Hollywood.

s. TEACHER: [Acknowledges Student 12 and moves hands
                  horizontally as though building a sentence]
                  En Hollywood#...
                  (In Hollywood#...)

3.0 sec.

t. STUDENT 15:   *#se*
                  (#is)

u. TEACHER: *se#...*

0.0 sec.

v. SEVERAL   *#habla.* [correct third singular suffix]
   STUDENTS: (#spoken)

w. TEACHER: *Habla—*

x. STUDENT 8:   [simultaneously] *Habla, habla,* blah, blah, blah.

y. TEACHER:	—*En Hollywood, se habla español. Oh, qué difícil. Y 'muchos idiomas'. Si hacemos la frase,* [Again, moving hands horizontally, as though building a sentence] *'En Hollywood, ba- ba- ba, muchos idiomas', ¿Qué?#*
	(Spoken. In Hollywood, Spanish is spoken. Oh, how difficult. And 'many languages'? If we make the sentence 'In Hollywood, many languages blah, blah, blah', what then?#)
0.5 sec.	
z. STUDENT 8:	#*Habla muchos idiomas.* [*se* omitted; incorrect singular suffix]
	(Speak many languages.)
aa. TEACHER:	*¿Habla?#*
	(Speak?#)
1.5 sec.	
bb. SEVERAL STUDENTS:	#*Se hablan.* [correct plural suffix]
	(Are spoken.)
cc. TEACHER:	*Se hablan. Perfecto. En Hollywood, se hablan muchos idiomas. Muy bien.*
	(Are spoken. Great. In Hollywood, many languages are spoken. Very good.)

Thus, with accurate communication a well-established goal and collaboration a familiar means to that end, the teacher in line (a) could easily question the grammaticality of Student 8's earlier utterance without introducing a costly topic shift that might have extended latencies. The short gaps and several learner responses in lines (b)–(h) demonstrate how readily many could respond to the prompt in (a) and feedback in (e). Student 8's unsolicited explanation for his answer in (h) then identified his difficulty in understanding *se* and verbal agreement. Rather than provide an explanation herself however, the teacher sought to construct that understanding by prompting peers in (k), (o), and (q) to demonstrate agreement contrasts between personal subjects like '*muchas personas*', and impersonal ones with *se*. The assisted, collaborative formulation of the sentence with *se* then built upon Student 12's unsolicited contribution of the topic 'Hollywood' in (l) and (r), with the teacher isolating the problematic portion in (s) and then reinforcing the learners' use of *se* with correct verbal agreement in (u) and (w). During this extended assistance episode, most latencies lasted less than 1 second, with the longest at 3.0 seconds before line (t), while learners worked on verb agreement. Finally in (y), the teacher initiated further L2 assistance by posing the plural subject '*muchos idiomas*' (many languages) with *se*, apparently to contrast agreement with singular '*español*'. As teacher gestures provided visual support for utterance formulation, several learners followed Student 8's erroneous answer in

(z) with an accurate model in (bb). Thus, whereas in Class A, the teacher's attempts to prioritize accuracy through implicit feedback contributed to the disfluencies often associated with TLD, in Class B, the teacher's more overt treatment of accuracy led not only to shorter latencies, but also more of the linguistic assistance that both cognitive and sociocultural L2 theories value.

Discussion

The striking differences between Classes A and B demonstrate that although TLD may sometimes be counter-productive, it is equally possible that well-managed TLD can facilitate L2 development. Still, successful TLD clearly requires complex decision-making at several interrelated levels, from broader discourse goals that link utterances together, to initiations and feedback that determine the range of addressees and the nature of desirable responses. Because this coordination can either strengthen or weaken the cohesion upon which discursive comprehension depends, relevance theory's account for how we infer intentions and decide what to say has implications for ensuring that TLD provides fertile sociocognitive conditions for effective L2 assistance.

Relevance theory and the sociocognition of latencies in TLD

To begin, the consistency of extended latencies following teachers' initial task instructions most strongly reflects relevance theory, as learners took time to hypothesize teacher intentions and formulate suitable responses within the limits of their L2 proficiency. Having activated relevant responses, Figure 11.1 shows that subsequent latencies in both classes immediately decreased as teachers followed initial learner answers with feedback or follow-ups, to which the same individuals usually responded quickly, building on the preceding discourse. In Class A, however, latencies continued spiking as the teacher changed the topical reference of questions, narrowly selected addressees, and mixed conversation with implicit correction, all of which would have affected the cognitive processing of relevant responses. However, given greater clarity over discourse goals in Class B, the clustering of latencies in Task 2—which were comparatively long but not as long as Class A—suggests the more isolated impact of topic shifts resulting from discrete informational questions. However, Task 3's latency profile demonstrates the more cohesive results of IRFs built into a socially collaborative task, where multiple learners took turns responding to the same initiation. Because learners understood target-structure accuracy to be as much an objective as accurate information, linguistic problem-solving could be introduced with little cost to latency. Thus, in both classes, latencies depended on a sociocognitive interplay between topical reference, discourse goals, and intended addressees.

Relevance, communication, and sociocognitively valid focus on form

Relevance theory would therefore suggest that for instructional discourse to be truly 'communicative', it must not merely reference real-world topics such as student pastimes or L2 culture, but rather it must use language to accomplish readily identifiable goals, such as analyzing, comparing, evaluating, and describing—even if the object of such work is L2 structure. Indeed, the disfluencies in Class A, where interaction was supposed to be conversational, stood in stark contrast to Class B, where less 'communicative' display questions were effectively organized into an accuracy-oriented matching task. Although such thinking about L2 pedagogy is indeed compatible with sociocultural concepts of language as meaningful 'activity' (Leont'ev 1978; Wertsch 1998) and cognitive proposals for 'task-based' instruction (Skehan 1998; Lee 2000; R. Ellis 2003), traditional attempts to address L2 accuracy within communicative methodology, as well as interactionist calls for an incidental 'focus on form' while ostensibly doing something else (e.g. Long 1991, 1996; Doughty 2001), suffer equally from a disassociation of accuracy from discursive intention. Both appear to assume that authentic communication treats topics other than L2 structure, and that linguistic development occurs most efficiently by overtly working toward some other goal while covertly or incidentally pursuing grammatical objectives. Given that this closely reflects what the Class A teacher tried to do, it would seem that such a dualistic view of grammar and communication could bring out the worst in whole-class interaction.

Recalling both Widdowson's (1978: 26) view of cohesion as propositional development, and Sperber and Wilson's (2002: 19) 'path of least effort' in construing discursive meaning, it seems unreasonable to expect that without clear cues, learners should readily recognize conversational questions as also intending that they produce target forms, or unobtrusive recasts as meaning that they should focus on form rather than on message. Indeed, such covert accuracy goals may violate the socio-pragmatic principles that underlie cognition, given Sperber and Wilson's assertion that 'the plausibility of [any] hypothesis about [a] speaker's meaning depends not only on its content but also on its accessibility' (ibid. 18). Wilson and Sperber (2004: 609) illustrate this point by comparing two possible answers to a hypothetical inquiry from a dinner guest about the evening's menu:

(a) We are serving chicken.
(b) Either we are serving chicken or (7^2-3) is not 46.

Although both utterances have the same truth value and provide the requested information, the second is less relevant to the hearer, given that it 'requires an additional effort of parsing and inference' to continue propositional development from the preceding question (ibid. 610). Thus, when teacher questions about topics other than L2 structure belie less overtly manifest concerns over accuracy, or when recasts suddenly but subtly turn conversation into correction, learners are put in a similar processing bind, in that either the incoming utterance or the preceding discourse fails as a 'least effort' cue for formulating a relevant, desirable response. By contrast, when formal accuracy is more overtly integrated into discourse, as in Class B's collective problem-solving, or the linguistically oriented L2 classrooms where recasts have proven effective, stronger cohesion more readily allows learners to engage in activities that benefit acquisition. In short, L2 feedback, models, assistance, and ultimately, output cannot easily occur in classroom discourse without an accessible, interpretative basis for doing so.

Relevance and sociocognition in collective turn-taking

Poor cohesion in Class A also evidently resulted from the teacher's mismanagement of discursive power, both in the sequencing of initiation and feedback moves and her selection of respondents. Often her initiations modified discourse goals within the same turn, as questions changed their topical focus and intended audience, leaving non-volunteers to perform with little support. In Class B however, the teacher's strategy of seeking multiple voluntary responses to widely posed initiations fostered a social environment of collaboration where collective problem-solving and spontaneous peer assistance produced generally brief latencies. Indeed, relevance theory supports this latter strategy, since, as listeners infer meaning from each teacher or peer utterance, the possibility that several responses could be relevant to the same prompt provides more individuals with opportunities to test their hypotheses before subsequent initiations render the thought process moot. Furthermore, if as Ohta (2001) suggests, whole-class learners actively attend to the turns of others, then the possibility that previous models and feedback could be relevant to a learner's forthcoming response enhances the developmental value of such assistance. Thus, the advantages of TLD as a collaborative task begin to accrue when accuracy in communication is clearly understood as a basis for interpreting what is being said and why.

Conclusion

This study thus strongly suggests that neither whole-class interaction nor expectations for grammatical accuracy are antithetical to the principles of form-focused, communicative language teaching. Instead, this work has demonstrated that clear communication of discourse goals and careful management of turn-taking can lead to facilitative sociocognitive conditions for L2 acquisition in whole-class contexts, and that Sperber and Wilson's theory of relevance provides some insights into how and why this may be so. Given the extremely limited scope of this data, however, broad generalizations about teacher-led discourse in all instructed L2 contexts are unwarranted. Nonetheless, the possibility that pursuing L2 accuracy within a collaborative task design may provide instructional conditions that both sociocultural and cognitive theory value is one that surely merits further investigation as we seek to better integrate linguistic development and communicative intention for maximal benefit to learners.

Appendix

Lesson Plan excerpt, Class A

Activity 1: Place the 10 laminated pictures from the previous lesson on the blackboard and ask students to identify which activities in the pictures they have done recently. Then ask students to make comparisons between their activities and those of someone who has already spoken, e.g.: *¿Cuál de las siguientes actividades has hecho esta semana? ¿Lo hiciste sólo o con otra gente? ¿Con quién lo hiciste?* After student answers, repeat in 2nd person: '*OK, te has bañado.*' Then try elicitation such as: '*¿Has hecho las mismas actividades que XXX?*' '*¿Qué actividades diferentes has hecho?*' '*¿Cómo han sido diferentes tus actividades de las de XXX?*'

Lesson Plan excerpt, Class B

Activity 1: After an informal warm-up, review use of *se* by writing the place names below on the board and asking the following questions:

Chicago	Wisconsin	Nueva York
Miami	Kansas	Alaska
Detroit	Maine	Hollywood
Florida	Idaho	El estado de Washington

¿Dónde...

Se producen muchos carros? *Se cultivan papas?* *Se cultivan manzanas?*
Se cultivan naranjas? *Se ven muchos edificios altos?* *Se produce mucho queso?*
Se pescan langostas? *Se filman películas?*

Acknowledgments

I am grateful to Sara Hagen, at the University of Wisconsin-Madison, for her assistance in transcribing and coding the data for this study. Sincere thanks are also due to Richard Young, of the University of Wisconsin-Madison, for his valuable comments and feedback on an earlier draft of this chapter. Finally, I am greatly indebted to the instructors and students at the University of Pittsburgh who participated in this research. I have learned much from working with them, and continue to gain insight from their experience as I reflect on my own good and bad days as a teacher.

Notes

1. Measurements included the teachers' repetition and paraphrasing of their initiations on the assumption that the perceived need for such clarification would be at least partly related to cohesion.
2. Although measured latencies could potentially include gaps purposefully extended by the instructor to allow greater 'wait time' for responses (J. White and Lightbown 1984, Rowe 1986), the video data indicated that neither teacher observably did so at any time, and that both systematically called on the first available learner throughout the two segments.
3. The researcher used the 2004 Macintosh version of Final Cut Pro HD, whose time stamp reads at 1/30 second intervals.
4. Likewise, within recommendations that teachers purposely extend the 'wait time' between their questions and student responses, it has been argued that 5 seconds is a maximally beneficial amount of time (Rowe 1986: 48).
5. The 6.5-second measurement corresponds to gap 28 for Class B in Figure 11.1. The preceding shorter gaps in Task 2 came from an informal exchange while the teacher was writing the place names on the board, before she posed task instructions to learners.

12

Interaction research: what can socially informed approaches offer to cognitivists (and vice versa)?

JENEFER PHILP AND ALISON MACKEY

Introduction

The field of second language acquisition is comprised of researchers from a variety of different academic backgrounds. Interdisciplinary insights and productive new avenues for research are continually emerging. Interaction research is a case in point. The interaction hypothesis of SLA was formulated in the early 1980s, and has been refined, extended, and updated several times since its inception, most recently by Long in 1996 and 2007a, and by Gass and Mackey in 2007. Long's original hypothesis emerged from observations about the contributions of conversation to learning. Today interaction is often seen as a window through which important cognitive aspects of the learning process can be viewed. In this chapter we suggest that the interaction approach might also be seen as a potential forum for combining some of the different perspectives that are emerging within the broader field of SLA, both the more cognitive and the more social. The interaction approach has always been dynamic, with a history of evolving in response to theoretical and methodological developments in SLA and related areas. The more cognitive areas include work emerging from cognitive psychology, for example, in relation to recent research on the relationship between working memory and language learning. The more social areas include, for example, work on how the role of the conversational partner and context might impact learning opportunities through interaction.

Interaction research has been primarily cognitive in nature to date. It has contributed to our understanding of second language learning. A strong base of empirical research has supported an association between interaction and L2 learning. The combined results of more than fifty studies have identified a variety of specific interactional features as facilitative of second language learning and this positive relationship between interaction and second language learning has been confirmed in recent meta-analyses by Keck et al. (2006), by Mackey and Goo (2007) and, in relation to corrective feedback, by Russell and Spada (2006). These are encouraging results, as is the fact that both meta-analyses and replications are becoming part of the maturing interaction research base. While on the one hand providing us with a 'bigger picture' view of the effects of interaction, such meta-analyses also reflect one of the main limitations of much of interaction research. A bigger picture view necessarily involves generalization. Some have critiqued one of the side effects of this, that less attention has been paid to the social contextual factors that are intrinsic to any interaction and its effects. This tension between seeking what is common, while recognizing the particular, is an old chestnut in the field (Gass and Mackey 2007). At the end of many of our cognitive-interactionist research papers, we point out that the context of the research was limited and should be extended, and we occasionally mention that social factors need to be considered. In this chapter we take up the challenge to consider social factors in more detail. We do this in order to further our research into how the relationship between cognitive and social factors might extend our understanding of SLA. It is important to note that we are starting from the perspective of cognitive SLA which is where our expertise lies. This initial discussion is intended to identify areas for potentially fruitful future collaboration between cognitive and social theorists.

How is the interaction research agenda developing? First, interaction researchers have begun calling for more rigorous operationalizations of the cognitive constructs we're using in our studies. These include, for example, working memory, attention, aptitude, and so on, as well as a more complete understanding of interactional features such as recasts and corrective feedback (Mackey 2006*b*). Second, there is increasing consideration of social and contextual factors together with discussion of the idea that the relationship between the cognitive, which is the traditional foci of interaction research, and the social might be helpful in furthering our understanding of SLA. For example, in a review of theories of SLA, Lourdes Ortega (2007*b*: 248) explains that social theories investigate

experience that is lived, made sense of, negotiated, contested, and claimed by learners in their physical, inter-personal, social, cultural, and historical context. If in the future, SLA researchers recognize the importance of theorizing learner experience, it may be possible to achieve a balance between linguistic, cognitive, psychological, and social explanations in our theories.

Interaction research is growing in each direction, both towards more careful understanding and measurement of concepts from psychology and cognitive science, as well as to a consideration of the advantages a more socially informed perspective might offer. This is a sign that the field is maturing, and moving towards a position of greater explanatory power. It's encouraging that researchers from two ends of the spectrum think that the interaction approach has enough to offer that it's worth pushing to be more inclusive and rigorous. As we seek to increase our understanding of the interaction–learning relationship, our research questions, and equally our methodologies, are evolving to incorporate both cognitive and social factors.

One of the questions that might be addressed is how researchers investigating the interaction–learning relationship from a cognitive perspective can begin carefully and rigorously to explore the kaleidoscope of social factors at play during interaction in a way that can help to address and refine our research questions and improve our analyses, understandings, and explanations of the interaction–learning relationship. In this chapter we illustrate this point through an analysis of data which takes some first steps towards pursuing social as well as cognitive factors when investigating the potential of corrective feedback. These data were collected from university students learning French in a foreign language context. The focus is corrective feedback and the extent to which learning outcomes of feedback might be affected by variables related to the student's prior knowledge, as well as aspects of the delivery of the feedback. This included, for example, whether the feedback was incidental or intentional, and whether it was initiated by the teacher or the student. Further, we investigate some of the social factors that impact the classroom interactions. We explore how learners' perceptions about their relationships with the teacher and each other might act to shape the interactions that took place in the class, the quality of the interaction, and its outcomes, focusing particularly on the provision and use of corrective feedback in group work. We illustrate the different aspects of interaction that come to light when we employ open-ended research questions and more heuristically oriented research instruments.

The study

Our research question was open-ended and initially exploratory: 'To what extent do social factors within the classroom impact interaction?'

Our data came from interviews with individual learners, where we played them excerpts of interaction from a class they had just participated in and asked them to reflect on aspects of the interactions. The excerpts were from the group and pair work in the classroom, and involved the learners and their classmates. Using a stimulus in an interview technique is a version of stimulated recall, which has been increasingly used in research in SLA (Gass and Mackey 2000) to uncover learners' perceptions about an event at the time it was taking place. Our study was designed to consider learners' views of the event when it took place, and also as it was being discussed, to learn about micro-contextual influences (Watson-Gegeo and Nielsen 2003). Thus, rather than traditional stimulated recall, which exclusively involves very specific questions such as 'what was going through your mind *at that time*', we used the excerpts as prompts for our interviews, and also included open-ended questions, such as: 'tell me more about that extract'; 'what was happening here?' So, in addition to the 'there and then' processing that is the goal of traditional stimulated recall interviews, our learners also provided information about their views and perceptions in the 'here and now'.

Participants

The research was situated in a university elective class offered to second- and third-year undergraduate students of French. There was a wide range of proficiency levels and of experience as language learners and French L2 users. This variability was reflected among the seven students out of a class of thirty who volunteered to participate in the study. Biographical details appear in Table 12.1 below, pseudonyms are given for all participants. Students are ranked according to proficiency level, beginning with the most proficient learner. Four of the seven had learnt French previously in high school, and three of these had been to France for a period. All four of the female participants spoke L1 Mandarin, and had varied proficiency in English. Some had attended 1–3 years of high school in New Zealand.

The course was 'French for Business' and involved four hour-long classes in French each week; its emphasis was oral/aural skills. The textbook was *Français.com* (Penfornis 2002) and included taped dialogues and activities for task-based interactions which were often role-play activities. Each week of lessons used a different chapter of the book, and each week was theme-based. The themes over the three-week period of the current study were: Hotels, Appointments, and Dining Out. The teacher, Patrick, was French, male, bilingual in French and English, and an experienced ESOL teacher and interpreter. This was his first year teaching French in a university setting in New Zealand.

Design

Daily observations and recordings were made of the classes over three weeks and each of the seven students took part in a prompted interview, described above, in the third week. By the third week, students were familiar with the interviewer (the first author), who had also been observing the classes, and were relaxed in talking to her about the class.

Pseudonym	Gender	L1	L2	French in high school	French at university (years)	Experience in French-speaking country
Gerard	M	English	Latin French	Yes	2.5	1 yr exchange
Ben	M	English	French	Yes	2.5	Holiday
Claude	M	English	French	Yes	2.5	None
Laurence	F	Mandarin	English French	Yes	1.5	Holiday
Eve	F	Mandarin	English French	No	2.5	None
Violette	F	Mandarin	English French	No	1.5	None
Yvonne	F	Mandarin	English French	No	1.5	None

Table 12.1 Biodata of participants

Classroom observation with detailed field notes was conducted for every class over the three weeks. All the classroom interaction of the individual participants, including the teacher, was digitally recorded via individual microphones. The data were transcribed by five L1 French speakers and subsequently coded for presence of peer- or teacher-provided corrective feedback, reformulation, and other responses to peer-and teacher feedback. Table 12.2 documents the group and pair work tasks in week 3. The prompts for the interviews consisted of excerpts from the classes in week 3.

During the prompted interviews, participants listened to digital audio recordings of particular segments of their oral interaction during group or pair work that had taken place that day or the previous day. These excerpts were chosen because they included episodes of comprehension or production difficulties, and provision or opportunity for corrective feedback. The excerpts were intended as a trigger for participants to provide insights into their perceptions of factors relating to their interactions. The interview took place in English and/or French according to the participant's preference. Only one participant (Ben) chose to use French in the interview sessions, seeing them as an opportunity for further practice.

The interviews included both non-directive questions, e.g. *so what's going on there?* as well as specific questions, e.g. *why did you say it in English first?* Participants were asked to reflect on the excerpts being played to them, but tangents were also encouraged if participants chose to reflect on other aspects of the class, or on previous episodes. The participants were prompted to reflect on: (*a*) choice of language at particular points in the class interaction (e.g. English, French, Mandarin); (*b*) what was happening at that point in the interaction; (*c*) what they were thinking about; (*d*) how they felt about talking with their particular partner(s) in the task; and (*e*) the goal of the particular task as they saw it.

Week 3	Task name	Task description	Task features
Day 1	*Dinner at Miss Lee's*	Collaborative reconstruction in pairs. Draw up a list of rules of etiquette in China following the description of Miss Lee's visit to a French family for dinner	Shared information Convergent
Day 1	*Booking into a hotel in person*	Role play between a receptionist and a guest	Two-way information gap. Convergent
Day 2	*Deciding what to order*	Discussion task. Choose the dishes for 2 people with specific requirements from the menu at *La Casserole*	No information gap Convergent
Day 3	*Ordering in a restaurant*	Group role play	Two-way information Divergent
Day 4	*Making a complaint*	Dialogue reconstruction based on a list of complaints	One-way information Divergent

Table 12.2 Interactional group work tasks

The first author and a co-researcher coded the transcripts of pair and group work for language-related episodes (LRE)s. LREs were identified as *'any part of a dialogue where language learners talk about the language they are producing, question their language use, or correct themselves or others'* (Swain and Lapkin 1998: 326). The source of each LRE (the error) was identified, according to whether it was self- or peer-initiated, and the LRE was then coded according to its linguistic focus; lexical, grammatical, or phonological. The number of conversational turns involving the LRE was also noted. Inter-rater reliability (IRR) was initially 84.9 percent. Following discussion of differences with a third rater, any episodes with unresolved consensus were excluded. Thus 100 percent agreement was reached. An example of a peer-initiated LRE with a lexical focus is given in Example 1.

(1)
STUDENT A: il y a uh uh il y a beaucoup de choisie choisie [*sic*]
            There's uh uh there's lots of chose chose
STUDENT B: choix ?
            choice?
STUDENT A: oui
            Yes

Results and discussion

In order to address the question 'To what extent do social factors within the classroom impact interaction?' we begin by briefly describing the task-based interaction upon which the prompted interviews were based. We then explore some social factors that appeared to impact aspects of interaction, including participation, and provision and use of feedback. These social factors include relationships with others in the class, shared or not shared histories in the individual experiences of class participants, their perceptions of one another's abilities, and approaches to the tasks.

The excerpts played for the prompted interviews were based on the third week of classes, and contained a sample of the fifteen LREs that took place in those three classes. Thirteen of the LREs involved lexical items as the linguistic focus, and two involved phonology and morphology respectively. Thirteen of these LREs were self-initiated and a peer and the teacher initiated one each. As noted above, the research question asked 'To what extent do social factors within the classroom impact interaction?'

The classroom itself was relatively narrow, and seating was arranged in two columns of rows, four abreast. Generally students sat in the same row in each class, and worked with those around them, with the teacher walking about to offer assistance as required. Task partners changed on occasion due to absentees or task requirements. The L1 Mandarin- and Korean-speaking women tended to sit together on one side of the class, while most of the New Zealand-born students, male and female, tended to sit on the left or at the back of the class. This was partly due to friendship groups and partly to the students' late arrival or quick departure due to the other classes they took.

Relationships between learners in the class

Regarding their participation in class, the students commented that they felt more comfortable speaking in small groups or pairs than in the whole class, and were more likely to take risks in the former context, as indicated by Eve and Violette (all names have been changed), in Examples 2 and 3, and by Ben, a more proficient speaker, in Example 4.

(2)
J: what in what way was [the pair-work task] useful?
E: I think it's uhm because that your neighbor is not she like she's not a teacher or something and I feel like more relaxed

(3)
J: and is it different between talking in front of the whole class and talking just in your pairs does that make a difference?
V: I think there's quite a huge difference because um when you're talking just in a small group you sort of I don't know it's easier to correct each other and it's more like a test trial instead of a formal situation where you're talking to the class.

Ben remarks that he is more relaxed among friends and is more careful about his French when speaking with his teacher, sticking to expressions he is comfortable with.

(4)
B: Ah uhm yeah I'm ah how do you say I'm more relaxed when I talk to people who are my real my close friends uhm I think perhaps it's much more natural for for people to to speak in a more relaxed way to a close friend and you do it in English you do it in French hey it's the fact that they're your friends uhm and they're not going to judge you by ah well if you you make mistakes or whatever when you talk uhm you're you're uhm not worried about making mistakes
J: hmhm
B: when you talk to someone who's more important uhm if I uhm ask the teacher something if I've asked him something ahhh I'm more hesitant but also I ah take a lot of care to make sure that I'm talking in an appropriate way and and make sure that I don't say don't make grammatical and pronunciation mistakes and so on and
J: Yeah

B: maybe maybe yeah I'm more uhm I use language I'm more comfortable with when I talk to him [the teacher] because they're expressions I know well and I don't often make mistakes with uhm that level of language

J: Yeah

B: but when I talk to close friends ah it doesn't bother me if I've made mistakes or or it doesn't bother me as much.

The participants varied in the degree to which they knew, and liked, the peers that they worked with on group and pair tasks. Within the class, there were certain combinations of students that appear to have led to uncollaborative or awkward group or pair interaction. The learners suggested reasons for this in their prompted interviews, either because students didn't know one another, as suggested in Example 5, or because they knew each other too well—and had formed negative associations through past experience, as seen in Example 18 in the next section.

(5)

J: is there anyone in the class that you feel nervous talking to?

V: the lecturer [laughter] uhm I don't know I haven't really talked to a lot of people but I found that I h I didn't really know how to talk to uhm this girl I think her name was Helen uhm she sits next to me sometimes and she has this expression like I don't understand you

J: oh ok

V: and so sometimes I feel quite nervous talking to her uhm like in a group situation as well because yeah like she just doesn't seem to understand and so I'll be thinking well is this my pronunciation problem or like am I saying this correctly or yeah [laughter]

These data suggest that both context (whether whole class or small group) and the relationships between the interlocutors make a difference to the extent to which learners may be willing to take risks in language use, as documented in other research (e.g. Cao 2009; Tarone 2009). A fruitful area for research may be to explore whether the potential of interaction for learning is mediated by the social relationships between peer interlocutors.

Provision of feedback

There was a relatively wide disparity in the class between students in terms of experience in learning French and in level of proficiency. Some members of the class seemed to be recognized by their peers as more expert than others. Some students appreciated the expertise that fellow learners brought and welcomed modeling and feedback from them, as seen in Eve's description of two partners, both heritage learners, in Examples 6 and 7.

(6)

J: what's good about working with them?

E: because Pierre and Robert they are like like lecturers yeah

J: you mean they're really good in their French

E: yes

J: yeah do they help you a lot

E: yeah because we know uhm one semester before in the we were in the same class.

(7)

E: uhm sometimes I think uhm Pierre and Robert they will like said *oh you are wrong* you need to say it XX and that but others I think it's like me they just don't care because they understand.

Although Pierre and Robert were not participants in the study and so their point of view is unknown here, from another participant, Claude, we see a similar scenario of help being given to a less proficient peer. In Examples 8 and 9, Claude provides scaffolding in English and through modeling. Claude usually worked with the same partner, as they were often both late arriving from other classes and sat at the back. In Example 8, Claude and his partner rehearsed the task in English first, then in French, then reenacted the whole thing, perfecting their lines. In Example 9, Claude models his partner's lines for him in French. These data suggest peer correction and modeling can be a useful resource in the class within unmatched proficiency pairing.

(8)

J: OK and do you two f= do you find it easier to work it out in English first and then say it in the French? Like how come you didn't say it just directly [in the French?

C: [in French? Um (laughs) I I think I was trying to make it clear for Matt because um he had told that it had been a while since he had done French [and um (.) um I was just trying to

J: [uhuh

C: make it a bit clear for him what I was asking him

(9)

J: [plays tape]

C: yeah so I said *à quelle heure* there and he says *à quelle heure*

J: yeah

[...]

C: um (. .) yeah that's me prompting Matt to ask me what time does the restaurant close

J: ah OK so you're wanting him= *he's* the one who's supposed to=

C: he yeah he's supposed to ask me er what time does the restaurant close.

However, several of the participants also reported reluctance to correct one another, particularly if the error did not impede understanding. This is expressed below by Violette in Example 10 and Ben in Example 11, each for different reasons: Violette, due to lack of confidence and Ben, because he doesn't feel it his role, as a peer, and because he wishes to maintain the guise of the task itself, continuing in French for as long as possible.

(10)
v: think most of the time uhm because we're still learning we don't
       really correct each other because we're afraid that we might be
       wrong ourselves
j: hmhm
v: and or maybe we have misinterpreted the meaning yeah.

(11)
j: When the others when the other students make mistakes for
       example the warriors they don't know how to say XX uhm do you
       correct them or ?
b: Ah sometimes but not that often I think uhm
j: do you notice it do you=
b: Normally yes normally it does throw me a bit but uhm I don't want
       to be uhm I make mistakes myself so uhm I don't want to say oh no
       no no you can't say it like that you're meant to say blablablablabla
       because I'm a stu...student too and I'm not better than them than
       them so uhm I don't want to be better than them.

Ben's reflection on another task, a role play between a hotel receptionist and guest, in which his partner's incorrect use of the language makes the discourse illogical, demonstrates his difficulty with the dual functions of language pedagogy: on the one hand a context for L2 use, in this case a role-play, and on the other a didactic context in which learners receive instruction on language form (Ulichny 1996; Breen 2001; see Batstone 2002). In reporting room availability, Ben's partner had translated the English 'a bit busy' incorrectly as 'peu occupé', literally, 'little occupied'. Ben realizes the error but is unsure how to respond. Although in the transcript of the class (Example 12 below), this conundrum barely shows up, Ben notes in the interview, Example 13, that the scene presented him with a conflict: whether to remain 'in the play', or to 'ruin the game' and rectify the error explicitly. His partner had not understood the error she had made, but recognized there was a problem and did ask Ben what 'peu occupé' meant once their role play was over, suggesting she too recognized a distinction between role-play discourse and classroom discourse (open for pedagogy).

(12)   Role play in a hotel: booking a room
s: bonjour monsieur
       Good day sir
b: bonjour...j'ai une réservation pour une nuit , mais je voudrais
       rester deux nuits, est-ce que c'est possible?

Good day... I've got a reservation for one night but I'd like to stay
for two nights. Is that possible?

S: un moment... désolée monsieur mais l'hôtel est peu occupé en ce
moment
Just a moment... I'm sorry sir but the hotel isn't full up at the
moment

B: peu occupé ? Alors pas grand chose si je veux rester deux nuits? *Not*
full up? So it's not a problem if I want to stay two nights?

S: XX

B: oui enfin (.) tout va bien alors
Yes so that's ok then?

B: Alors si l'hôtel est peu occupé je peux enfin rester deux nuits
Look if the hotel's not full I can stay two nights then?

(13)

B: I think that she that she made a little mistake in uhm her mind
and she got a bit confused she says sorry sir it's not full it's not
full sir and that and yeah and that stopped the conversation a bit
and I don't know exactly uhm what to do to re... re... restart the
conversation because I was like I I can't know what she means
because I don't have if you p... if you play along if you play along
and you can't look at what's written over there in the book and you
believe you're really in a hotel and you say yeah I'd like to stay 2
nights XX and the receptionist says sorry the hotel isn't busy, I'm
thinking hey? [...] well for me it was quite difficult to decide if I
should ruin the game a bit and say uhm *peu occupé* that means uhm
not many people.

Most learners in this small group of seven reported feeling comfortable
testing hypotheses, trying out new language, and potentially making errors.
However, only a couple of learners felt comfortable providing feedback to
their peers. Their comments provide reasons for why this might be the case,
suggesting that their relationships with one another, their histories with their
peers, and their own orientation to the task all impact the interaction and
the provision of feedback. The distinction between the pedagogic roles that
learners can take in interaction, for example, negotiator, corrector, clarifier,
and so on, and their social roles is also important. In both experimental and
classroom-based research carried out in the interaction paradigm, mutual
comprehension is foregrounded, with less emphasis on learners' social roles
and relationships. These data suggest it may sometimes be worth considering such social issues. In the classroom context, they also serve to illustrate
conflicting relationships between social roles and pedagogic roles as pointed
out by Allwright (1996: 210–11),

there is an inherent conflict between the social and the pedagogic pressures that obtain
in the classroom... new material must itself, almost by definition, pose challenges for

learners...and such challenges must hold the risk of upsetting the social equilibrium in a classroom group, because any difficulty learners may have in coping with the new material is potentially embarrassing to such learners...this may be why...teachers and their learners may prefer even to conspire with each other, covertly, to allow social considerations to outweigh the pedagogic ones.

The comments made by learners in our study support Allwright's arguments in this respect.

Learners' perceptions about the tasks, their group, and pairwork

We found considerable variation among the seven participants in terms of how they viewed a particular task. This impacted the nature of their performance, and the provision and use of feedback. In the previous section, we saw how two learners differed in the extent to which they felt it was appropriate to provide feedback to their partner or to scaffold their performance through modeling. In the following excerpts, we also see differences in the way they perceive and approach the task. Most participants reported that tasks provided a chance for them to practice the target forms, or to use phrases from the textbook in a partially authentic context. For example, for a role play involving ordering food in a restaurant, Ben states that he used the textbook as his resource, Example 14.

(14)

B: and yes I try to use phrases er er from the text er I had my book in front of me and I found some things in it which are like er *je vais prendre une salade* [I'll have a salad] blah blah blah and [teacher] told us to try and use the things so I saw them and I thought why not I er (..) borrowed that way of saying *je vais prendre une salade de tomates* [I'll have a tomato salad].

By contrast, however, Gerard, a very confident and fluent speaker of French, orients quite differently to the task and does not look at the book at all. Rather, Gerard and his friend see the task as an opportunity to act out a different persona: '*I was playing up the annoyed customer*'. It is clear that Gerard considers the task a chance to play-act 'being French' (not just using French); he uses as his reference point not the textbook, as other students do, but his own experiences of living with a host family over one year in France. This is seen in Example 15 in which Gerard recalls what he was thinking about at the time of the role play he enacted with his friend and a third student, Robert, as he listens to a recording of it.

(15)

G: Robert wasn't in the best of moods so he wasn't into mucking round too much...I was thinking of a good wine to recommend

G: I was thinking about how my host brother was always very proud of the Côtes de Rhone wine and so at the dinner table he would always say oh we should have the Côtes de Rhone wine

J: you all sounded like you were at a restaurant

G: I was playing up the annoyed customer and I was like 'eh garçon' I was ordering formally for us (. . .) cos that's the way the French do it

G: [I was thinking about] just going out with my host family and . . . only one person orders.

Examples 16 and 17 provide excerpts of the task interaction itself. Robert is cast as the waiter and plays a minimal role, taking infrequent turns compared to the others. In the task transcript, Robert plays his role very seriously, follows the textbook script, for the most part produces accurate and appropriately formal language throughout as a waiter, but has difficulty taking an order from Gerard and Florence, who, by contrast, joke and laugh, take their time to order and engage in extended banter about wine and cheese, switching to English at times.

(16)

R: = Vous avez fait votre choix mesdames, messieurs?=
      Have you made your choice mesdames, messieurs?

R: [Tu prends quoi] monsieur?
      [You'll take what] monsieur?

G: Côtes du Rhône?

F: C'est bon(>) mais euh:: tu penses qu'ils ont le Min, euh: le Dom Pérignon mille neuf cent (.) quatre-vingt:quatre ?
      Thats good but ah you think they have the Min the Dom Pérignon 1984?

R: Hummmm

G: Pour des apéritifs ?
      And for aperitifs ?

R: Euh, alors
      well

F: C'est une bonne année ?
      Is it a good year ?

G: Bon, éc, ecoutez-moi(>) [petit rire] (.) On veut une bouteille de Dom Pérignon(>)
      Right, listen, [laughs] We'd like a bottle of Dom Pérignon

R: Qu'est-ce que vous prenez en entrée?
      What will you have as entrée?

G: Euh: on n'a pas choisi [rire] (.) nos repas
      Ah, we haven't decided [laughs] on our dinner

F: Is it a good vintage?

G: Dom Pérignon [brou]???

F: Oui(>) le::, no like, what's the word for vintage

G: Yeah I'd say vintage in (.) [—]
F: [Singing]
G: [Laughs] [talks in English about wine and the difficulty of knowing wine from different countries]
R: You would like to order or::?
G: Oui, d'accord(>) [rire des filles] Pour les poissons, ma chère dame, veut:: une verre du: moitié Vodka ou:: =
   Yes, all right [girls laughing] For fish, my dear lady wa:nts a half glass of Vodka o::r

(17)
R: Oui (>), comme plat principal, qu'est-ce que vous prenez?
   Yes, what would you like as a main course?
G: Je prends le coq au vin(>). La dame ici: elle veut bien::
   I'll have the coq au vin. The lady here: she'd like::
R: Euh:, désolé monsieur =
   Uhm sorry sir
G: =Il dit [voix comique et feignant l'exaspération] ici, y a un entre nous(.) qui peut commander
   He says [putting on a comical voice and pretending to be annoyed] here, there is one among us(.) able to order.
R: Excusez-nous monsieur, euh :, il n'y a plus de coq au vin(>)
   I'm terribly sorry, sir, ah : we've run out of coq au vin
G: Ah [d'un air déçu] il n'y a plus de coq au vin!
   Oh [sounding disappointed] there's no more coq au vin!
F: Ah, mince alors!
   Oh, damn it!

In Example 18 from the prompted interview following this task, Gerard comments on this role-play sequence conducted with his close friend, Florence, and Robert. All three had been in classes together in previous years and all had high levels of fluency in French. However Gerard reported believing that Robert disliked him and his partner, as did other members of the class. Referring to a previous year, Gerard recounts *'we got told that we scoffed and made other students feel uncomfortable'*. Gerard, for his part, perceives Robert's behavior as rather surly and attributes it to Robert's dislike for his partners, and general disinterest/fatigue.

(18)
G: [hear tape 'oui d'accord'] that's Robert 'just fucking order it. Stop [m]ucking around like Kiwis'.
J: OK [tape]. So what's going on there?
G: That's me ordering formally again like 'cos he's… Robert prompted me so he said ok the way he does (…) skadaaa:::
J: Yeah

G: 'are you guys actually gonna tell me the drinks' and because
      Messieurs/dames
J: And you're laughing?
G: And because its because Florence has also lived in France you
      wouldn't= that's more of a drink you'd go and have at a club rather
      than with dinner because it's a lot of vodka to have in a glass= and
      then the teacher said Ah, you're being very formal over there kind
      of thing so (...) *formel hein* so I was like (...) drinking vodka (...)
      it's not quite the point
      [Tape playing]
G: That's Florence.
J: So what's going on there?
G: Uhm, I ordered the drinks...ah so I ordered ah the wine and then
      Florence wanted cheese with her vodka as you do round small parts
      of Russia uhm and (...) and so she wanted to know which cheese.
      And like Robert was like 'oh yeah really fuck I don't care'. Sorry
      if I'm being uhm he wasn't really into the whole exercise and um
      Florence didn't want to was just playing it more and more saying
      oh well...I want something strong and well you can always get the
      [Roquefort] and Florence was sort of like taken back and going like
      oh yeah 'really getting into this' and I'm like 'oh yeah so inspiring'
      [sarcastically] 'really getting into this aren't you?'

What we see here is a relationally mismatched group. Although their proficiency in French is congruent, they differ in how they carry out the task
(Robert follows the script, while Gerard and Florence put on an act and
'get into it' more), and their past experiences in previous classes appear to
have led to a mutual distrust. Gerard and Florence are close friends, both
part of drama groups, both enjoy play-acting. Gerard criticizes Robert
for 'not getting into it'. The relationship between the three, and their
past histories in previous classes, likely impact on the participation of
each. In a study of university students learning FL Arabic, Mackey et al.
(2007) similarly point out the effect of a learner's dislike of their partner
and subsequent unwillingness to listen to him/her, and, thus, to benefit
from feedback, as seen in Examples 19 and 20. On a close examination of
stimulated recall data, Mackey et al. found six learners mentioned reasons
for why they were *not* listening to corrective feedback directed at their
classmates.

(19)
*I wasn't even trying to understand cause whenever Graham says
anything I just kind of try to pretend that he doesn't exist. So yeah in
my head I was saying, 'shut up Graham, shut up Graham.' But I guess
I wasn't really paying attention which is I guess a basic pattern in this
class.*

(20)

*I was maybe just angry at Martha. Yeah, I remember actually trying to
follow what she was saying and then kind of ... stopping, just tired of
listening to her.*

A further analysis of the data in the Mackey et al. study showed that, under-
standably, when learners provided reasons why they were not listening, their
perceptions about the linguistic target of the episodes overlapped with the
teachers' intentions when providing the feedback only 11 percent of the
time.

The Mackey et al. data, and those from our study reported here, clearly
point to the idea that social relationships can influence learners' perceptions
and use of feedback in task-based interaction. Since perception and use of
feedback has been shown to impact learning, it can logically be suggested that
the social relationships might be impacting opportunities to learn.

Learners' perceptions about the teacher's expectations

In the assessment for this class, students were awarded marks for class participation and were thus under some pressure to perform orally. In Example 21,
Yvonne, an immigrant from China, and one of the least proficient students in
the class, reflects on an excerpt which was the follow-up to the restaurant role-
play task (illustrated in Examples 16 and 17). The teacher had invited anyone
in the class to present their role play in front of the class. After several increasingly awkward moments of silence, Gerard and Ben (from separate groups)
volunteered. While listening to a replay of the interaction, the researcher asks
Yvonne if she had considered volunteering. Yvonne reflects on her reasons
for not taking the opportunity to participate in a role play, in spite of a desire
to do so. She and, by her report, her classmates, perceive the teacher as not
seeking their participation at this point.

(21)

J: did you think of volunteering?
Y: ah I I want to but I we all got XX we all got the same opinion that
      because our teacher prefers student who can speak fluent French ah
      he doesn't really encourage us
J: hmhm why do you think that?
Y: mmm [laughter] he never look at XX XX he just look at some
      student are fluent like Girard.

Later in the same session, Yvonne recalls another incident in class that
prompted her unwillingness to volunteer in whole class sessions. In that
incident, which had occurred two weeks previously, Yvonne volunteered
an answer during a class discussion on why tourists choose to go on tours.
The teacher had difficulty understanding Yvonne's suggestion and had to ask
her several times to repeat herself, finally abandoning the topic. Neither the

teacher nor the student realized the problem: Yvonne had wanted to explain that people prefer tours in order to avoid getting lost, but used the verb *se tromper* (to make a mistake) instead of *se perdre* (to get lost).

(22)
J: so when he asks for a volunteer what do you think then do you=
Y: =ah= I just want to raise my hand and speak but XX XX one time
      I speak why I he said why people pay for like not join tourist group I
      said oh one advantage is they don't get lost but [laughter] he didn't
      understand me as soon as yes so I several times I write down the
      XX XX I was so embarrassed I didn't want to do.

This episode was also commented on by other participants. In Example 23 below, another student comments on her dislike of talking in class, preferring to remain silent rather than risk embarrassment.

(23)
J: so first do you think about whether you feel you can do this or not
      before you volunteer?
E: yeah because er I remember when Patrick [the teacher] asked some
      volunteers and a girl sit in front and she she said something and
      I didn't understand and I think um Patrick he didn't understand
      and I think the girl is like 'oh'
J: oh yeah yeah yeah
E: yeah so I don't want to be that
J: (laughs) so you're afraid to make a mistake like that [in case he
      doesn't
E: [yeah
J: understand you [or something like that yeah
E: [yeah   yeah

These data indicate that shared experiences within the class impact on learners' perceptions of themselves and of their teacher's perceptions. In this way, these experiences appear to sculpt their behavior in the class and the degree to which they interact. Since interaction provides learning opportunities, it is potentially the case that learners' social roles within the class impact their provision and use of these opportunities, and possibly their L2 developmental outcomes. Previous work has looked at learner interpretations (for example, Mackey, Gass, and McDonough 2000) but not from a social perspective. This chapter shows that taking a closer look at the data can shed even more light on how learners interpret the input they receive.

Conclusion

The interviews in this study reveal an interesting blend of the personal and the social which underlie the nature of learners' participation in interaction, including their provision and use of feedback. Learners reported feeling generally more comfortable speaking with their peers in pair or group work than in the whole class, and being more likely to take risks in small group settings. Second, with regard to provision of feedback, learners noted an inherent conflict between achieving accuracy and authenticity of the task. Provision of feedback to peers was also seen as problematic by some learners, who felt it negated positions of equality between peers. In a few cases, where a level of friendship had already been established and there was a history of one peer helping another, feedback was provided without embarrassment and welcomed. Finally, variation in how students approached tasks in group and pair work seemed in part a function of their proficiency, past experiences, and personalities. In role-play situations, for example, some learners approached the task as a script to be perfected, planning it in English before rehearsing it in French, and modeling parts for partners of weaker proficiency. Others acted out the script as a play, using formulaic sequences from the textbook script, yet refraining from overt feedback or requests for help which might belie the central activity of the role play. Some participants looked at each activity as a chance to shift identity and play at 'being French', using past experiences in France as a guide rather than the textbook itself. Relationships between participants, and their shared histories, impacted their participation, motivation, and even reports about how much enjoyment they got out of task-based interaction. Mackey and Polio (2009: 5), discussing the major tenets of the interaction approach, suggest that 'social factors, including motivation, can affect access to input, type and frequency of feedback, and willingness to produce output, as well as the attention learners pay to language'. Long's 1996 version of the interaction hypothesis took account of then-new work demonstrating the importance of cognitive resources, particularly attention, and working memory capacity, in processing language during interaction. Mackey and Polio (2009) build on Gass and Mackey (2007) to acknowledge the potential for social considerations to mediate the processes and outcomes of interaction as part of the hypothesis. The next logical step for empirical research is to consider to what extent social factors impact on learning, directly or indirectly, and to explore this range of 'social factors' (motivation, identities, relationships, past histories). Similarly, the next step in theory development is to better articulate the hypothesis. In other words, we believe that future research could profitably investigate the interplay between cognitive and social factors and how these, individually and in concert might impact the developmental outcomes of interaction in instructional contexts. Investigating how social factors can impact not just interaction but how the interrelationships, in turn, might impact learning, is a central issue for interaction research and if a relationship can reliably be found, it should lead to an update of the interaction approach. It is hoped that this edited collection, bringing together social theorists and cognitivists, will foster such research and make testable links that will help broaden all our horizons.

Bibliography

Adjémian, C. 1976. 'On the nature of interlanguage systems'. *Language Learning* 26: 297–320.

Ainsworth, S. and A. T. Loizou. 2003. 'The effects of self-explaining when learning with texts or diagrams'. *Cognitive Science* 27: 669–81.

Aleven, V. A. and K. R. Koedinger. 2002. 'An effective metacognitive strategy: learning by doing and explaining with a computer-based cognitive tutor'. *Cognitive Science* 26: 147–79.

Alibali, M. W., M. Bassok, K. O. Solomon, S. E. Syc, and S. Goldin-Meadow. 1999. 'Illuminating mental representations through speech and gesture'. *Psychological Science* 10: 327–33.

Aljaafreh, A. and J. P. Lantolf. 1994. 'Negative feedback as regulation and second language learning in the Zone of Proximal Development'. *The Modern Language Journal* 78: 465–83.

Allen, L. Q. 1995. 'The effects of emblematic gestures on the development and access of mental representations of French expressions'. *The Modern Language Journal* 79: 521–9.

Allen, L. Q. 2000. 'Nonverbal accommodations in foreign language teacher talk'. *Applied Language Learning* 11: 155–76.

Allwright, D. 1996. 'Social and pedagogic pressures in the language classroom: the role of socialization' in H. Coleman (ed.): *Society and the Language Classroom*. Cambridge: Cambridge University Press.

Andersen, R. (ed.). 1983. *Pidginization and Creolization as Language Acquisition*. Rowley, Mass.: Newbury House.

Andersen, R. 1984. 'The one to one principle of interlanguage construction'. *Language Learning* 34/4: 77–95.

Antón, M. 1999. 'The discourse of a learner-centered classroom: sociocultural perspectives on teacher-learner interaction in the second-language classroom'. *The Modern Language Journal* 83: 303–18.

Antón, M. and F. DiCamilla. 1999. 'Socio-cognitive functions of L1 collaborative interaction in the L2 classroom'. *The Modern Language Journal* 83/2: 233–47.

Arievitch, I. M. 2003. 'A potential for an integrated view of development and learning: Galperin's contribution to sociocultural psychology'. *Mind, Culture, and Activity* 10: 278–88.

Atkinson, D. 2002. 'Toward a sociocognitive approach to second language acquisition'. *The Modern Language Journal* 86: 525–45.

Atkinson, D. 2008. 'A sociocognitive approach to language acquisition: how mind, body, and world work together in SLA'. Unpublished manuscript.

Atkinson, D. Forthcoming *a*. 'Introduction' in D. Atkinson (ed.) forthcoming *c*.

Atkinson, D. Forthcoming *b*. 'A sociocognitive approach to second language acquisition: how mind, body, and world work together in SLA' in Atkinson (ed.) forthcoming *c*.

Atkinson, D. (ed.). Forthcoming *c*. *Alternative Approaches to Second Language Acquisition*. London: Routledge.

Atkinson, D. Forthcoming *d*. 'Extended, embodied cognition and second language acquisition'. *Applied Linguistics*.

Atkinson, D., E. Churchill, T. Nishino, and H. Okada. 2007. 'Alignment and interaction in a sociocognitive approach to second language acquisition'. *The Modern Language Journal* 91/2: 169–88.

Bachman, L. and A. S. Palmer. 1993. *Language Testing in Practice*. Oxford: Oxford University Press.

Bakhtin, M. M. 1929/1984. *Problems in Dostoevsky's Poetic*, ed. and trans. C. Emerson and M. Holquist. Minneapolis: University of Minnesota Press.

Bakhtin, M. M. 1981. *The Dialogic Imagination*. Austin: University of Texas Press. (Original work published 1975).

Bakhtin, M. M. 1986. *Speech Genres and Other Later Essays*. Austin: University of Texas Press. (Original work published 1979).

Barselou, L. 2008. 'Grounded cognition'. *Annual Review of Psychology* 59: 617–45.

Bateson, G. 1972. *Steps to an Ecology of Mind*. Chicago: University of Chicago Press.

Batstone, R. 2002. 'Contexts of engagement: a discourse perspective on "intake" and "pushed output" '. *System* 30: 1–14.

Batstone, R. 2006. 'Recontextualizing focus on form' in S. Fotos and H. Nassaji (eds.): *Form-Focused Instruction and Teacher Education: Studies in Honour of Rod Ellis*. Oxford: Oxford University Press.

Batstone, R. 2007. 'A role for discourse frames and learner interpretation in focus on form'. *New Zealand Studies in Applied Linguistics* 13/1: 55–68.

Bayley, R. and J. Langman. 2004. 'Variation in the group and the individual: evidence from second language acquisition'. *International Review of Applied Linguistics* 42: 303–18.

Bayley, R. and D. Preston (eds.). 1996. *Second Language Acquisition and Linguistic Variation*. Amsterdam: John Benjamins.

Bayley, R. and S. R. Schecter (eds.). 2003. *Language Socialization in Bilingual and Multilingual Societies*. Clevedon: Multilingual Matters.

Bayley, R. and E. Tarone. Forthcoming. 'Variationist perspectives' in S. Gass and A. Mackey (eds.): *Handbook of Second Language Acquisition*. New York: Routledge.

Beebe, L. 1977. 'The influence of the listener on code-switching'. *Language Learning* 27: 331–9.

Beebe, L. 1980. 'Sociolinguistic variation and style-shifting in second language acquisition'. *Language Learning* 30: 433–47.

Beebe, L. and H. Giles. 1984. 'Speech accommodation theories: a discussion in terms of second language acquisition'. *International Journal of Sociology of Language* 46: 5–32.

Bell, A. 1984. 'Language style as audience design'. *Language in Society* 13: 145–204.

Benet-Martinez, V. and J. Haritatos. 2005. 'Bicultural identity integration (BII): components and psychological antecedents'. *Journal of Personality* 73/4: 1015–49.

Bigelow, M. and E. Tarone. 2004. 'The role of literacy level in SLA: doesn't *who* we study determine *what* we know?' *TESOL Quarterly* 38/4: 689–700.

Bigelow, M., R. delMas, K. Hansen, and E. Tarone. 2005. 'Literacy and the processing of oral recasts in SLA'. Paper given at AILA, Madison, Wisconsin, USA.

Bigelow, M., R. delMas, K. Hansen, and E. Tarone. 2006. 'Literacy and the processing of oral recasts in SLA'. *TESOL Quarterly* 40: 1–25.

Birdwhistell, R. L. 1970. *Kinesics and Context: Essays on Body Motion Communication*. Philadelphia: University of Pennsylvania Press.

Bitchener, J., S. Young, and D. Cameron. 2005. 'The effect of different types of corrective feedback on ESL student writing'. *Journal of Second Language Writing* 14: 191–205.

Block, D. 2003. *The Social Turn in Second Language Acquisition*. Edinburgh: Edinburgh University Press.

Block, D. 2006. *Multilingual Identities in a Global City: London Stories*. London: Palgrave.

Bloome, D. 1994. 'Reading as a social process in a middle school classroom' in D. Graddol, J. Maybin, and B. Stierer (eds.): *Researching Language and Literacy in Social Context*. Clevedon: Multilingual Matters.

Bondevik, S. G. 1996. 'Foreigner talk: when does it occur and why?' Paper presented at the Eleventh World Congress, AILA. Jyvaskyla, Finland.

Bourdieu, P. 1977. *Outline of a Theory of Practice*. Cambridge: Cambridge University Press.

Breen, M. 2001. 'The social context for language learning: a neglected situation' in C. Candlin and N. Mercer (eds.): *English Language in its Social Context: A Reader*. London: Routledge.

Bremer, K., C. Roberts, M. Vasseur, M. Simonot, and P. Broeder. 1996. *Achieving Understanding: Discourse in Intercultural Encounters*. Harlow: Longman.

Brock, C. 1986. 'The effects of referential questions on ESL classroom discourse'. *TESOL Quarterly* 20: 47–59.

Broner, M. 2001. 'Impact of interlocutor and task on first and second language use in a Spanish Immersion program'. *CARLA Working Paper* 18. Minneapolis: CARLA. Summarized in: <http://www.carla.umn.edu/immersion/broner.html>

Broner, M. and E. Tarone. 2001. 'Is it fun? Language play in a fifth grade Spanish immersion classroom'. *Modern Language Journal* 85: 363–79.

Brooks, F. B. 1993. 'Some problems and caveats in "communicative" discourse: toward a conceptualization of the foreign language classroom'. *Foreign Language Annals* 26: 231–42.

Brooks, F. B. and R. Donato. 1994. 'Vygotskyan approaches to understanding foreign language discourse during communicative tasks'. *Hispania* 77: 262–74.

Brooks, F. B., R. Donato, and J. V. McGlone. 1997. 'When are they going to say "it" right? Understanding learner talk during pair-work activity'. *Foreign Language Annals* 30: 524–41.

Brooks, L., M. Swain, S. Lapkin, and I. Knouzi. Forthcoming. 'Mediating between scientific and spontaneous concepts through languaging'. *Language Awareness*.

Brown, J. S., A. Collins, and P. Duguid. 1989. 'Situated cognition and the culture of learning'. *Educational Researcher* 18/1: 32–42.

Brown, R. 1973. *A First Language*. Cambridge, Mass.: Harvard University Press.

Bruner, J. S. 1996. 'Frames for thinking: ways of making meaning' in D. Olson and N. Torrance (eds.): *Modes of Thought: Explorations in Culture and Cognition*. New York: Cambridge University Press.

Butcher, K. R. 2006. 'Learning from text with diagrams: promoting mental model development and inference generation'. *Journal of Educational Psychology* 98: 182–97.

Byrne, D. 2002. *Interpreting Quantitative Data*. London: Sage.

Cameron, L. and A. Deignan. 2006. 'The emergence of metaphor in discourse'. *Applied Linguistics* 27/4: 671–90.

Campbell, W. J., B. J. Barnett, and M. McMeniman. 1984. *A review of the Commonwealth English as a Second Language (ESL) Program*. Canberra: Commonwealth Schools Commission.

Canale, M. and M. Swain. 1980. 'Theoretical bases of communicative approaches to second language teaching and testing'. *Applied Linguistics* 1/1: 1–47.

Cao, Y. 2009. 'Understanding the notion of interdependence, and the dynamics of willingness to communicate'. Unpublished doctoral dissertation, University of Auckland, New Zealand.

Carr, T. and T. Curren. 1994. 'Cognitive factors in learning about structured sequences: applications to syntax'. *Studies in Second Language Acquisition* 16: 205–30.

Carrier, K. 1999. 'The social environment of second language listening: does status play a role in comprehension?' *The Modern Language Journal* 83: 65–79.

Carroll, S. 2001. *Input and Evidence: The Raw Material of Second Language Acquisition*. Amsterdam: John Benjamins.

Cathcart, R. and J. Olsen. 1976. 'Teachers' and students' preferences for correction of classroom errors' in J. Fanselow and R. Crymes (eds.): *ON TESOL '76*. Washington DC: TESOL.

Cazden, C. B. 2001. *Classroom discourse: The Language of Teaching and Learning* (2nd edn.). Portsmouth, NH: Heinemann.

Centeno-Cortés, B. and A. Jiménez-Jiménez. 2004. 'Problem-solving tasks in a foreign language: the importance of the L1 in private verbal thinking'. *International Journal of Applied Linguistics* 14: 7–35.

Chandler, J. 2003. 'The efficacy of various kinds of error feedback for improvement in the accuracy and fluency of L2 student writing'. *Journal of Second Language Writing* 12/3: 267–96.

Chaudron, C. 1988. *Second Language Classrooms: Research on Teaching and Learning.* Cambridge: Cambridge University Press.

Chi, M. T. H. 2000. 'Self-explaining expository texts: the dual processes of generating inferences and repairing mental models' in R. Glaser (ed.): *Advances in Instructional Psychology.* Mahwah, NJ: Lawrence Erlbaum.

Chi, M. T. H., N. D. Leeuw, M. Chiu, and C. Lavancher. 1994. 'Eliciting self-explanations improves understanding'. *Cognitive Science* 18: 439–77.

Chi, M. T. H., M. Bassok, M. W. Lewis, P. Reimann, and R. Glaser. 1989. 'Self-explanations: how students study and use examples in learning to solve problems'. *Cognitive Science* 13: 145–82.

Chi, M. T. H., S. A. Siler, H. Jeong, T. Yamanouchi, and R. G. Hausmann. 2001. 'Learning from human tutoring'. *Cognitive Science* 25: 471–533.

Chun, A., R. Day, A. Chenoweth, and S. Luppescu. 1982. 'Errors, interaction, and correction: a study of non-native conversations'. *TESOL Quarterly* 16: 537–47.

Churchill, E., T. Nishino, H. Okada, and D. Atkinson. In press. 'Symbiotic gestures and the visibility of grammar in a sociocognitive approach to second language acquisition'. *The Modern Language Journal* 94: 2.

Clark, A. 1999. 'Embodied, situated, and distributed cognition' in W. Betchel and G. Graham (eds.): *A Companion to Cognitive Science.* Malden, Mass.: Blackwell.

Clark, A. 2001. *Mindware: An Introduction to the Philosophy of Cognitive Science.* Oxford: Oxford University Press.

Clark, A. and D. Chalmers. 1998. 'The extended mind'. *Analysis* 58: 7–19.

Clark, H. H. 2006. 'Social actions, social commitments' in Enfield and Levinson (eds.).

Collentine, J. and B. Freed (eds.). 2004. *Studies in Second Language Acquisition, Special Issue: Learning Context and its Effects on Second Language Acquisition* 26: 153–356.

Collins, R. 2004. *Interaction Ritual Chains.* Princeton: Princeton University Press.

Cooper, D. 1999. *Linguistic Attractors: The Cognitive Dynamics of Language Acquisition and Change.* Amsterdam: John Benjamins.

Corder, S. P. 1967. 'The significance of learners' errors'. *International Review of Applied Linguistics* 5: 161–70.

Corder, S. P. 1967/1981. *Error Analysis and Interlanguage.* Oxford: Oxford University Press.

Coughlan, P. and P. Duff. 1994. 'Same task, different activities: analysis of an SLA task from an activity theory perspective' in J. P. Lantolf and G. Appel (eds.): *Vygotskian Approaches to Second Language Research.* Norwood, NJ: Ablex.

Cumming, A., M. Busch, and A. Zhou. 2002. 'Investigating learners' goals in the context of adult second language writing' in S. Ransdell and M. Barbier (eds.): *New Directions for Research for L2 Writing.* Dordrecht: Kluwer.

Dale, R. and M. Spivey. 2006. 'Unraveling the dyad: using recurrence analysis to explore patterns of syntactic coordination between children and caregivers in conversation'. *Language Learning* 56/3: 391–430.

Davis, E. A. 2003. 'Promoting middle school science students for productive reflection: generic and direct prompts'. *The Journal of the Learning Science* 12: 91–142.

Day, R. (ed.). 1986. *Talking to Learn: Conversation in Second Language Acquisition.* Rowley, Mass.: Newbury House.

de Bot, K., W. Lowie, and M. Verspoor. 2007. 'A dynamic systems theory approach to second language acquisition'. *Bilingualism: Language and Cognition* 10/1: 7–21.

Dewaele, J. M. 2004. 'Vous or tu? Native and non-native speakers of French on a sociolinguistic tightrope'. *International Review of Applied Linguistics* 42: 383–402.

Dewey, J. 1896. 'The reflex arc concept in psychology'. *Psychological Review* 3: 357–70.

Dewey, J. 1985/1917. 'The need for social psychology' in J. A. Boydston (ed.): *John Dewey: The Middle Works, 1899–1924,* x. Carbondale: Southern Illinois University Press.

Dias, P. 2000. 'Writing classrooms as activity systems' in P. Dias and A. Paré (eds.): *Transitions: Writing in Academic and Work Place Settings.* Cresskill, NJ: Hampton.

Dickerson, L. 1974. 'Internal and external patterning of phonological variability in the speech of Japanese learners of English'. Unpublished Ph.D. thesis, University of Illinois.

Doehler, S. P. 2002. 'Mediation revisited: the interactive organization of mediation in learning environments'. *Mind, Culture, and Activity* 9: 21–42.

Donato, R. 1994. 'Collective scaffolding in second language learning' in J. Lantolf and G. Appel (eds.): *Vygotskian Approaches to Second Language Research*. Norwood, NJ: Ablex.

Donato, R. and F. B. Brooks. 2004. 'Literary discussions and advanced speaking functions: researching the (dis)connection'. *Foreign Language Annals* 37/2: 183–99.

Dörnyei, Z. 2005. *The Psychology of the Language Learner*. Mahwah, NJ: Lawrence Erlbaum.

Dörnyei, Z. and E. Ushioda (eds.). 2009. *Motivation, Language Identity and the L2 Self*. Bristol: Multilingual Matters.

Doughty, C. 2001. 'Cognitive underpinnings of focus on form' in P. Robinson (ed.): *Cognition and Second Language Instruction*. Cambridge: Cambridge University Press.

Doughty, C. 2003. 'Instructed SLA: constraints, compensations, and enhancement' in Doughty and Long (eds.).

Doughty, C. and M. Long (eds.). 2003. *The Handbook of Second Language Acquisition*. London: Blackwell.

Doughty, C. and J. Williams (eds.). 1998. *Focus on Form in Classroom Second Language Acquisition*. Cambridge: Cambridge University Press.

Douglas, D. 2004. 'Discourse domains: the cognitive context of speaking' in D. Boxer and A. D. Cohen (eds.): *Studying Speaking to Inform Second Language Learning*. Clevedon: Multilingual Matters.

Duff, P. A. 1995. 'An ethnography of communication in immersion classrooms in Hungary'. *TESOL Quarterly* 25: 505–37.

Duff, P. A. 2002. 'The discursive construction of knowledge, identity, and difference: an ethnography of communication in the high school mainstream'. *Applied Linguistics* 23: 289–322.

Duff, P. A. 2003. 'New directions and issues in second language socialization research'. Plenary talk presented at the Annual Meeting of the American Association for Applied Linguistics, Arlington, Virginia. Also appears in: *Korean Journal of English Language and Linguistics* 3: 309–39.

Duff, P. A. 2004. 'Intertextuality and hybrid discourses: the infusion of pop culture in educational discourse'. *Linguistics and Education* 14: 231–76.

Duff, P. A. 2007a. 'Language socialization as sociocultural theory: insights and issues'. *Language Teaching* 40/4: 309–19.

Duff, P. A. 2007b. 'Problematising academic discourse socialisation' in H. Marriott, T. Moore, and R. Spence-Brown (eds.): *Discourses of Learning and Learning of Discourses*. Sydney: Monash University e-Press/University of Sydney Press.

Duff, P. A. 2008a. 'Language socialization, higher education, and work' in P. Duff and N. Hornberger (eds.): *Encyclopedia of Language and Education*, viii. *Language Socialization*. New York: Springer.

Duff, P. A. 2008b. 'Language socialization, participation and identity: ethnographic approaches' in M. Martin-Jones, M. de Mejia, and N. Hornberger (eds.): *Encyclopedia of Language and Education*, iii. *Discourse and Education*. New York: Springer.

Duff, P. A. 2009. 'Language socialization in a Canadian secondary school: talking about current events' in R. Barnard and M. Torres-Guzman (eds.): *Creating Classroom Communities of Learning: International Case Studies and Perspectives*. Clevedon: Multilingual Matters.

Duff, P. A. Forthcoming a. 'Language socialization and academic discourse'. *Annual Review of Applied Linguistics*.

Duff, P. A. Forthcoming b. 'Language socialization' in N. H. Hornberger and S. McKay (eds.): *Sociolinguistics and Language Education*. Clevedon: Multilingual Matters.

Duff, P. A. Forthcoming c. 'Second language socialization' in A. Duranti, E. Ochs, and B. B. Schieffelin (eds.): *Handbook of Language Socialization*. Malden, Mass.: Blackwell.

Duff, P. A. and N. H. Hornberger (eds.). 2008. *Language Socialization. Encyclopedia of Language and Education*, viii. New York: Springer.

Dulay, H. and M. Burt. 1973. 'Should we teach children syntax?' *Language Learning* 23: 245–58.

Dulay, H. and M. Burt. 1974. 'Natural sequences in child second language acquisition'. *Language Learning* 24: 37–53.

Eisenstein, M. (ed.). 1989. *The Dynamic Interlanguage: Empirical Studies in Second Language Variation*. New York: Plenum.

Elio, R. and J. R. Anderson. 1981. 'The effects of category generalizations and instance similarity on schema abstraction'. *Journal of Experimental Psychology: Human Learning and Memory* 7/6: 397–417.

Elio, R. and J. R. Anderson. 1984. 'The effects of information order and learning mode on schema abstraction'. *Memory and Cognition* 12: 20–30.

Ellis, N. 1998. 'Emergentism, connectionism, and language learning'. *Language Learning* 48: 631–64.

Ellis, N. 2002. 'Frequency effects in language processing: a review with implications for theories of implicit and explicit language acquisition'. *Studies in Second Language Acquisition* 24/2: 143–88.

Ellis, N. and F. Ferreira-Junior. 2009. 'Construction learning as a function of frequency, frequency distribution, and function'. *The Modern Language Journal* 93/3: 370–85.

Ellis, N. and D. Larsen-Freeman. 2006. 'Language emergence: implications for applied linguistics. Introduction to the special issue'. *Applied Linguistics* 27/4: 558–89.

Ellis, N. and D. Larsen-Freeman (eds.). 2009. *Language as a Complex Adaptive System*. *Language Learning* 59 (Supplement 1).

Ellis, R. 2003. *Task-based Language Learning and Teaching*. Oxford: Oxford University Press.

Ellis, R. Forthcoming. 'Theoretical pluralism in SLA: is there a way forward?' in P. Seedhouse, S. Walsh, and C. Jenks, *Conceptualising 'Learning' in Applied Linguistics*. Basingstoke: Palgrave Macmillan.

Ellis, R., H. Basturkmen, and S. Loewen. 2001. 'Learner uptake in communicative ESL lessons'. *Language Learning* 51: 281–318.

Ellis, R., S. Loewen, and R. Erlam. 2006. 'Implicit and explicit corrective feedback and the acquisition of L2 grammar'. *Studies in Second Language Acquisition* 28: 339–68.

Ellis, R. and Y. Sheen. 2006. 'Re-examining the role of recasts in SLA'. *Studies in Second Language Acquisition* 28: 575–600.

Enfield, N. J. and S. C. Levinson (eds.). 2006. *Roots of Human Sociality*. Oxford: Berg.

Erickson, F. 1986. 'Qualitative methods in research on teaching' in M. C. Wittrock (ed.): *Handbook of Research on Teaching* (3rd edn.). London: Macmillan.

Ericsson, K. A. and H. A. Simon. 1998. 'How to study thinking in everyday life: contrasting think-aloud protocols with descriptions and explanations of thinking'. *Mind, Culture, and Activity* 5: 178–86.

Erlich, S. 1997. 'Gender as social practice: implications for second language acquisition'. *Studies in Second Language Acquisition* 19: 421–46.

Evans, J. 2007. 'The emergence of language: A dynamical systems account' in E. Hoff and M. Shatz (eds.): *Handbook of Language Development*. Malden, Mass.: Blackwell.

Everett, D. L. 2005. 'Cultural constraints on grammar and cognition in Piraha: another look at the design features of human language'. *Current Anthropology* 46: 612–46.

Everett, D. L. 2009. 'Piraha culture and grammar: a response to some criticisms'. *Language* 85: 405–42.

Fasold, R. and D. Preston. 2007. 'The psycholinguistic unity of inherent variability: old Occam whips out his razor' in R. Bayley and C. Lucas (eds.): *Sociolinguistic Variation: Theory, Methods, and Applications*. Cambridge: Cambridge University Press.

Fauconier, G. and M. Turner. 2002. *The Way We Think: Conceptual Blending and the Mind's Hidden Complexities*. New York: Basic Books.

Ferris, D. 2002. *Treatment of Error in Second Language Student Writing*. Ann Arbor: University of Michigan Press.

Ferris, D. 2006. 'Does error feedback help student writers? New evidence on the short- and long-term effects of written error corrections' in K. Hyland and F. Hyland (eds.): *Feedback in Second Language Writing. Contexts and Issues.* Cambridge: Cambridge University Press.

Firth, A. 2009. 'Doing *not* being a foreign language learner: English as a *lingua franca* in the workplace and (some) implications for SLA'. *International Review of Applied Linguistics* 47: 127–56.

Firth, A. and J. Wagner. 1997. 'On discourse, communication, and (some) fundamental concepts in SLA research'. *The Modern Language Journal* 81: 285–300.

Fogel, A. 1993. *Developing through Relationships: Origins of Communication, Self, and Culture.* Chicago: University of Chicago Press.

Foster, P. 1998. 'A Classroom Perspective on the Negotiation of Meaning'. *Applied Linguistics* 19/1: 1–23.

Garrett, P. B. and P. Baquedano-Lopez. 2002. 'Language socialization: reproduction and continuity, transformation and change'. *Annual Review of Anthropology* 31: 339–61.

Gass, S. 1997. *Input, Interaction, and the Second Language Learner.* Mahwah, NJ: Lawrence Erlbaum.

Gass, S. 1998. 'Apples and oranges: or, why apples are not oranges and don't need to be'. *The Modern Language Journal* 82/1: 83–90.

Gass, S. 2003. 'Input and interaction' in Doughty and Long (eds.).

Gass, S. and A. Mackey. 2000. *Stimulated Recall Methodology in Second Language Research.* Mahwah, NJ: Lawrence Erlbaum.

Gass, S. and A. Mackey. 2007. *Data Elicitation for Second and Foreign Language Research.* Mahwah, NJ: Lawrence Erlbaum.

Gatbonton, E., P. Trofimovich, and M. Magid. 2005. 'Learners' ethnic group affiliation and L2 pronunciation accuracy: a sociolinguistic investigation'. *TESOL Quarterly* 39: 489–511.

Geeslin, K. 2003. 'A comparison of copula choice: native Spanish speakers and advanced learners'. *Language Learning* 53: 703–64.

Geeslin, K. and P. Guijarro-Fuentes. 2006. 'Second language acquisition of variable structures in Spanish by Portuguese speakers'. *Language Learning* 56: 53–107.

Gibbs, R. W. 1994. *The Poetics of Mind: Figurative Thought, Language and Understanding.* Cambridge: Cambridge University Press.

Gibbs, R. W. 2005. *Embodiment and Cognitive Science.* Cambridge: Cambridge University Press.

Gibson, J. J. 1979. *The Ecological Approach to Visual Perception.* New York: Houghton Mifflin.

Giles, H. and T. Ogay. 2007. 'Communication accommodation theory' in B. B. Whaley (ed.): *Explaining Communication: Contemporary Theories and Exemplars.* Mahwah, NJ: Lawrence Erlbaum.

Gleick, J. 1987. *Chaos: Making a New Science.* New York: Penguin.

Gleitman, L., E. Newport, and H. Gleitman. 1984. 'The current state of the motherese hypothesis'. *Journal of Child Language* 11: 43–79.

Goffman, E. 1972. 'The neglected situation' in P. P. Giglioli (ed.): *Language and Social Context.* Harmondsworth: Penguin.

Goffman, E. 1974/1986. *Frame Analysis: An Essay on the Organization of Experience.* Boston: Northeastern University Press.

Goldberg, A. 2006. *Constructions at Work: The Nature of Generalization in Language.* Oxford: Oxford University Press.

Goldin-Meadow, S. 2005. 'The two faces of gesture: language and thought'. *Gesture* 5: 241–57.

Goldin-Meadow, S. and M. Singer. 2003. 'From children's hands to adults' ears: gestures' role in teaching and learning'. *Developmental Psychology* 39: 509–20.

Goldin-Meadow, S., M. W. Alibali, and R. Breckinridge Church. 1993. 'Transitions in concept acquisition: using the hand to read the mind'. *Psychological Review* 100: 279–97.

Goldin-Meadow, S., H. Nusbaum, K. Spencer, and S. Wagner. 2001. 'Explaining math: gesturing lightens the load'. *Psychological Science* 12: 516–22.

Goldman, S. R. 2008. 'A sociocognitive perspective on the discourse of classroom literacy lesson' in D. Bloome, S. P. Carter, B. M. Christian, S. Madrid, S. Otto, N. Shuart-Faris, and M. Smith (eds.): *Discourse Analysis in Classrooms*. New York: Teachers College Press.

Goldschneider, J. and R. DeKeyser. 2001. 'Explaining the "natural order of L2 morpheme acquisition" in English: a meta-analysis of multiple determinants'. *Language Learning* 51/1: 1–50.

Goldstein, L. 2001. 'For Kyla: what does research say about responding to ESL writers' in T. Silva and P. Matsuda (eds.): *On Second Language Writing*. Mahwah NJ: Lawrence Erlbaum.

Goldstein, L. 2004. 'Questions and answers about teacher written commentary and student revision: teachers and students working together'. *Journal of Second Language Writing* 13/1: 63–80.

Goodwin, C. 1980. 'Restarts, pauses, and the achievement of a state of mutual gaze at turn-beginning'. *Sociological Inquiry* 50: 272–302.

Goodwin, C. 1981. *Conversational Organization: Interaction between Speakers and Hearers*. New York: Academic Press.

Goodwin, C. 2000. 'Action and embodiment within situated human interaction'. *Journal of Pragmatics* 32: 1489–522.

Goodwin, C. 2003. 'The body in action' in J. Coupland and R. Gwin (eds.): *Discourse, the Body, and Identity*. Basingstoke: Palgrave-Macmillan.

Goodwin, C. 2006. 'Human sociality as mutual orientation in a rich interactive environment: multimodal utterances and pointing in aphasia' in Enfield and Levinson (eds.).

Greeno, J. G. 1989. 'A perspective on thinking'. *American Psychologist* 44: 134–41.

Greeno, J. G. 2006. 'Authoritative, accountable positioning and connected, general knowing: progressive themes in understanding transfer'. *Journal of the Learning Sciences* 15/4: 539–50.

Gregg, K. R., M. H. Long, G. Jordan, and A. Beretta. 1997. 'Rationality and its discontents in SLA. *Applied Linguistics* 18/4: 538–58.

Grice, H. P. 1975. 'Logic and conversation' in P. Cole and J. Morgan (eds.): *Syntax and Semantics*, iii. *Speech Acts*. New York: Academic Press.

Guénette, D. 2007. 'Is feedback pedagogically correct? Research design issues in studies of feedback on writing'. *Journal of Second Language Writing* 16: 40–53.

Gumperz, J. J. (ed.). 1982. *Language and Social Identity*. Cambridge: Cambridge University Press.

Haenen, J. 1996. *Piotr Gal'perin: Psychologist in Vygotsky's Footsteps*. New York: Nova Science.

Hall, J. K. 1995*a*. '(Re)creating our worlds with words: a sociohistorical perspective of face-to-face interaction'. *Applied Linguistics* 16/2: 216–32.

Hall, J. K. 1995*b*. ' "Aw man, where you goin'?": interaction and the development of L2 interactional competence'. *Issues in Applied Linguistics*. 6: 37–62.

Hall, J. K. 1997. 'A consideration of SLA as a theory of practice: a response to Firth and Wagner'. *The Modern Language Journal* 81/3: 301–6.

Hall, J. K. 2004. ' "Practicing speaking" in Spanish: lessons from a high school foreign language classroom' in D. Boxer and A. D. Cohen (eds.): *Studying Speaking to Inform Second Language Learning*. Clevedon: Multilingual Matters.

Halliday, M. 1990. 'New ways of meaning: the challenge to applied linguistics'. *Journal of Applied Linguistics* 6: 7–36.

Han, Z. 2002. 'A study of the impact of recasts on tense consistency in L2 output'. *TESOL Quarterly* 36: 543–72.

Harris, R. 1996. *Signs, Language and Communication*. London: Routledge.

Harris, R. 2003. 'On redefining linguistics' in H. G. Davis and T. J. Taylor (eds.): *Rethinking Linguistics*. London: Routledge.

Haugeland, J. 1998. *Having Thought: Essays in the Metaphysics of Mind*. Cambridge, Mass.: Harvard University Press.

Hauser, M.D., N. Chomsky, and W. T. Fitch. 2002. 'The faculty of language: What is it, who has it, and how did it evolve?' *Science* 298: 1569–79.

Hicks, D. 1996. 'Contextual inquiries: a discourse-oriented study of classroom learning' in D. Hicks (ed.): *Discourse, Learning, and Schooling*. New York: Cambridge University Press.

Hopper, P. 1998. 'Emergent grammar' in M. Tomasello (ed.): *The New Psychology of Language*. Mahwah, NJ: Lawrence Erlbaum.

Howard, M. 2004. 'On the interactional effect of linguistic constraints on interlanguage variation: the case of past time marking'. *International Review of Applied Linguistics* 42: 319–34.

Hyland, F. 2000. 'ESL writers and feedback: giving more autonomy to students'. *Language Teaching Research* 4: 33–54.

Hyland, K. and F. Hyland. 2006. 'Feedback on second language students' writing'. *Language Teaching* 39: 83–101.

Hyltenstam, K. and N. Abrahamsson. 2003. 'Maturational constraints in SLA' in Doughty and Long (eds.).

Hymes, D. 1972. 'On communicative competence' in Pride and Holmes (eds.).

Iacoboni, M. 2009. 'Imitation, empathy, and mirror neurons'. *Annual Review of Psychology* 60: 653–70.

Ivanic, R. 2006. 'Language, learning and identification'. *British Studies in Applied Linguistics* 21: 7–29.

Johnson, M. 2004. *A Philosophy of Second Language Acquisition*. New Haven, Conn.: Yale University Press.

Kanno, Y. 2000. 'Bilingualism and identity: the stories of Japanese returnees'. *International Journal of Bilingual Education and Bilingualism* 3/1: 1–18.

Kasper, G. 1997. ' "A" stands for acquisition: a response to Firth and Wagner'. *The Modern Language Journal* 81/3: 307–12.

Keck, C. M., G. Iberri-Shea, N. Tracy-Ventura, and S. Wa-Mbaleka. 2006. 'Investigating the empirical link between task-based interaction and acquisition: a meta-analysis' in Norris and Ortega (eds.).

Kim, J. 2004. 'Issues of corrective feedback in second language acquisition'. *Teachers College, Columbia University Working Papers in TESOL and Applied Linguistics* 4: 1–24.

Kim, Y. Y. 1989. 'Personal, social and economic adaptation: 1975–1979 arrivals in Illinois' in D. W. Haines (ed.): *Refugees as Immigrants: Cambodians, Laotians and Vietnamese in America*. Totowa, NJ: Rowman & Littlefield.

Kingstone, A., D. Smilek, and J. D. Eastwood. 2008. 'Cognitive ethnology: a new approach for studying human cognition'. *British Journal of Psychology* 99: 317–40.

Kinsbourne, M. and J. S. Jordan. 2009. 'Embodied anticipation: a neurodevelopmental interpretation'. *Discourse Processes* 46: 103–26.

Klein, W. 1998. 'The contribution of second language acquisition research'. *Language Learning* 48/4: 527–50.

Knouzi, I., M. Swain, S. Lapkin, and L. Brooks. Forthcoming. 'Self-scaffolding mediated by languaging: microgenetic analysis of high and low performers'. *International Journal of Applied Linguistics*.

Kobayashi, M. 2003. 'The role of peer support in ESL students' accomplishment of oral academic tasks'. *The Canadian Modern Language Review* 59: 337–68.

Kobayashi, M. 2004. 'A sociocultural study of second language tasks: activity, agency, and language socialization'. Unpublished doctoral dissertation, University of British Columbia, Vancouver, BC, Canada.

Kobayashi, M. 2006. 'Second language socialization through an oral project presentation' in G. H. Beckett and P. C. Miller (eds.): *Project-Based Second and Foreign Language Education: Past, Present, and Future*. Greenwich, Conn.: Information Age.

Koch, C. and N. Tsuchiya. 2006. 'Attention and consciousness: two distinct brain processes'. *Trends in Cognitive Science* 11: 16–22.

Kormos, J. 1999. 'Monitoring and self-repair in a second language'. *Language Learning* 49: 303–42.

Kövesces, Z. 2006. *Language, Mind, and Culture: A Practical Introduction*. Oxford: Oxford University Press.

Kowal, M. and M. Swain. 1997. 'From semantic to syntactic processing: how can we promote it in the immersion classroom?' in M. Swain and R. K. Johnson (eds.): *Immersion Education: International Perspectives*. Cambridge: Cambridge University Press.

Kramsch, C. (ed.). 2002. *Language Acquisition and Language Socialization: Ecological Perspectives*. London: Continuum.

Kramsch, C. 2008. 'Ecological perspectives on foreign language education'. *Language Teaching* 41/3: 389–408.

Kramsch, C. and A. Whiteside. 2008. 'Language ecology in multilingual settings. Towards a theory of symbolic competence'. *Applied Linguistics* 29/4: 645–71.

Labov, W. 1972. *Sociolinguistic Patterns*. Philadelphia: University of Pennsylvania.

Lafford, B. 2006. 'The effects of study abroad vs. classroom contexts on Spanish SLA: old assumptions, new insights and future research directions' in C. A. Klee and T. L. Face (eds.): *Selected Proceedings of the 7th Conference on the Acquisition of Spanish and Portuguese as First and Second Languages*. Somerville, Mass.: Cascadilla Proceedings Project.

Lafford, B. (ed.). 2007. *The Modern Language Journal, Focus Volume on the Impact of Firth and Wagner (1997)* 91: 5.

Lakoff, G. and M. Johnson. 1980. *Metaphors We Live By*. Chicago: University of Chicago Press.

Lakoff, G. and M. Turner. 1989. *More Than Cool Reason: A Field Guide to Poetic Metaphor*. Chicago: University of Chicago Press.

Lalande, J. F. 1982. 'Reducing composition errors: an experiment'. *The Modern Language Journal* 66: 140–9.

Lantolf, J. P. (ed.). 2000. *Sociocultural Theory and Second Language Learning*. Oxford: Oxford University Press.

Lantolf, J. P. 2003. 'Intrapersonal communication and internalization in the second language classroom' in A. Kozulin, V. S. Ageev, S. Miller, and B. Gindis (eds.): *Vygotsky's Educational Theory in Cultural Context*. Cambridge: Cambridge University Press.

Lantolf, J. P. 2005. 'Sociocultural and second language learning research: an exegesis' in E. Hinkel (ed.): *Handbook of Research on Second Language Teaching and Learning*. Mahwah, NJ: Lawrence Erlbaum.

Lantolf, J. P. 2006. 'Sociocultural theory and second language learning: state of the art'. *Studies in Second Language Acquisition* 28: 67–109.

Lantolf, J. P. 2007. 'Dialectics and L2 proficiency'. Paper presented at the pre-symposium workshop of the Symposium on Socio-cognitive Approaches to L2 Development. University of Auckland. 11 April 2007. Auckland, NZ.

Lantolf, J. P. and A. Aljaafreh. 1995. 'Second language learning in the zone of proximal development: a revolutionary experience'. *International Journal of Educational Research* 23: 619–32.

Lantolf, J. P. and M. E. Poehner. 2007. *Dynamic Assessment in the Foreign Language Classroom: A Teacher's Guide*: 149 pp. and Video DVD version 1.0. University Park, Pa.: CALPER.

Lantolf, J. P. and M. E. Poehner (eds.). 2008. *Sociocultural Theory and the Teaching of Second Languages*. London: Equinox.

Lantolf, J. P. and S. L. Thorne. 2006. *Sociocultural Theory and the Genesis of Second Language Development*. Oxford: Oxford University Press.

Lapkin, S., M. Swain, and I. Knouzi. 2008. 'Postsecondary French as a second language students learn the grammatical concept of voice: study design, materials development, and pilot data' in J. P. Lantolf and M. Poehner (eds.): *Sociocultural Theory and the Teaching of Second Languages*. London: Equinox.

Larsen-Freeman, D. 1976. 'An explanation for the acquisition order of second language learners'. *Language Learning* 26: 125–34.

Larsen-Freeman, D. 1997. 'Chaos/complexity science and second language acquisition'. *Applied Linguistics* 18/2: 141–65.

Larsen-Freeman, D. 2002. 'Language acquisition and language use from a chaos/complexity theory perspective' in C. Kramsch (ed.): *Language Acquisition and Language Socialization.* London: Continuum.

Larsen-Freeman, D. 2003. *Teaching Language: From Grammar to Grammaring.* Boston, Mass.: Thomson/Heinle.

Larsen-Freeman, D. 2006. 'The emergence of complexity, fluency, and accuracy in the oral and written production of five Chinese learners of English'. *Applied Linguistics* 27/4: 590–619.

Larsen-Freeman, D. 2007. 'Reflecting on the cognitive-social debate in second language acquisition'. *The Modern Language Journal* 91 (Focus Issue): 773–87.

Larsen-Freeman, D. and L. Cameron. 2008. *Complex Systems and Applied Linguistics.* Oxford: Oxford University Press.

Larsen-Freeman, D. and M. Long. 1991. *An Introduction to Second Language Acquisition Research.* London: Longman.

Lave, J. and E. Wenger. 1991. *Situated Learning: Legitimate Peripheral Participation.* Cambridge: Cambridge University Press.

Lavelli, M., A. P. F. Pantoja, H. Hsu, D. Messinger, and A. Fogel. 2004. 'Using microgenetic designs to study change processes' in D. M. Teti (ed.): *Handbook of Research Methods in Developmental Psychology.* Baltimore: Blackwell.

Lazaraton, A. 2004. 'Gesture and speech in the vocabulary explanations of one ESL teacher: a microanalytic inquiry'. *Language Learning* 54: 79–117.

Leather, J. and J. van Dam (eds.). 2003. *Ecology of Language Acquisition.* Dordrecht: Kluwer.

Lee, J. F. 2000. *Tasks and Communicating in Language Classrooms.* New York: McGraw-Hill.

Lee, N., L. Mikesell, A. D. L. Joaquin, A. W. Mates, and J. H. Schumann. 2009. *The Interactional Instinct: The Evolution and Acquisition of Language.* Oxford: Oxford University Press.

Leeman, J. 2003. 'Recasts and L2 development: beyond negative evidence'. *Studies in Second Language Acquisition* 25: 37–63.

Leeuw, N. and M. T. H. Chi. 2003. 'The role of self-explanation in conceptual change learning' in G. Sinatra and P. Pintrich (eds.): *Intentional Conceptual Change*: 55–78. Mahwah, NJ: Lawrence Erlbaum.

Leki, I. 1991. 'The preferences of ESL students for error correction in college level writing classes'. *Foreign Language Annals* 24: 203–18.

Leki, I. 2001. ' "A narrow thinking system". Nonnative-English-speaking students in group projects across the curriculum'. *TESOL Quarterly* 35: 39–67.

Lemke, J. 2000. 'Across the scales of time: artifacts, activities, and meanings in ecosocial systems'. *Mind, Culture and Activity* 7: 273–90.

Lemke, J. 2002. 'Language development and identity: multiple timescales in the social ecology of learning' in Kramsch (ed.).

Leon, D. 1995. *Death and Judgment.* New York: Penguin.

Leont'ev, A. N. 1978. *Activity, Consciousness, and Personality.* Englewood Cliffs, NJ: Prentice Hall.

Leont'ev, A. N. 1981. 'The problem of activity in psychology' in J. V. Wertsch (ed. and trans.): *The Concept of Activity in Soviet Psychology.* Armonk, NJ: M. E. Sharpe.

Levinson, S. C. 2006. 'On the human "interaction engine" ' in Enfield and Levinson (eds.).

Lightbown, P. 1985. 'Can language acquisition be altered by instruction?' in K. Hyltenstam and M. Pienemann (eds.): *Modelling and Assessing Second language Acquisition.* Clevedon: Multilingual Matters.

Liu, G. 1991. 'Interaction and second language acquisition: a case study of a Chinese child's acquisition of English as a second language'. Unpublished manuscript, Deakin University, Melbourne, Australia.

Loewen, S. 2005. 'Incidental focus on form and second language learning'. *Studies in Second Language Acquisition* 27: 361–86.

Loewen, S. and J. Philp. 2006. 'Recasts in the adult English L2 classroom: characteristics, explictness, and effectiveness'. *The Modern Language Journal* 90: 536–56.

Long, M. 1980. 'Input, interaction and second language acquisition'. Unpublished Ph.D. dissertation, UCLA.

Long, M. 1991. 'Focus on form: a design feature in language teaching methodology' in K. de Bot, R. Ginsberg, and C. Kramsch (eds.): *Foreign Language Research in Cross-Cultural Perspective*. Amsterdam: John Benjamins.

Long, M. 1996. 'The role of the linguistic environment in second language acquisition' in W. C. Ritchie and T. K. Bhatia (eds.): *Handbook of Language Acquisition*, ii. *Second Language Acquisition*. New York: Academic Press.

Long, M. 1997. 'Construct validity in SLA research: a response to Firth and Wagner'. *The Modern Language Journal* 81: 318–23.

Long, M. 1998. 'SLA: Breaking the siege'. *University of Hawai'i Working Papers in ESL* 17: 79–129.

Long, M. 2007a. 'Recasts in SLA: the story so far' in Long (2007b).

Long, M. 2007b. *Problems in SLA*. Mahwah, NJ: Lawrence Erlbaum.

Long, M. and C. Doughty. 2003. 'SLA and cognitive science' in Doughty and Long (eds.).

Long, M. and P. Robinson. 1998. 'Focus on form: theory, research and practice' in Doughty and Williams (eds.).

Luria, A. R. 1982. *Language and Cognitive Development*. New York: John Wiley & Sons.

Lybeck, K. 2002. 'Cultural identification and second language pronunciation of Americans in Norway'. *The Modern Language Journal* 86: 174–91.

Lyster, R. 1998. 'Recasts, repetition and ambiguity in L2 classroom discourse'. *Studies in Second Language Acquisition* 20/1: 51–81.

Lyster, R. 2002. 'The importance of differentiating negotiation of form and meaning in classroom interaction' in P. Burmeister, T. Piske, and A Rohde (eds.): *An Integrated View of Language Development: Papers in Honor of Henning Wode*. Trier: Wissenschaftlicher.

Lyster, R. 2004. 'Differential Effects of Prompts and Recasts in Form-Focused Instruction'. *Studies in Second Language Acquisition* 26: 399–432.

Lyster, R. 2007. *Learning and Teaching Languages through Content: A Counterbalanced Approach*. Amsterdam: John Benjamins.

Lyster, R. and H. Mori. 2006. 'Interactional feedback and instructional counterbalance'. *Studies in Second Language Acquisition* 28: 269–300.

Lyster, R. and L. Ranta. 1997. 'Corrective feedback and learner uptake: negotiation of form in communicative classrooms'. *Studies in Second Language Acquisition* 19: 37–66.

McCafferty, S. G. 1998. 'Non-verbal expression and L2 private speech'. *Applied Linguistics* 19: 73–96.

McCafferty, S. G. 2004. 'Space for cognition: gesture and second language learning'. *International Journal of Applied Linguistics* 14: 148–65.

McCafferty, S. G. and G. Stam (eds.). 2008. *Gesture: Second Language Acquisition and Classroom Research*. Mahwah, NJ: Ablex.

McCormick, D. E., and R. Donato. 2000. 'Teacher questions as scaffolded assistance in an ESL classroom' in J. K. Hall and L. S. Verplaetse (eds.): *Second and Foreign Language Learning through Classroom Interaction*. Mahwah, NJ: Lawrence Erlbaum Associates.

McKay, P. (ed.). 1994a. *ESL Development: Language and Literacy in Schools*, i. *Teachers' Manual* (2nd edn.). Canberra: NLLIA.

McKay, P. (ed.). 1994b. *ESL Development: Language and Literacy in Schools*, ii. *Documents on Bandscale Development and Language Acquisition* (2nd edn.). Canberra: NLLIA.

Mackay, S. and S. C. Wong. 1996. 'Multiple discourses, multiple identities: investment and agency in second-language learning among Chinese adolescent immigrant students'. *Harvard Educational Review* 66/3: 577–608.

Mackey, A. 2006a. 'Feedback, noticing and instructed second language learning'. *Applied Linguistics* 27: 405–30.

Mackey, A. 2006*b*. 'From introspections, brain scans, and memory tests to the role of social context: advancing research on interaction and learning'. *Studies in Second Language Acquisition* 28/2: 369–79.

Mackey, A., S. M. Gass, and K. McDonough. 2000. 'How do learners perceive interactional feedback?' *Studies in Second Language Acquisition* 22/4: 471–97.

Mackey, A. and J. Goo. 2007. 'Interaction research: a meta-analysis and research synthesis' in A. Mackey (ed.): *Conversational Interaction in Second Language Acquisition: A Collection of Empirical Studies*. New York: Oxford University Press.

Mackey, A., M. Al-Khalil, G. Atanassova, M. Hama, A. Logan-Terry, and K. Nakatsukasa. 2007. 'Teachers' intentions and learners' perceptions about corrective feedback in the L2 classroom'. *Innovations in Language Learning and Teaching* 1/1: 129–52.

Mackey, A. and C. Polio. 2009. 'Introduction' in A. Mackey and C. Polio (eds.): *Multiple Perspectives on Interaction*. New York: Routledge.

McNeill, D. 1992. *Hand and Mind: What the Hands Reveal about Thought*. Chicago: University of Chicago Press.

McNeill, D. 2003. 'Pointing and morality in Chicago' in S. Kita (ed.): *Pointing: Where Language, Culture, and Cognition Meet*. Mahwah, NJ: Lawrence Erlbaum.

McNeill, D. 2005. *Gesture and Thought*. Chicago: University of Chicago Press.

McNeill, D. and S. Duncan. 2000. 'Growth points in thinking for speaking' in D. McNeill (ed.): *Language and Gesture*. New York: Cambridge University Press.

Markee, N. and G. Kasper (eds.). 2004. 'The special issue: classroom talks'. *The Modern Language Journal* 88/4: 491–500.

Marr, D. 1982. *Vision: A Computational Investigation into the Human Representation and Processing of Visual Information*. New York: W. H. Freeman.

Mead, G. H. 1934. *Mind, Self and Society*. Chicago: University of Chicago Press.

Mehan, H. 1979. *Learning Lessons: Social Organization in the Classroom*. Cambridge, Mass.: Harvard University Press.

Meisel, J., H. Clahsen, and M. Pienemann. 1981. 'On determining developmental stages in second language acquisition'. *Studies in Second Language Acquisition* 3: 109–35.

Miller, J. 2000. 'Language use, identity and social interaction'. *Research on Language and Social Interaction* 33/1: 69–100.

Miller, J. 2003. *Audible Difference: ESL and Social Identity in Schools*. Clevedon: Multilingual Matters.

Milroy, L. 1980. *Language and Social Networks*. Oxford: Basil Blackwell.

Mohanan, K. P. 1992. 'Emergence of complexity in phonological development' in C. Ferguson, L. Menn, and C. Stoel-Gammon (eds.): *Phonological Development*. Timonium, Md.: York.

Morita, N. 2000. 'Discourse socialization through oral classroom activities in a TESL graduate program'. *TESOL Quarterly* 34: 279–310.

Morita, N. 2004. 'Negotiating participation and identity in second language academic communities'. *TESOL Quarterly* 38: 573–603.

Morita, N. and M. Kobayashi. 2008. 'Academic discourse socialization in a second language' in P. Duff and N. Hornberger (eds.): *Language Socialization. Encyclopedia of Language and Education*, viii. 243–55. New York: Springer.

Mougeon, R. and J. M. Dewaele (eds.). 2004. *International Review of Applied Linguistics, Special Issue on Interlanguage Variation* 42: 295–402.

Mwangi, W. and J. Sweller. 1998. 'Learning to solve compare word problems: the effects of example format and generation self-explanations'. *Cognition and Instruction* 16: 173–99.

Nassaji, H. and A. Cumming. 2000. 'What's in a ZPD? A case study of a young ESL student and teacher interacting through dialogue journals'. *Language Teaching Research* 4: 95–121.

Nassaji, H. and M. Swain. 2000. 'A Vygotskian perspective on corrective feedback in L2: the effect of random versus negotiated help in the learning of English articles'. *Language Awareness* 9: 34–51.

Nassaji, H. and G. Wells. 2000. 'What's the use of "Triadic Dialogue"?: an investigation of teacher-student interaction'. *Applied Linguistics* 21/3: 376–406.

Negueruela, E. 2003. 'A sociocultural approach to the teaching-learning of second languages: systemic-theoretical instruction and L2 development'. Unpublished Ph.D. dissertation, Penn State University. University Park, Pa.

Negueruela, E. and J. P. Lantolf. 2006. 'Concept-based pedagogy and the acquisition of L2 Spanish' in R. Salaberry and R. Lafford (eds.): *The Art of Teaching Spanish: Second Language Acquisition from Research to Praxis*. Washington DC: Georgetown University Press.

Negueruela, E., J. P. Lantolf, S. Jordan, and J. Gelabert. 2004. 'The "private function" of gesture in second language speaking activity: a study of motion verbs and gesturing in English and Spanish'. *International Journal of Applied Linguistics* 14: 113–47.

Nichol, L. (ed.). 2003. *The Essential David Bohm*. London: Routledge.

Nicholas, H., P. Lightbown, and N. Spada. 2001. 'Recasts as feedback to language learners'. *Language Learning* 51: 719–58.

Ninio, A. 2006. 'Syntactic development: lessons from complexity theory'. Paper presented at the Eighth Annual Gregynog/Nant Gwrtheyrn Conference on Child Language, April.

Norris, J. M. and L. Ortega (eds.). 2006. *Synthesizing Research on Language Learning and Teaching*. Amsterdam: John Benjamins.

Norris, J. M. and L. Ortega. 2000. 'Effectiveness of L2 instruction: a research synthesis and quantitative meta-analysis'. *Language Learning* 50: 417–528.

Norton, B. 2000a. *Identity and Language Learning: Gender, Ethnicity and Educational Change*. Harlow: Longman.

Norton, B. 2000b. *Language and Identity*. London: Longman/Pearson.

Ochs, E., E. A. Schegloff, and S. A. Thompson (eds.). 1996. *Interaction and Grammar*. Cambridge: Cambridge University Press.

Ochs, E. and B. B. Schieffelin. 2008. 'Language socialization: an historical overview' in Duff and Hornberger (eds.): 3–15.

Ohta, A. S. 2001. *Second Language Acquisition Processes in the Classroom: Learning Japanese*. Mahwah, NJ: Lawrence Erlbaum.

Oliver, R. and A. Mackey. 2003. 'Interactional context and feedback in child ESL classrooms'. *The Modern Language Journal* 87: 519–33.

Ortega, L. 2007a. 'Meaningful L2 practice in foreign language classrooms: a cognitive-interactionist perspective' in R. M. DeKeyser (ed.): *Practice in a Second Language: Perspectives from Applied Linguistics and Cognitive Psychology*. Cambridge: Cambridge University Press.

Ortega, L. 2007b. 'Second language learning explained? SLA across nine contemporary theories' in B. VanPatten and J. Williams (eds.): *Theories in Second Language Acquisition: An Introduction*. Mahwah, NJ: Lawrence Erlbaum.

Pavlenko, A. and A. Blackledge (eds.). 2004. *Negotiation of Identities in Multilingual Settings*. Clevedon: Multilingual Matters.

Pavlenko, A. and J. P. Lantolf. 2000. 'Second language learning as participation and the (re)construction of selves' in Lantolf (ed.).

Penfornis, J. 2002. *Français.com: Méthode de Français Professional et des Affaires*. Paris: CLE International.

Pienemann, M. 1991. 'COALA: a computational system for interlanguage analysis'. *LARC Occasional Paper* 1.

Pienemann, M. and M. Johnston. 1987. 'Factors influencing the development of language proficiency' in D. Nunan (ed.): *Applying Second Language Acquisition Research*. Adelaide: National Curriculum Resource Centre.

Pienemann, M., M. Johnston, and G. Brindley. 1988. 'Constructing an acquisition-based procedure for assessing second language acquisition'. *Studies in Second Language Acquisition* 10: 217–43.

Poole, D. 1992. 'Language socialization in the second language classroom'. *Language Learning* 42: 593–616.

Preston, D. 2000. 'Three kinds of sociolinguistics and SLA: a psycholinguistic perspective' in B. Swierzbin, F. Morris, M. Anderson, C. Klee, and E. Tarone (eds.): *Social and Cognitive*

Factors in Second Language Acquisition: Selected Proceedings of the 1999 Second Language Research Forum. Somerville, Mass.: Cascadilla.

Preston, D. 1989. *Sociolinguistics and Second Language Acquisition*. New York: Basil Blackwell.

Preston, D. 2002. 'A variationist perspective on SLA: psycholinguistic concerns' in R. Kaplan (ed.): *Oxford Handbook of Applied Linguistics*. Oxford: Oxford University Press.

Pride, J. B. and J. Holmes (eds.). 1972. *Sociolinguistics*. Harmondsworth: Penguin.

Qi, D. S. and S. Lapkin. 2001. 'Exploring the role of noticing in a three-stage second language writing task'. *Journal of Second Language Writing* 10: 277–303.

Rampton, B. 1995. *Crossing: Language and Ethnicity among Adolescents*. London: Longman.

Rau, D. V., H. A. Chang, and E. Tarone. 2009. 'Think or sink: Chinese learners' acquisition of the English interdental fricative'. *Language Learning* 59: 581–621.

Reddy, M. 1979. 'The conduit metaphor' in A. Ortony (ed.): *Metaphor and Thought*. Cambridge: Cambridge University Press.

Regan, V. 2004. 'The relationship between the group and the individual and the acquisition of native speaker variation patterns: a preliminary study'. *International Review of Applied Linguistics* 42: 335–48.

Rehner, K. 2002. 'The development of aspects of linguistic and discourse competence by advanced second language learners of French'. Ph.D. dissertation, Toronto: OISE/University of Toronto.

Rehner, K., R. Mougeon, and T. Nadasdi. 2003. 'The learning of sociolinguistic variation by advanced FSL learners: the case of nous vs. on in immersion French'. *Studies in Second Language Acquisition* 25: 127–56.

Reinders, H. and R. Ellis. 2009. 'The effects of two types of input on the acquisition of L2 implicit and explicit knowledge' in R. Ellis, S. Loewen, C. Elder, R. Erlam, J. Philp, and H. Reinders. *Implicit and Explicit Knowledge in Second Language Learning and Teaching*. Clevedon: Multilingual Matters.

Renkl, A. 1997. 'Learning from worked-out examples: a study on individual differences'. *Cognitive Science* 21: 1–29.

Rider, K. 2005. ' "We found this verb, but what do we do with it now?" The collaborative dialogue of two adult learners of Italian as a foreign language'. MA Qualifying Paper, English as a Second Language Program, University of Minnesota.

Ritchie, W. and T. Bhatia (eds.). 1996. *Handbook on Language Acquisition*. New York: Academic Press.

Rittle-Johnson, B. 2006. 'Promoting transfer: effects of self-explanation and direct instruction'. *Child Development* 77: 1–15.

Rizzolatti, G. and L. Craighero. 2004. 'The mirror-neuron system'. *Annual Review of Neuroscience* 27: 169–92.

Robb, T., S. Ross, and I. Shortreed. 1986. 'Salience of feedback on error and its effect on EFL writing quality'. *TESOL Quarterly* 20: 83–91.

Robinson, P. 2001a. 'Task complexity, cognitive resources, and syllabus design: a triadic framework for examining task influences on SLA' in Robinson (ed.).

Robinson, P. (ed.). 2001b. *Cognition and Second Language Instruction*. Cambridge: Cambridge University Press.

Robinson, P. and N. Ellis (eds.). 2008. *Handbook of Cognitive Linguistics and Second Language Acquisition*. London: Routledge.

Roebuck, R. 2000. 'Subjects speak out: how learners position themselves in a psycholinguistic task' in J. Lantolf (ed.).

Rogers, R. (ed.). 2004. *A Critical Discourse Analysis of Literate Identities across Contexts: Alignment and Conflict*. Mahwah, NJ: Lawrence Erlbaum.

Rogoff, B. 1990. *Apprenticeship in Thinking: Cognitive Development in Social Context*. New York: Oxford University Press.

Rogoff, B. 1995. 'Observing sociocultural activity on three planes: participatory appropriation, guided participation, and apprenticeship' in J. V. Wertsch, P. D. Rio, and A. Alvarez (eds.): *Sociocultural Studies of Mind*. New York: Cambridge University Press.

Rogoff, B. 1998. 'Cognition as a collaborative process' in D. Kuhn and R. S. Siegler (eds.): *Handbook of Child Psychology*, ii. New York: Wiley.

Rogoff, B. 2003. *The Cultural Nature of Human Development*. New York: Oxford University Press.

Rommetveit, R. 1979. 'On the architecture of intersubjectivity' in R. Rommetveit and R. Blakar (eds.): *Studies of Language, Thought, and Verbal Communication*. New York: Academic Press.

Rowe, M. B. 1986. 'Wait times: slowing down may be a way of speeding up'. *Journal of Teacher Education* 37/1: 43–50.

Rumelhart, D. and J. McClelland. 1986. 'On learning the past tenses of English verbs' in D. Rumelhart, J. McClelland, and University of California San Diego PDP Research Group (eds.): *Parallel Distributed Processing: Explorations in the Microstructure of Cognition*, ii. *Psychological and Biological Models*. Cambridge, Mass.: MIT.

Russell, J. and N. Spada. 2006. 'The effectiveness of corrective feedback for the acquisition of L2 grammar: a meta-analysis of the research' in Norris and Ortega (eds.).

Sachs, R. and C. Polio. 2007. 'Learners' uses of two types of written feedback on a L2 writing revision task'. *Studies in Second Language Acquisition* 29: 67–100.

Sanaoui, R. 1984. 'The use of reformulation in teaching writing to ESL students'. *Carleton Papers in Applied Language Studies* 1: 139–46.

Schegloff, E. M., H. Sacks, and G. Jefferson. 1977. 'The preference for self-correction in the organization of repair in conversation'. *Language* 53: 361–82.

Schieffelin, B. B. and E. Ochs. 1986. *Language Socialization across Cultures*. Cambridge: Cambridge University Press.

Schmidt, R. W. 1983. 'Interaction, acculturation, and the acquisition of communicative competence' in N. Wolfson and E. Judd (eds.): *Sociolinguistics and Language Acquisition*. Rowley, Mass.: Newbury House.

Schmidt, R. W. 1990. 'The role of consciousness in second language learning'. *Applied Linguistics* 11: 129–57.

Schmidt, R. W. 1993. 'Awareness and second language acquisition'. *Annual Review of Applied Linguistics* 13: 206–26.

Schmidt, R. W. 2001. 'Attention' in P. Robinson (ed.): *Cognition and Second Language Instruction*, 3–32. New York: Cambridge University Press.

Schmidt, R. W. and S. N. Frota. 1986. 'Developing basic conversational ability in a second language: a case study of an adult learner of Portuguese' in R. Day (ed.): *Talking to Learn: Conversation in Second Language Acquisition*. Rowley, Mass.: Newbury House.

Schulz, R. 2001. 'Cultural differences in student and teacher perceptions concerning the role of grammar instruction'. *The Modern Language Journal* 85: 244–58.

Schumann, J. 1978a. 'The acculturation model for second language acquisition' in R. Gingras (ed.): *Second Language Acquisition and Foreign Language Teaching*. Arlington, Va.: Center for Applied Linguistics.

Schumann, J. 1978b. 'The relationship of pidiginization, creolization, and decreolization in second language acquisition'. *Language Learning* 28/2: 367–79.

Schwartz, B. 1993. 'On explicit and negative data effecting and affecting competence and linguistic behaviour'. *Studies in Second Language Acquisition* 15: 147–63.

Seedhouse, P. 2004. *The Interactional Architecture of the Language Classroom: A Conversation Analysis Perspective*. Malden, Mass.: Blackwell.

Seedhouse, P. 2005. ' "Task" as research construct'. *Language Learning* 55/3: 533–70.

Segalowitz, N. and B. Freed. 2004. 'Context, contact, and cognition in oral fluency acquisition: learning Spanish in at home and study abroad contexts'. *Studies in Second Language Acquisition* 26: 173–200.

Seidenberg, M. S. and M. C. MacDonald. 1999. 'A probabilistic constraints approach to language acquisition and processing'. *Cognitive Science* 23: 569–88.

Selinker, L. and D. Douglas. 1985. 'Wrestling with "context" in interlanguage theory'. *Applied Linguistics* 6: 190–204.

Semin, G. R. and E. R. Smith (eds.). 2008. *Embodied Grounding*. Cambridge: Cambridge University Press.

Semin, G. R. and J. T. Cacioppo. 2008. 'Grounding social cognition: synchronization, coordination, and co-regulation' in Semin and Smith (eds.).

Sfard, A. 1998. 'On two metaphors for learning and the dangers of choosing just one'. *Educational Researchers* 27: 4–13.

Sheen, Y. 2004. 'Corrective feedback and learner uptake in communicative classrooms across instructional settings'. *Language Teaching Research* 8: 263–300.

Sheen, Y. 2006a. 'Exploring the relationship between characteristics of recasts and learner uptake'. *Language Teaching Research* 10: 361-92.

Sheen, Y. 2006b. 'Corrective feedback, individual differences and the acquisition of articles by second language learners'. Unpublished Ph.D. thesis, University of Nottingham.

Siegler, R. S. 2002. 'Microgenetic studies of self-explanations' in N. Granott and J. Parziale (eds.): *Microdevelopment: Transition Processes in Development and Learning*, 31–58. New York: Cambridge University Press.

Sinclair, J. M., and R. M. Coulthard. 1975. *Toward an Analysis of Discourse: The English Used by Teachers and Pupils*. London: Oxford University Press.

Skehan, P. 1998. *A Cognitive Approach to Language Learning*. Oxford: Oxford University Press.

Slembrouck, S. 2006. 'What is meant by "discourse analysis?" '. <http://bank.rug.ac.be/da/da.htm>, accessed 2 Dec. 2009. English Department, Ghent University, Belgium.

Slobin, D. I. 1996. 'From "thought and language" to "thinking for speaking" ' in S. Gumperz and S. Levinson (eds.): *Rethinking Linguistic Relativity*. Cambridge: Cambridge University Press.

Slobin, D. I. 2003. 'Language and thought online: cognitive consequences of linguistic relativity' in D. Gentner and S. Goldin-Meadow (eds.): *Language in Mind: Advances in the Study of Language*. Cambridge, Mass.: MIT.

Smagorinsky, P. 1998. 'Thinking and speech and protocol analysis'. *Mind, Culture, and Activity* 5: 157–77.

Sperber, D. and D. Wilson. 1995. *Relevance: Communication and Cognition* (2nd edn.). Oxford: Blackwell.

Sperber, D. and D. Wilson. 2002. 'Pragmatics, modularity and mind-reading'. *Mind and Language* 17/1 & 2: 3–23.

Stefanowitsch, A. and S. Gries. 2003. 'Collostructions: investigating the interaction of words and constructions'. *International Journal of Corpus Linguistics* 8: 209–43.

Stoller, F. L. 2002. 'Project work: a means to promote language and content' in J. C. Richards and W. A. Renandya (eds.): *Methodology in Language Teaching: An Anthology of Current Practice*. Cambridge: Cambridge University Press.

Suzuki, W. 2009. 'Languaging, direct correction, and second language writing: Japanese university students of English'. Ph.D. dissertation, University of Toronto.

Swain, M. 2000. 'The output hypothesis and beyond: mediating acquisition through collaborative dialogue' in Lantolf (ed.).

Swain, M. 2005a. 'Languaging, agency and collaboration'. Plenary paper presented at the Applied Linguistics Association of Australia (ALAA), University of Melbourne, Australia, 26 September 2005.

Swain, M. 2005b. 'The output hypothesis: theory and research' in E. Hinkel (ed.): *The Handbook of Research in Second Language Teaching and Learning*. Mahwah, NJ: Lawrence Erlbaum.

Swain, M. 2006a. 'Languaging, agency and collaboration in advanced language proficiency' in H. Byrnes (ed.): *Advanced Language Learning: The Contribution of Halliday and Vygotsky*. London: Continuum.

Swain, M. 2006b. 'Verbal protocols: what does it mean for research to use speaking as a data collection tool?' in M. Chalhoub-Deville, M. Chapelle, and P. Duff (eds.): *Inference and Generalizability in Applied Linguistics: Multiple Research Perspectives*. Amsterdam: John Benjamins.

Swain, M. and P. Deters. 2007. ' "New" mainstream SLA theory: expanded and enriched'. *The Modern Language Journal* 91 (Focus Issue): 820–36.

Swain, M. and S. Lapkin. 1998. 'Interaction and second language learning: two adolescent French immersion students working together'. *The Modern Language Journal* 82: 320–37.

Swain, M. and S. Lapkin. 2000. 'Task-based second language learning: the uses of the first language'. *Language Teaching Research* 4: 251–74.

Swain, M. and S. Lapkin. 2001. 'Focus on form through collaborative dialogue: exploring task effects' in M. Bygate, P. Skehan, and M. Swain (eds.): *Researching Pedagogic Tasks: Second Language Learning, Teaching and Testing*. London: Longman.

Swain, M. and S. Lapkin. 2002. 'Talking it through: two French immersion learners' response to reformulation'. *International Journal of Educational Research* 37: 285–304.

Swain, M. and S. Lapkin. 2007. 'The distributed nature of second language learning: Neil's perspective' in S. Fotos and H. Nassaji (eds.): *Form-focused Instruction and Teacher Education: Studies in Honour of Rod Ellis*. Oxford: Oxford University Press.

Swain, M. and S. Lapkin. 2008. ' "Oh, I get it now!" From production to comprehension in second language learning' in D. M. Brinton and O. Kagan (eds.): *Heritage Language Acquisition: A New Field Emerging*. Mahwah, NJ: Lawrence Erlbaum.

Swain, M., S. Lapkin, I. Knouzi, W. Suzuki, and L. Brooks. 2009. 'Languaging: university students learn the grammatical concept of voice in French'. *The Modern Language Journal* 93: 5–29.

Talmy, S. 2008. 'The cultural productions of ESL student at Tradewinds High: contingency, multidirectionality, and identity in L2 socialization'. *Applied Linguistics* 29: 619–44.

Talyzina, N. 1981. *The Psychology of Learning*. Moscow: Progress.

Tardy, C. 2006. 'Appropriation, ownership, and agency: negotiating teacher feedback in academic settings' in K. Hyland and F. Hyland (eds.): *Feedback in Second Language Writing: Contexts and Issues*. New York: Cambridge University Press.

Tarone, E. 1979. 'Interlanguage as chameleon'. *Language Learning* 29: 181–91.

Tarone, E. 1982. 'Systematicity and attention in interlanguage'. *Language Learning* 32/1: 69–84.

Tarone, E. 1988. *Variation in Interlanguage*. London: Edward Arnold.

Tarone, E. 2000a. 'Still wrestling with "context" in interlanguage theory'. *Annual Review of Applied Linguistics* 20: 182–98.

Tarone, E. 2000b. 'Getting serious about language play: language play, interlanguage variation and second language acquisition' in B. Swierzbin, F. Morris, M. Anderson, C. Klee, and E. Tarone (eds.): *Social and Cognitive Factors in SLA: Proceedings of the 1999 Second Language Research Forum*. Somerville, Mass.: Cascadilla.

Tarone, E. 2007a. 'Social and Cognitive Aspects of Second Language Learning and Teaching'. Plenary Speech at the Social and cognitive aspects of second language learning conference, University of Auckland, New Zealand, 12–14 April 2007.

Tarone, E. 2007b. 'Sociolinguistic approaches to second language acquisition research, 1997–2007'. *The Modern Language Journal* 91 (Focus Issue): 837–48.

Tarone, E. 2009. 'A sociolinguistic perspective on interaction in SLA' in A. Mackey and C. Polio (eds.): *Multiple Perspectives on Interaction: Second Language Research in Honor of Susan M. Gass*. New York: Routledge.

Tarone, E., M. Bigelow, and K. Hansen. 2009. *Literacy and Second Language Oracy*. Oxford: Oxford University Press.

Tarone, E. and G. Liu. 1995. 'Situational context, variation, and second language acquisition theory' in G. Cook and B. Seidlhofer (eds.): *Principle and Practice in Applied Linguistics*. Oxford: Oxford University Press.

Tarone, E. and M. Swain. 1995. 'A sociolinguistic perspective on second-language use in immersion classrooms'. *The Modern Language Journal* 79: 166–78.

Teutsch-Dwyer, M. 2001. '(Re)constructing masculinity in a new linguistic reality' in A. Pavlenko, A. Blackledge, I. Piller and M. Teutsch Dwyer (eds.): *Multilingualism, Second Language Learning, and Gender*. Berlin: Mouton de Gruyter.

Thelen, E. and L. Smith. 1994. *A Dynamic Systems Approach to the Development of Cognition and Action*. Cambridge, Mass.: MIT.

Thomas, A. 2004. 'Phonetic norm versus usage in advanced French as a second language'. *International Review of Applied Linguistics* 42: 365–82.

Thornbury, S. 1991. *Uncovering Grammar*. Oxford: Macmillan Heinemann.

Thornbury, S. 1997. 'Reformulation and reconstruction: tasks that promote "noticing"'. *ELT Journal* 51: 326–35.

Tocalli-Beller, A. and M. Swain. 2005. 'Reformulation: the cognitive conflict and L2 learning it generates'. *International Journal of Applied Linguistics* 15: 5–28.

Tomasello, M. 2003. *Constructing a Language*. Cambridge, Mass.: Harvard University Press.

Tomasello, M. 2008. *Origins of Human Communication*. Cambridge, Mass.: MIT.

Toohey, K. 1999. 'Comments on Kelleen Toohey's "Breaking them up, taking them away: ESL students in Grade 1": the author responds'. *TESOL Quarterly* 33/1: 132–6.

Toth, P. D. 2004. 'When grammar instruction undermines cohesion in L2 Spanish classroom discourse'. *The Modern Language Journal* 88: 14–30.

Toth, P. D. 2008. 'Teacher- and learner-led discourse in task-based grammar instruction: providing procedural assistance for L2 morphosyntactic development'. *Language Learning* 58/2: 237–83.

Toth, P. D. and A. Garritano. 2008. 'La retroalimentación implícita por medio de "contraejemplos" en una clase de español como lengua extranjera [Implicit feedback through recasts in a foreign language Spanish class]'. *Hispania* 91: 123–37.

Truscott, J. 1996. 'The case against grammar correction in L2 writing classes'. *Language Learning* 46: 327–69.

Truscott, J. 1999. 'What's wrong with oral grammar correction'. *Canadian Modern Language Review* 55: 437–55.

Tucker, M. and K. Hirsch-Pasek. 1993. 'Systems and language: implications for acquisition' in L. Smith and E. Thelen (eds.): *A Dynamic Systems Approach to Development: Applications*. Cambridge, Mass.: MIT.

Ulichny, P. 1996. 'Performed conversations in an ESL classroom'. *TESOL Quarterly* 30/4: 739–64.

Uritescu, D., R. Mougeon, K. Rehner, and T. Nadasdi. 2004. 'Acquisition of the internal and external constraints of variable schwa deletion by French immersion students'. *International Review of Applied Linguistics* 42: 349–64.

van Baaren, R. B., T. G. Horgan, T. L. Chartrand, and M. Dijkmans. 2004. 'The forest, the trees, and the chameleon: context dependence and mimicry'. *Journal of Personality and Social Psychology* 86: 453–9.

van Geert, P. and H. Steenbeek. 2005. 'Explaining "after" by "before": basic aspects of a dynamic systems approach to the study of development'. *Developmental Review* 25: 408–42.

van Lier, L. 1996. *Interaction in the Language Curriculum: Awareness, Autonomy, and Authenticity*. London: Longman.

van Lier, L. 2000. 'From input to affordances: social-interactive learning from an ecological perspective' in Lantolf (ed.).

van Lier, L. 2004. *The Ecology and Semiotics of Language Learning: A Sociocultural Perspective*. Norwell, Mass.: Kluwer.

VanPatten, B. 1996. *Input Processing and Grammar Instruction: Theory and Research*. Norwood, NJ: Ablex.

Varela, F., E. Thompson, and E. Rosch. 1991. *The Embodied Mind: Cognitive Science and Human Experience*. Cambridge, Mass.: MIT.

Varonis, E. and S. Gass. 1985. 'Non-native/non-native conversations: a model for negotiation of meaning'. *Applied Linguistics* 6: 71–90.

Vickers, C. H. 2007. 'Second language socialization through team interaction among electrical and computer engineering students'. *The Modern Language Journal* 91: 621–40.

Vuchinich, S. 1977. 'Elements of cohesion between turns in ordinary conversation'. *Semiotics* 20: 227–57.

Vygotsky, L. S. 1978. *Mind in Society*. Cambridge: Mass.: Harvard University Press.

Vygotsky, L. S. 1986. *Thought and Language*. Cambridge, Mass.: MIT.

Vygotsky, L. S. 1987. *The Collected Works of L. S. Vygotsky*, i. *Problems of General Psychology. Including the Volume Thinking and Speech* (ed. R. W. Reiber and A. S. Carton). New York: Plenum.

Wagner, J. 2004. 'The classroom and beyond'. *Modern Language Journal* 88/4: 612–16.

Wang, X-L, R. Bernas, and P. Eberhard. 2004. 'Engaging ADHD students in tasks with hand gestures: a pedagogical possibility for teachers'. *Educational Studies* 30: 217–29.

Watanabe, Y. 2004. 'Collaborative dialogue between ESL learners of different proficiency levels: linguistic and affective outcomes'. Unpublished MA thesis, OISE, University of Toronto.

Watson-Gegeo, K. 2004. 'Mind, language, and epistemology: toward a language socialization paradigm for SLA'. *The Modern Language Journal* 88/3: 331–50.

Watson-Gegeo, K. and S. Nielsen. 2003. 'Language socialization in SLA' in Doughty and Long (eds.).

Waxman, P. 2000. 'The impact of English language proficiency on the adjustment of recently arrived Iraqi, Bosnian and Afghan refugees in Sydney'. *Prospect: A Journal of Australian TESOL* 15/1: 4–22.

Weber, M. 1922/1978. 'The nature of social activity' in W. C. Runciman (ed.): *Weber: Selections in Translation*. Cambridge: Cambridge University Press.

Wells, G. 1996. 'Using the tool-kit of discourse in the activity of learning and teaching'. *Mind, Culture, and Activity* 3/2: 74–101.

Wells, G. 1999. *Dialogic Inquiry. Toward a Sociocultural Theory and Practice of Education*. Cambridge: Cambridge University Press.

Wenger, E. 1998. *Communities of Practice: Learning, Meaning, and Identity*. Cambridge: Cambridge University Press.

Wertsch, J. V. 1985. *Vygotsky and the Social Formation of Mind*. Cambridge, Mass.: Harvard University Press.

Wertsch, J. V. 1991. *Voices of the Mind: A Sociocultural Approach to Mediated Action*. Cambridge, Mass.: Harvard University Press.

Wertsch, J. V. 1998. *Mind as Action*. Oxford: Oxford University Press.

White, J. and P. Lightbown. 1984. 'Asking and answering in ESL classes'. *Canadian Modern Language Review* 40: 228–44.

White, L. 1989. *Universal Grammar and Second Language Acquisition*. Amsterdam: John Benjamins.

Widdowson, H. G. 1978. *Teaching Language as Communication*. Oxford: Oxford University Press.

Widdowson, H. G. 1989. 'Knowledge of language and ability for use'. *Applied Linguistics* 10: 128–37.

Wigglesworth, G. 2005. 'Current approaches to researching second language learner processes'. *Annual Review of Applied Linguistics* 25: 98–111

Wigglesworth, G. and N. Storch. 2007. 'The effect of different forms of feedback on learners' writing'. Paper presented at the Social and cognitive aspects of second language learning conference, Auckland University, NZ, April 2007.

Wilson, D. and D. Sperber. 2004. 'Relevance theory' in L. R. Horn and G. Ward (eds.): *The Handbook of Pragmatics*. Oxford: Blackwell.

Wong, W. 2005. *Input Enhancement*. New York: McGraw-Hill.

Wortham, S. E. F. 2005. 'Socialization beyond the speech event'. *Journal of Linguistic Anthropology* 15: 95–112.

Xu, Y. Z. 1997. 'Interlanguage development and interaction: a longitudinal study of three adult learners of Chinese as a foreign language with particular reference to adverbials and negation'. Unpublished Ph.D. thesis, La Trobe University, Melbourne.

Yates, L. and A. Williams. 2003. 'Turning the kaleidoscope: perceptions of learning and teaching in the AMEP' in G. Wigglesworth (ed.): *The Kaleidoscope of Adult Second Language Learning: Learner, Teacher and Researcher Perspectives*. Sydney: NCELTR.

Young, R. 1990. *Variation in Interlanguage Morphology*. New York: Peter Lang.
Young, R. 1999. 'Sociolinguistic approaches to SLA'. *Annual Review of Applied Linguistics* 19: 105–32.
Young, R. and E. R. Miller. 2004. 'Learning as changing participation: discourse roles in ESL writing conferences'. *The Modern Language Journal* 88/4: 519–35.
Yule, G. 1990. 'Interactive conflict resolution in English'. *World Englishes* 9: 53–62.
Yule, G. and D. Macdonald 1990. 'Resolving referential conflicts in L2 interaction: the effect of proficiency and interactive role'. *Language Learning* 40: 539–56.
Yule, G., M. Powers, and D. Macdonald 1992. 'The variable effects of some task-based learning procedures on L2 communicative effectiveness'. *Language Learning* 42: 249–77.
Zappa-Hollman, S. 2007. 'Academic presentations across post-secondary contexts: the discourse socialization of non-native English speakers.' *The Canadian Modern Language Review* 63: 455–85.
Zipf, G. K. 1935. *The Psycho-biology of Language*. Boston, Mass.: Houghton Mifflin.
Zlatev, J., T. Racine, C. Sinha, and E. Itoken (eds.). 2008. *The Shared Mind: Perspectives on Intersubjectivity*. Amsterdam: John Benjamins.
Zuengler, J. and K. Cole. 2005. 'Language socialization and L2 learning' in E. Hinkel (ed.): *Handbook of Research in Second Language Teaching and Learning*. Mahwah, NJ: Lawrence Erlbaum.
Zuengler, J. and E. Miller. 2006. 'Cognitive and sociocultural perspectives: two parallel SLA worlds?' *TESOL Quarterly* 40: 35–58.
Zukow-Goldring, P. and K. R. Ferko. 1994. 'An ecological approach to the emergence of the lexicon: socializing attention' in V. John-Steiner, C. P. Panofsky, and L. W. Smith (eds.): *Sociocultural Approaches to Language and Literacy*. Cambridge: Cambridge University Press.

Index